# How Power Corrupts

# How Power Corrupts

## Cognition and Democracy in Organisations

Ricardo Blaug
*Reader in Democracy and Political Theory, University of Westminster, UK*

First published 2010 by
PALGRAVE MACMILLAN

First published in paperback 2014 by
PALGRAVE MACMILLAN

Palgrave Macmillan in the UK is an imprint of Macmillan Publishers Limited, registered in England, company number 785998, of Houndmills, Basingstoke, Hampshire RG21 6XS.

Palgrave Macmillan in the US is a division of St Martin's Press LLC, 175 Fifth Avenue, New York, NY 10010.

Palgrave Macmillan is the global academic imprint of the above companies and has companies and representatives throughout the world.

Palgrave® and Macmillan® are registered trademarks in the United States, the United Kingdom, Europe and other countries

ISBN: 978-0-230-21854-3 hardback
ISBN: 978-1-137-38468-3 paperback

This book is printed on paper suitable for recycling and made from fully managed and sustained forest sources. Logging, pulping and manufacturing processes are expected to conform to the environmental regulations of the country of origin.

A catalogue record for this book is available from the British Library.

A catalog record for this book is available from the Library of Congress.

*All special privilege in some way limits the outlook of those who possess it.*

*John Dewey*

# Contents

# List of Figures

# Acknowledgements

My love and thanks to Amy Kenyon and Isaac Blaug. The roots of this book lie in work conducted with Gene Orro, Robert Paul Wolff and Rohit Lekhi – to all, I am indebted. Finally, I wish to thank Janet McIntosh for her page 560.

Ricardo Blaug

# Introduction

For democrats, we do not manage our leaders well. Be they investment bankers or parliamentarians, they endlessly misbehave. Ask anyone if they agree with Lord Acton's observation that 'power corrupts', and they will nod knowingly. Then they will offer other examples, and perhaps a caveat, and before long they are holding forth on one of the classic problems of politics.

Corruption by power occurs so frequently we are barely surprised by it. Mad kings, psychotic dictators, insane warlords, unhinged corporate executives and politicians who never understood what they did wrong, all attest to our collective inability to manage elevated power. The regularity with which occupying armies engage in arbitrary violence against civilians, and governments turn a blind eye to torture, shows again our strong tendency to abuse it. On a smaller scale, and across our daily organisational lives, most families have their martinet, most offices their petty tyrants and most playgrounds their mini mountebank emperors.[1]

Corruption by power causes widespread individual suffering, organisational mission drift, wasted effort, ineffectiveness and inefficiency. It is characterised by arbitrary abuses, damaged lives and organisational sclerosis. As such, we have developed a variety of methods to better control it. In the liberal democracies, for example, we insist on a range of what Claus Offe has called institutional 'bindings, shackles and brakes' to head-off dangerous concentrations of power. These include the separation of state powers and the fixed duration of public offices.[2] Corruption is also guarded against by custom, practice and organisational *ethos*.[3] In the ancient Roman

1

Republic, for example, triumphant generals were accompanied by a slave, who, among the adulation and tumult, repeatedly whispered a simple phrase in their ear: 'remember you are mortal'. This was clearly intended to counter the strong tendency to imagine that triumph made you *immortal*. The management of corruption by power is thus a recurrent theme in the history of political thought.

Despite its long history – and evident contribution to many of our current problems – the manner in which power corrupts has received surprisingly little study. Acton's quote is commonly cited as an explanation for political failure, but only a handful of social scientists have engaged with it directly. Where such research has been undertaken, it has largely concentrated on *whether or not* power corrupts, rather than *how* it does so. No cause or trigger has been identified; no mechanism by which power corrupts has been fully examined. This is partly because, upon asking how power corrupts, we immediately encounter certain difficulties.

First, though Acton's phrase has undeniable predictive accuracy, it is by no means clear that 'corruption' signifies a common and defining set of behaviours. The tendency may manifest itself with great frequency, but it can take many different forms. The problem of identifying a common and defining element arises when we move from the general claim – that power corrupts – to levelling the accusation at a particular individual. Is *this* person corrupted by power? What *are* the symptoms? Could the behaviour be brought about by some other cause? Was Hitler, for example, corrupted by power, or had he always been barking mad?[4]

The second difficulty arises because the word 'corruption' has undergone considerable change in usage over time. Acton's quote in fact makes little reference to modern understandings of the term. Nowadays, corruption denotes personal financial gain, kick-backs and nepotism. Acton's phrase, however, appeals to an altogether more ancient – and indeed, republican – conception; one in which 'corruption' signifies a general failure to orient to the common good, a crisis of moral judgement and an aggrandised and *hubristic* distortion of individual thinking. Mad autocrats are thus corrupted by power in this ancient sense, for they have suffered nothing short of a moral collapse and a failure of *virtue* that has impoverished their thought and judgement. Corruption here more closely resembles its current usage in information technology – as in a 'corrupted' file – where it denotes a mistake, a line of broken code buried deep; a recurrent source of error. 'Ancient' or Actonian corruption thus appears as a pervasive disorder of the leader's character.

A third hindrance to studying how power corrupts is that changes in the usage of 'corruption' are accompanied by an even more rapid evolution of our understanding of 'power'. Originally seen as a direct capacity to make someone do things he would not otherwise do, power has received considerable clarification in recent social and political thought and is now regarded as multidimensional.[5] Notions of a simple capacity, or force, have thus been augmented by more indirect forms of power; particularly, power over what is being decided upon and the power inherent in the very structure of institutions. The work of Michel Foucault adds a still greater understanding of the subtleties of power, its manifestations in the very language we use to describe the world and its active *creation* of meaning. When we ask how power corrupts, we need to be clear about what is doing the corrupting.

Fourth, with corruption signifying a disorder of judgement, and power conceived as creative of meaning, it should come as no surprise to observe that corruption by power occurs beneath the awareness of afflicted individuals. They behave badly but tell you everything's fine. This is a condition in which the symptoms are invisible to the sufferer. Even when we swear blind to ourselves that power will not affect us; it all too often does. Individuals who become corrupt are not kidding when they claim that they alone know what is good for others. They really do think all their subordinates are fools. This is not a lie. Rather, it is the inability to see. As Gandhi observed, 'possession of power makes men blind and deaf'.[6] What we are considering here, therefore, is a *perceptual* failure, a distortion of experience itself. Unbeknown to the afflicted, the very way they make meaning has become corrupted, and their elevated status within an organisational hierarchy has affected both how and what they perceive. Corruption by power thus posits a false consciousness, with all the classic difficulties and pitfalls such a charge entails.

The fifth obstacle we face is one of the great myths of modern individualism: the belief that our thoughts are all our own. It is widely imagined that we think for ourselves; that we are autonomous. Yet this claim sits uneasily beside contemporary developments in social theory, which show that humans make meaning in social contexts and that we are strongly influenced in our thinking by the groups, organisations and institutions among which we live and work. Individuals join and interact in organisations and, to varying degrees, absorb their norms, rules and categories of thought. Again, however, this influence largely occurs beneath our awareness. As a result, when we join organisations, we become like centaurs: part human; part organisation.[7] Plead with a man in uniform, whether at the ticket barrier or the end of a gun, and we appeal to his human side. His reply: that he is 'only doing his job', signifies that we have failed. We are individuals, but our identities and thoughts are *also* the product of social and organisational processes. It is likely, therefore, that corruption by power is what might be called a 'boundary' pathology; occurring as it does deep within the interaction of self and organisation. To address so complex a relationship requires us to cross the disciplinary walls that separate the social sciences, and to seek insights from political theory, social psychology and organisational studies.

Finally, as if these many difficulties in examining how power corrupts are not enough, we must acknowledge one further obstacle: that we are *all* variously corrupted by power – if not as leaders, then as subordinates. This observation is central to ancient and republican accounts of corruption by power. Indeed, two of the greatest students of corruption: Niccolo Machiavelli and Jean-Jacques Rousseau, constantly refer to examples gleaned from the ancient republics, and make much of the damaging effects of corruption upon citizens themselves. Whereas for leaders, corruption manifests itself as aggrandisement and insularity; for subordinates and citizens, common symptoms are dependence, apathy and blind obedience. Early republicanism and its modern variants see corrupt citizens as unable to control their leaders and, therefore, as incapable of preserving their own freedom.

We can then recognise the importance of understanding how power corrupts for contemporary democratic politics. The current crisis of elites is accompanied by significant initiatives to deepen democracy. If we are to extend public engagement, devolve power and renew our public institutions, we must gain a better understanding of corruption by power and develop the means to guard against it. Democrats should thus give more help to their leaders, for they suffer from a chronic, and indeed historic, perceptual disorder.

*How*, then, does power corrupt? David Owen, in a recent book almost on the subject, labels the tendency 'The Hubris Syndrome'.[8] Having speculated that Tony Blair and Margaret Thatcher may have suffered from it, however, he does not drill down. There is little here on the causes of corruption, and nothing on the corruption of subordinates. We know it happens to elites – and *hubris* is certainly an old and good word for it – but to guard against such a 'syndrome', we need to know how it actually works. How do individual thinking and organisational structure collude to distort the leader's judgement? Owen usefully terms *hubris* an 'illness of position'.[9] And though he does not enquire into how it comes about, what he does – as a medical doctor – is to step confidently over our contemporary nervousness about pathologising difference to assert that corruption by power is a form of mental illness.[10] Given the extraordinary damage it has done across our history, and its likely continuation in future, this seems a more than reasonable claim. If psychiatry cannot identify corruption by power as pathology, this is a serious *clinical* failure. Certainly, we are currently in dire need of improved diagnostics and treatments.

To identify and study how power corrupts, this book draws upon fundamental debates in social science and the history of political thought. Primarily a work of social and political theory, it also makes use of analytic tools arising from the study of human cognition and neurobiology – a burgeoning area of research with increasing sophistication and profound implications across the social sciences.[11] At the core of cognitive science is the premise that individual minds are perpetually engaged in the active processing of information to construct meaning. All humans have a cognitive apparatus, a hard-wired structure that has evolved over time; a common chassis, indeed, for thinking.

Right away, most social scientists would balk at such a claim. To accept it, they would demand a careful introduction to these alleged advances in cognitive science. Then they would want their suspicions about determinism and universal claims allayed. As an example of doing this well, the philosopher John Searle's work on the relationship between freedom and neurobiology may be unique.[12] Certainly, cognitive scientists have usually struggled to translate their developing knowledge into forms that other social scientists can use. They have not addressed important political objections and have failed to communicate effectively with their (impressively) suspicious audience.

At the same time, however, cognitive psychologists claim that their work is not being adequately taken on board by other social sciences. James Anderson insists that 'cognitive psychology studies the foundation on which all other social sciences stand',[13] and Mark Turner goes so far as to liken the current status of social scientific explanation (without cognition) to that of biology prior to the discovery of genetics.[14]

This is a serious charge, for it asserts that social science, by not drawing upon developments in cognitive psychology, is unable to identify underlying causal mechanisms and so confines itself to merely 'functional' explanations of its objects. A functional explanation is a provisional claim to have identified a causal connection, without yet being able to stipulate that mechanism.[15] An example might be a sociological study of the relation between criminality and poverty, where the relation can be empirically demonstrated but the precise causal mechanism evades our understanding. Functional explanations are always, in this sense, second best; simply because they might turn out to be wrong. Once revealed, the causal mechanism(s) might be something quite different. As Turner knows, the classic functional explanation that came good was Darwin's theory of evolution. Darwin knew it happened but didn't know how. Only when Mandel discovered the genetic mechanism some thirty years later was the causal connection 'filled-in'. It is unlikely that many functional explanations, especially in social science, can hope to fare so well.

Power corrupts; not always, but often. If we follow Turner's advice, we can ask: what can cognitive psychology tell us about *how* power corrupts? Can it reveal how the mechanism actually works – cognitively? Can we use the insights provided by cognitive social psychology to move beyond a merely functional explanation and begin to fill in the parts which remain hidden? This book presents and uses cognitive psychology for political research; here on the question of how power corrupts.

Where social scientists have used cognitive tools – mostly in economics and public policy – they have often focused on the failures of human thinking, and our strong tendency to make knowledge processing mistakes. Most recently, for example, bias and irrationality have featured in the emerging 'science of persuasion', particularly in marketing and advertising. 'Choice architectures'[16] designed to exploit the cognitive mistakes we regularly make are also gaining influence in policy arenas, where they are being applied to a wide range of problems. These have included inducing the illusion of excessive speed by painting lines across the road, calibration of home heating thermostats to show cost and the placing of fruit at eye level in shops in order to induce healthy eating. Here, for our own good, our natural failings are to be corrected by a helpful cognitive 'nudge' from government. In Thaler and Sunstein, this is boldly justified by an appeal to 'libertarian paternalism'.[17] Let us merely note, however, yet another instance in which cognitive science is being used to assist governing elites. As a politician, Owen shows a similar orientation, and it is perhaps for this reason that he ignores subordinate corruption completely. Surely, the analytic tools made available by cognitive science could be used towards more democratic ends, particularly in regard to managing our leaders.

This book explores the psychological and organisational processes by which power corrupts. As such it is a critical and cognitive examination of the hierarchic organisational form, and an attempt to assist with the problem of its democratic management. If power corrupts, it is surely up to democrats to make sure it does not do so absolutely.

We here stand before a dangerous and destructive condition: a disorder of meaning, a mixing of self and organisation, a madness that is in part collective. To enquire into how it works is to momentarily illuminate the usually hidden power struggle in organisations over what we think.

# 1

# Corruption, Power and Democracy

It happened to Caligula, Tiberius, Robespierre, Hitler and Stalin, and perhaps also to Mugabe, Thatcher, Bush and Blair. But there was no question about Richard Keys. In his case, it took a curiously protracted form. Promoted first to middle management and then to managing director, Keys moved slowly from popular and enthusiastic office worker to gruff and impatient boss. Confined to his parochial empire on the edge of an industrial estate near Swindon, Keys evinced all the classic indicators of corruption by power; so much so that at last, his erstwhile friends used a telling everyday phrase to describe him to new recruits: power, they said, had 'gone to his head'.

When we look back over the entirely fictional career of Richard Keys, we can discern a number of changes in his behaviour that serve to reveal the ways in which power corrupts. We can also note the many difficulties encountered in trying to find a good example of such corruption. Hitler, Stalin, Caligula, etc., all turn out to be problematic examples. Indeed, corruption by power may simultaneously be a general claim of considerable predictive accuracy, while at the same time, an accusation almost impossible to make stick to a particular individual.

Clearly, it entails a discernible change in behaviour and personality; one that is readily noted by colleagues and remarked upon behind the back of the afflicted. So, for example, upon promotion, we can observe, in Richard Keys, an increase in self-confidence and a renewed dedication to organisational goals. Gradually, he was transformed into a maker of decisions. His belief in the importance

8

of leadership grew also, as did his increased appreciation of the difficulties that accompany such roles. Whereas before he was part of the team, he came at last to stand aside and above; sometimes wearied by responsibility, sometimes impatient with subordinates. Increasingly able to cut through excessive and unproductive discussion and overcome resistance to change, he made bold decisions that relied on his instincts. Indeed, in Keys' case, the capacity to dismiss nay-sayers and to value his own perspective over those of others was a growing source of pride in himself and alarm in his colleagues. Increasingly, the latter found themselves sidelined, seen as ditherers, resistors, shirkers and free-riders.

Now, only he could see. Only he knew what was good for the team. Only he had the exceptional skills needed to run the organisation. Here, then, a subtle melding of private interest with that of the collective occurred, so that at last he became psychologically entangled with the organisation itself; at once its guardian, touchstone and keeper. Richard Keys' self had, as it were, expanded. As a consequence, the goals of the organisation drifted towards the satisfaction of his needs. Its activities changed. Indeed, from this point on, the organisation existed for one overriding purpose: to serve Richard Keys.

Former colleagues learned to tread with care, for they knew that 'the change' had occurred: his power has become arbitrary, unpredictable and unaccountable. If they spoke against their now corrupted leader, they risked his wrath, and perhaps being labelled as incapable or in need of discipline. And so they spoke less, resented him, looked busy and kept away. His only interactions were with people who agreed with him, and the result was a gradual separation between the leader and the led. Richard Keys thus became progressively isolated, and his world began to shrink. By the end, he was its only inhabitant.

In order to preserve his power, Keys was increasingly prepared to commit any act of recklessness and cruelty, to bend any rule and tell any lie. And all the while, he insisted it was for the good of all. He believed it. To that distorted end, he sought to propagate his view of the world and maintain his control. When this attitude hardened further still, he became increasingly defensive, so that at last even the smallest symbolic act of resistance drew punishment or exclusion. Interestingly, he always – very carefully and almost inadvertently

– worked to make sure his subordinates did not get together and talk. Even the idea was abhorrent to him. When, in the end, the business failed, it did so because *he* could not adapt.

If this description of the symptomology of corruption captures, even in part, the process by which it occurs, we can note a number of concerns about directing the accusation at a specific individual. First, if we are to say that an individual is corrupted, we need to establish that they were not corrupt before their promotion, and that significant behavioural change occurred following that promotion. The charge of corruption thus requires a reasonably beneficent and sane individual to morph into an evil and insane one. It is for this reason that Hitler is perhaps a rather poor example of corruption, for he was of dubious sanity well before he gained power. Against this, however, one might assert that because power does not *always* corrupt, it would seem to affect only those individuals who are particularly 'susceptible' – in other words – those of dubious sanity at the outset. We could then assert that Hitler was vulnerable to corruption by power, whereas, for example, George Washington (famously) was not.

The example of the Roman Emperor Caligula is instructive here also, for he is, at first glance, a classic example of corruption by power. Initially of pleasant enough character, he lost his sanity upon taking the Purple; whereupon he indulged in the arbitrary exercise of power and wild fantasies of sex and violence. In fact, however, Caligula did not undergo the characteristic changes in personality associated with the corruption by power until a terrifying attempt was made on his life. From this point on, he was so fearful of conspiracy – here, apparently, with good reason – that he saw it all around him.[1] Once triggered by trauma, of course, the form of his psychotic break was utterly changed by his social status. But his symptoms of corruption could have been the same even if he was not the Emperor. Anyone can stand in rags and scream alone in a dungeon. Perhaps, then, Caligula is not a good example of corruption by power as, given the right trigger, he was likely to fall apart anyway.

One final attempt to identify a good example of corruption by power might be to point at Robert Mugabe. Formerly a revolutionary leader and resistance fighter, Mugabe became president of Zimbabwe – whereupon he morphed into a tyrant. Violent, blind to the suffering of his people, defensive and isolated, he certainly showed many of the classic symptoms. Particularly characteristic was his willingness to sacrifice everything to retain his position, and to fight not only actual threats to his control, but also to those that were merely symbolic. To really make the charge stick, however, would require a detailed analysis of Mugabe's behaviour prior to his corruption and a careful charting of the changes wrought upon him by elevation to power. Such a task would, indeed, take up the remainder of this book.

Clear examples of corruption by power are thus hard to come by. It is equally difficult to ascertain whether power *always* corrupts, and more difficult still to discern the actual *mechanisms* by which it does so. Such an undertaking clearly requires us to examine corruption and, indeed, the nature of power, with considerably more care than has so far been the case in such debates.

## Corruption as an effect of power

Despite the evident predictive accuracy of Acton's quote, and the extraordinary cost of corruption across our history, its causes, symptoms and treatments are almost completely unstudied. A mere handful of social scientists and journalists, and perhaps three philosophers, have attended to it in any real detail. One contemporary social psychologist who has studied the effects of holding power, however, is David Kipnis, who himself notes the extraordinary lack of research available on the topic.[2]

In order to ascertain whether power does indeed corrupt, and to begin to study the forms such corruption might take, Kipnis conducted careful empirical research into behavioural sales techniques. He was particularly interested in successful sales interactions – in other words, where one individual succeeded in influencing another – and the effects of this success on the 'influencing agent'. Kipnis's work showed that when individuals succeeded in influencing others, they quickly 'viewed target persons as less worthy than themselves'. This was evidenced in the way influencing agents 'moved away from [target persons] socially and psychologically'.[3] Kipnis sought to explain this effect by suggesting that success in influencing others prompts us to see them as no longer in control of their own behaviour, and thus to 'evaluate them unfavourably'.

Kipnis labelled this a 'metamorphic effect of power', and concluded that 'the successful use of influence transforms the influencing agent's view of self and others'.[4] Corruption is surely, then, a 'metamorphic effect of power', and one of its symptoms is a disparagement of subordinates.

The tendency of power-holders to adopt a negative assessment of those with lower status is confirmed by the work of another team of social psychologists. Dacher Keltner and his colleagues, in their own empirical studies, show that high social status stimulates the perception that subordinates are chronic shirkers of responsibility who require constant supervision and motivation.[5] Yet Keltner also stresses the many benefits of holding a high status role and the general 'affirmation' of the self that it affords.[6] Holding power thus provides a self-image tinged with pride, and a constant series of interactions with subordinates that serve to confirm the effect of your status on others. There is a subtle reorientation of all such engagements *towards you,* towards *your* needs and *your* psychological processes.[7] This reorientation presents what amounts to repeated opportunities for narcissistic self-indulgence. Keltner is thus able to show that high relative status removes social controls upon the leader's behaviour. Power, it seems, serves to remove the boundaries on the self; it gives the leader greater freedom; it disinhibits.

Personal affirmation, disinhibition and the growing invisibility of subordinate competence all encourage the power-holder to, in effect; *substitute his own interests* for those of the collective.[8] Seeing no other responsible actor, no possibility for coordination other than his own leadership and no other world but his own, the leader gradually turns the organisation[9] towards his personal concerns. Usually, there is little self-awareness of this change, for it quickly plunges into the depths and disappears, leaving the occupant of the high status role quite unable to distinguish his own self-interest from that of the organisation. Martha Minow, the constitutional legal scholar, has accurately termed this process one of 'privileging subjectivity'.[10] It entails the emergence of an over-estimated self. Now there is just one set of concerns, just one possible solution to problems, one source of organisational advantage: the corrupt individual himself.

While inflation of the self is an important indicator of corruption by power, we should not miss its tendency to progressively separate the leader and the led. Corrupt leadership builds a sealed and self-confirming world. Populated by sycophants and 'yes men', it is increasingly isolated. Unable to learn, it will, eventually, fall.

Though studies of corruption by power are decidedly thin on the ground, we can, nevertheless, provisionally identify a series of recurrent behavioural changes that begins to outline the ways in which power corrupts. Ian Shapiro lists the creeping expansion of self-belief, negative evaluation of subordinates, mission drift and a tendency to atrophy.[11] Subsequently, he adds the penchant for insularity.[12] David Owen starts his own list with narcissism, excessive identification and confidence, and he also notes progressive isolation.[13] Later in the book he mentions 'contempt',[14] but this is not included in his original list. Once again, the difficulty of settling on a definitive set of symptoms presents itself. But a provisional symptomology for corruption by power arising from our investigation so far might include:

| | |
|---|---|
| 1. | *Self Inflation* : growing self-confidence; aggrandisement; subordination of the public good to own interests; narcissism, arrogance and disinhibition. |
| 2. | *Devaluation of Subordinates* : low assessment of subordinate capacities; seeing subordinates as free-riding and as having abnegated decision-making responsibility; dehumanisation of subordinates; contempt and arbitrary cruelty. |
| 3. | *Separation* : growing inability to take other perspectives on board; selection of advisors who support leader's views; shrinking sources of knowledge; progressive isolation. |
| 4. | *Invisibility* : the above three behavioural changes take place outside the conscious awareness of affected individuals. |

*Figure 1.1*   Provisional Clinical Indicators for Corruption by Power

This necessarily tentative list – to which we will add flesh as our investigation continues – is of course compatible with the notion that certain individuals, and perhaps certain character types, might be more susceptible to corruption than others. Indeed, it is quite possible to imagine individuals suffering only the mildest of such behavioural changes, and perhaps even managing them with some degree of conscious awareness. Others, however, can be trusted to tumble headlong into what amounts to a psychological trap.

Aggrandised, dismissive, isolated and unaware, such individuals are corrupted in direct proportion to the power they hold, with absolute power tending towards absolute corruption. The outcome is then a loss of organisational effectiveness, wasted knowledge and, always, arbitrary cruelty.

Though contemporary social scientific research is strikingly thin, the history of political thought does offer insights that both add to our list of symptoms and identify those at greatest risk of affliction. In particular, the issue of corruption by power has long been an important theme in republican thought, and is a central concern in the work of both Niccolo Machiavelli and Jean-Jacques Rousseau.

Machiavelli was a great student of leadership, and it is only recently that his reputation has been recovered from merely being a 'teacher of evil' to tyrants. *The Prince*, his best known work, is still widely read, and indeed, is one of only two 'old' books available in the business section of airport bookshops (the other being Sun Tui's *Art of War*). Yet *The Prince* was, in fact, a job application, and an unsuccessful one at that. Far more representative of his political theory was his *Discourse on Livy* – a series of notes penned while reading Titus Livy's tumultuous *History of Early Rome*. It is here that we find the republican heart of Machiavelli, his radical populism, his use of historical example and his deep analysis of corruption by power. It is here also that we first expand our understanding of such corruption to include not only leaders, but also their subordinates – and republican citizens in particular.

In *The Prince*, Machiavelli attempts to gain the tyrant's interest by placing him among the great actors of history. Recounting the glorious deeds of leaders from the past, Machiavelli here draws heavily on the Renaissance tradition of 'advice to Kings'.[15] He thus adopts the time-honoured role of supplicant, averting his eyes from the leader while genuflecting and humbly offering counsel. Yet even in *The Prince*, he shows his concern with the tendency of power to corrupt. For as with so many other examples of 'advice to Kings', Machiavelli is careful to include a series of concealed controls over the leader's behaviour. In effect, he presents the Prince with the subtle threat of public judgement. Should he lose his *virtu* and succumb to fortune, the Prince will be judged by his peers, by history and by the populace of his city. The first will rejoice at his failure and take his kingdom; the second will remember him as a fool and a tyrant, while the third will take his life. To be corrupted by power is thus shown to be an endemic danger for all leaders. Even when successful, aggrandised, dismissive, isolated and unaware, the corrupted Prince still faces constraints on his behaviour. It is perhaps for this reason that Machiavelli did not get the job, though the other reason was clearly his association with the previous republican regime.

It takes a special leader indeed to resist corruption. Machiavelli recounts one story from Livy that not only illustrates the characteristics of such a leader, but also serves to encourage citizens to be vigilant about their freedom and to ensure their chosen leaders in fact possess these characteristics. He thus uses the story of Cincinnatus to show an uncorrupted citizenry in action.[16]

Livy tells of an attack on the city of Rome by a(nother) barbarian tribe. Because the city is a republic, the citizens are sovereign and closely involved with decision-making. There is a lengthy public debate, after which they conclude that the city will only survive if they focus their energies behind a dictator. Their choice is Cincinnatus, an elderly General, known to be tired of public life and with little interest in glory. That night, the people go in their thousands to Cincinnatus's farm outside the city. There they plead with him as he works in his field. Eventually, and reluctantly, he agrees to be their dictator.

In the Roman Republic, the office of dictator was often used in times of crisis and was limited in law to a duration of six months. Cincinnatus was a successful dictator, for under his leadership the army expelled the invaders. Livy then describes a series of meetings with young patricians who sought to persuade him to exert his authority and stay on as dictator. Yet Cincinnatus refused, and after his allotted six months, returned to tend his fields.

In the *Discourses*, Machiavelli ruminates upon this example. On the one hand, he is impressed by the humility of Cincinnatus, and seeks to valorise his disinterest in power. Indeed, Machiavelli makes much of Cincinnatus's poverty, suggesting that this somehow immunises him from corruption. Far more important here, however, is the suggestion that the citizenry showed excellent political judgement, or *virtu:* for they carefully selected a dictator who they *knew* would not be corrupted by power. The story thus serves to illustrate that free citizens require extraordinarily vigilance if they are to survive as a republican entity and retain their freedom. They must, for example, be able to recognise the periodic and situational need for a dictator, yet also to ensure this never becomes a permanent arrangement.

Machiavelli's use of Cincinnatus shows his own solution to the problem of finding good examples: he takes them from ancient history; this being a common rhetorical tactic during the Renaissance.[17] Unencumbered by historical accuracy, he is thus free to use Cincinnatus to develop the central thesis of his *Discourses* – that in a republic, citizens must defend their freedom with *virtu* or lose it entirely. They must control their leaders or be controlled by them. It is then a short step to asserting that where citizens are not virtuous, are lazy in their defence of freedom, become diverted by the pursuit of luxury, let leaders decide, become dependent, passive, weak and resentful – they are themselves corrupted.[18] Machiavelli thereby demonstrates that power corrupts not only leaders but also their subordinates.

Some three centuries later, this theme was taken up by Rousseau, who not only extended our understanding of citizen corruption but also began to identify, with some precision, *how* power corrupts the leader. For Rousseau, the process by which the leader becomes corrupted is, again, a process of self-inflation and personal aggrandisement. Leaders slowly increase their estimation of their own importance until they at last come to substitute their own self-interest for that of the collective. Each of us, Rousseau argued, has within us a self-interested 'particular will', as well as a notion of the good of all, or the 'general will'.[19] Good judgement here amounts to finding the General Will in the self. He was additionally concerned with the tendency of officials and ministers to orient towards their group interests – or what he called their 'corporate will' – for here again their privileged position resulted in a loss of contact with the General Will. As we have seen, this has subsequently been confirmed by the empirical work of social psychologists like Kipnis and Keltner.

Rousseau saw politics as a process of rising above self-interest to grasp the good of all. The primary role of political institutions was thus to encourage citizens and leaders to find the General Will and act upon it. He was quite aware, however, that for the most part, self or group interests prevailed, and self interest was activity stimulated by the absolutist institutions of his time. Repeated experiences of subordination, luxury and passivity made it harder for citizens and their ministers to find, within themselves, the good of all. Corruption, for Rousseau, was a loss of the General Will, both in politics and inside oneself. It made the General Will, literally, inconceivable. Corruption by power is here described as a process of *substitution*: in which self-interest and group-interest gradually displaces the public interest. As such, corruption (again) affects both leaders and citizens.

Rousseau was unusual for a social contract theorist, for he saw human nature as malleable, as responsive to experience and as an expression of the times. His tight narration of our moral and physical degeneration in the *Discourse on the Origins of Inequality* shows us to be strongly influenced by our existing hierarchic organisations. It is not human nature, but long experience of illegitimate and ineffective hierarchies, that gradually turn us into mere bundles of Hobbesian rational self-interest. This, indeed, was his celebrated critique of Hobbes: that the latter assumed human nature to be *essentially* acquisitive, whereas in fact, he argued, such behaviour is the *product* of hierarchic society, rather than its cause.[20]

Moreover, Rousseau reiterates the destructive impact of excessive power on subordinates. Steeped in the history of civic republicanism,[21] and himself an admiring reader of Machiavelli, he sees corruption as affecting *all* participants in the hierarchic organisation, and as involving a diversion of energy away from collective concerns and towards the psychological processes of the leader. All too often, the organisation 'drifts' into what Machiavelli and Rousseau would call tyranny. It is for this reason that they both assert that hierarchies should be carefully constrained and actively managed by a vigilant, and uncorrupted, republican citizenry.

In all these conceptions of corruption by power, the constitutive relationship and object of study is one of domination and subordination, of asymmetrical power, of organisational hierarchy. In the work of a third philosopher, we find this relationship examined directly; and with such subtlety that, no sooner have we focused upon its apparent simplicity, than it comes apart in our hands. Hegel's examination of the relationship between master and slave[22] serves at once to confirm the corrupting effects of asymmetrical power and to alert us to the complexity of power itself.

Hegel uses the relationship between master and slave to show how the divided perspectives of dominance and subordination affect individual thinking, and how they do so in distinct ways. One such difference lies in what each party needs to know. For the master, knowing about the individuality of the slave is of little importance. The stability of the relationship does not require such knowledge, and there is much room for the master to 'exist only for himself'.[23] As we have already noted, one effect of asymmetrical power is the reorientation of interactions with subordinates towards *you*, so that they increasingly reflect your needs and your psychological processes.[24] From the slave's perspective, however, it is of considerable importance to have good knowledge of the master, for without it the slave will not survive. Hegel thus states that, 'servitude has the lord for its essential reality'.[25]

Yet the distinct knowledge requirement of each role has an unexpected outcome: that of a growing dependence, here of the *master upon the slave*.[26] Hegel moves up a gear when he points out that the master achieves the recognition of his power in the eyes of the slave. As this confirmation becomes habituated and integral to the master's identity, he cannot endure without it. Now intoxicated, the master must constantly inspect the eyes of the slave for the recognition he craves.[27] We have already noted, in the work of Machiavelli and Rousseau, the claim that subordinates need greater vigilance than dominant elites. Here repeated and deepened by Hegel, this claim is again confirmed by modern psychological research.[28] So, for example, Depret and Fiske have demonstrated that high status individuals are more likely to use stereotypes in their judgement of others,[29] while Snodgrass and her colleagues have attributed women's greater ability to read non-verbal communication to their relative subordination.[30] Gamson goes so far as to suggest that subordinate groups are motivated to engage in a more reflective and wide-ranging style of political discussion.[31]

When we recognise that corruption by power affects both leaders and followers, we begin to see it as a series of effects of hierarchic social relations more generally. While corruption by power has received comparatively little study, a great deal more attention has been paid to the effects of organisational hierarchy and the occupation of asymmetrical status roles in organisations. Indeed, when approached in this way, the analysis of corruption by power can draw upon advances in both organisational studies and social psychology. In the following chapter, we will examine the psychological effects of hierarchy in some detail. Here, however, in order to clarify *what it is that does the corrupting*, we must grasp the most apparent institutional manifestation of power – that of organisational hierarchy.

## Hierarchic power and democracy

We are increasingly aware that power can be complex, subtle and indirect. Yet this does not negate its frequent appearance in stark and material forms. Before we explore recent scholarship in political and social theory that both expands and undermines our traditional conception of power, we should begin with its most direct, visible and traditional form. Let us not mince words; when it comes to power, some people have more than others. We can thus safely speak of power *'over'*: of domination and subordination, of institutionalised relations characterised by asymmetrical power and of social and organisational structures that are hierarchic.[32]

Indeed, the prevalence of organisational hierarchy is remarkable.[33] Transcending historical and cultural contexts, it has shown itself to be durable, even when concerted effort is expended to limit it. The social psychologists Sidanius and Pratto go so far as to assert that 'every attempt to abolish... group-based hierarchy within societies of economic surplus have, without exception, failed'.[34] So important is this organisational form that one historian has asserted that, 'the history of hierarchy is the history of Occidental thought'.[35]

An organisational hierarchy is a set of frozen social relations bearing a strong family resemblance: all are arranged as a 'ranked tree'.[36] Hierarchy is thus a stack of power asymmetries, featuring different levels of status; layered, as it were, one above the other.[37] Such a family covers a wide range of practical arrangements, and is variously embedded in distinct organisational contexts. Some instances of hierarchy resist clear characterisation as a lexical stack of relative power relations. So, for example, where decision-makers are elected by those who then become their subordinates – as is the case in a representative democracy – hierarchy can itself be more complex than simply 'power over'.[38] Yet the hierarchic family resemblance is strong; and even among these distant relations, most members are easily recognised. As long as we recall that particular hierarchies differ significantly, and take many forms, we can proceed to analyse the general case of hierarchy as a ranked tree of asymmetrical power relations. Indeed, reasons given for the occurrence of hierarchy in general are widely used to justify particular hierarchies, and to defend their continued existence here and now.

With hierarchy so readily observable in nature, in food chains, in the very structure of plants and even among the heavenly bodies, ancient philosophers constructed analogous classificatory hierarchies for human affairs. The social world was seen to mirror relations in nature.[39] Everything from the smallest insect to the divine being himself was arranged in ranked 'degrees' of relative status. Zeus's 'Golden Chain'[40] and Jacob's 'Ladder' both reached from heaven all the way to earth,[41] and the world seemed a 'Great Chain of Being', in which each organism had its rightful place.[42] While the Reformation began the long process of undermining the notion that hierarchy is divinely-sanctioned, the idea that the material world was constructed of chains, links and layers continued to influence, even when Europe's Enlightenment sought to replace God's will with science. Indeed, the more science taught us about the nature of the world, the more it seemed that its very physical structures served to dictate what happens when individuals seek to coordinate their actions.[43]

Of course, the apparent hierarchical arrangements of the physical world, such as, for example, the evident domination of grass by caribou, and then of caribou by wolves, is not, in fact, so straight-forward. One could easily argue that grass benefits from caribou grazing and that caribou 'use' wolves to weed out the weak and thus improve their gene pool. Is a queen bee the apex or the servant of the hive? In other words, the widespread perception of hierarchy in nature, and its subsequent mimicry in (and justification of) hier-archic social relations, could be read the other way. If this were the case, then we might want to suggest that hierarchies in human rela-tions came first, and then served to encourage the widespread per-ception that the natural world was similarly hierarchical. Murray Bookchin, for example, uses just this argument to critique hierarchic social relations and to defend anarchist modes of organisation.[44]

To survive and prosper, humans must work together. Collective action needs to be effective, and, apparently mirroring the material world, this was assumed to be best achieved by leadership and hier-archy. In an environment dominated by scarcity and competition, for example, human relations take on the hierarchic form in order to appropriate effectively, generate and distribute scant resources. In a battle, a ship needs a captain.[45] In a firm or a factory, productive efficiency is improved by a hierarchic division of labour.[46] Even in democratic politics, effective decisions are achieved only by the hierarchic division of *political* labour into an active executive and a relatively passive populace.[47] Hierarchies are thus seen to emerge because of their unique organisational effectiveness.[48] The first hierarchies may have arisen around biological differences such as physical strength or gender.[49] Subsequently, more complex examples arose as political and economic conditions changed.[50] While hierarchy boasts many of humanity's greatest achievements, so must we acknowledge – to those of democratic persuasion – that as an organisational form, it has costs. Among them are the excessive concentration of power, chronic exclusion and a sclerotic inability to learn.[51] Hierarchy incurs significant health costs for its participants,[52] enforcement costs[53] and a range of deleterious psychological effects, including dehumanisation,[54] learned helplessness[55] and, of course, corruption by power. Such costs have taught democrats to manage carefully this most compelling and dangerous of organisational forms.

Yet those of more 'elitist' (or 'realist') persuasion can appeal to the commonly held belief that hierarchy is necessary for effective decision-making; that its occurrence is somehow 'natural' in human affairs and that it is, therefore, inevitable.[56] Organisations will always resemble pyramids; there will always be inequality and, sometimes, tyranny also. In the end, we simply do need leaders. Such views are extraordinarily widespread; meaning that they are frequently expressed, not only by democratic theorists,[57] but also in our everyday understanding of organisations. There is, therefore, a long ideological debate around whether or not hierarchy is natural and uniquely effective as an organisational form.[58] After all, a hierarchy that can claim to be necessary has the struggle for legitimacy all but won.[59] A second debate then follows from the first: for if hierarchy is natural, uniquely effective and thus inescapable, how can we hope to make our societies more democratic?

Any discussion of how a deeper democracy is to be organised must acknowledge that whenever humans coordinate their actions, there is a strong tendency, and perhaps even need, for hierarchy to emerge, for power to become concentrated in a group or individual, and for that power to corrupt that person or group. This tight circle of concern has always loomed over the design of democratic institutions, and we have already noted its influence in the development of constitutional separations of power and time limits on the occupation of public office. Its importance continues for participatory democrats in the public, private, voluntary and protest organisations of today. Current direct action protests show a marked suspicion of institutionalised politics, concern about the dangers of charismatic leadership and a growing awareness of the costs of hierarchy. Strongly influenced by anarchism, situationism and a healthy cynicism, grassroots democratic initiatives have sought to flatten their hierarchies[60] and distribute the functions of leadership. Yet such movements themselves face the need to articulate a viable organisational project, one that can be more widely seen to balance increased participation with effective decision-making; use hierarchy when necessary and yet aggressively minimise and manage its negative effects.[61]

Certainly, if we are to have more participation, we must address the *organisational* problem of effective decision-making. In a liberal representative democracy, effectiveness is delivered by an executive that is necessarily small in number, expert in governance and autonomous in judgement. Our political system thus uses a division of labour; here of political labour, in which a few proxy politicians decide 'on behalf of' the many citizens.[62] Representative government uses this hierarchy to attain effective organisation. Democracy, of course, demands that decision-makers receive public consent, whether by vote, constitutional convention or social contract.[63] How, then, would a more participatory democracy achieve organisational effectiveness? Can it use hierarchy, and if so, how much? How can the costs and dangers of hierarchy – among them the tendency of power to corrupt – be adequately managed?

Most people diagnose our inability to involve large numbers of citizens in governance by appealing to a notion akin to that of Robert Michels's 'Iron Law of Oligarchy'.[64] Michels claimed that all organisations inevitably generate leadership and hierarchy. As technical conditions become more complex,[65] he argues, there is an increasing need for 'a certain amount of Ceasarism'.[66] Slowly but surely, those who are particularly able will gain status and hang onto it as a vehicle of their own self-interest.[67] It happens all the time, and as he so compellingly demonstrates, it happened in particular in the Social Democratic party in pre-war Germany.

Yet Michels provides no real explanation for *why* this occurs. He stipulates no mechanisms by which hierarchy is able to achieve its unique effectiveness. In the absence of such an explanation, his general claim for the necessity of hierarchy is largely (if powerfully) rhetorical. What his particular empirical study *does* show, however, is that the emergence of hierarchy can occur even when an organisation is genuinely committed to *reducing* hierarchy. Michels thus forcefully expresses the concern that there is something inescapable, inherent and structural about collective action; something that means we will always and everywhere be subject to the will of another. Even if the claim is too strong, and is not a law at all,[68] and even if he cannot enlighten us as to the structural mechanisms by which hierarchy achieves effectiveness, he presents more participatory approaches to democracy with a stinging challenge, clearly articulating what, for most of us, is merely an unexamined assumption.

When we look over the long debates about how organisational hierarchy achieves effectiveness, it is striking how often appeal is made to its capacity to streamline and focus decision-making. Democracy is thus seen as a disorganised and inefficient clamour of different voices; while authority is clear, simple and definite. The capacity of authority to focus, simplify and *reduce* the flow of information is a recurrent theme in claims for the unique effectiveness of hierarchy, and seems to turn on a notion akin to an information bottleneck. In such a conception, information moves within and between organisations,[69] yet as these flows increase, so, at a certain scale, do they threaten to overload the organisation and limit its effectiveness. Decision-making is thus seen to require a reduction in complexity, one that allows a (nevertheless) restricted flow of information to pass through the bottleneck.[70] Hierarchy thus provides effectiveness by a process of simplification. It simplifies the knowledge environment, limits processes of communication, lowers costs[71] and systematises tasks.[72] Following Karl Popper's tactic of putting the opposition's position in its strongest form, we might therefore say that hierarchy is uniquely effective because the material world is a complex informational environment that humans need to simplify. By virtue of its ability to achieve precisely this end, hierarchy is necessary, inescapable and justified.

Yet if hierarchies are inescapable and necessary, we would regularly observe them removing themselves as their necessity passed. Complex informational environments and crises call for massive simplification, but when that degree of simplification is no longer required, hierarchy should diminish. But this barely occurs. Instead, hierarchies are usually maintained even though conditions have changed in such a way as to render them unnecessary.[73] Indeed, one of the characteristics of hierarchy is its durability, and tendency to cling to power with increasing desperation. This is how hierarchies get stuck. Having outlived its (alleged) original necessity, it is now artificially preserved for *other* reasons.[74] Whether we conceive of the 'stickiness' of hierarchy in terms of unconscious habituation,[75] or with concepts like 'lock-in',[76] 'path-dependency' or 'reification' – or a simple human desire to hang on to power – we now move beyond material explanations for hierarchy and confront what amount to ideological reasons for its persistence. Indeed, so regularly do hierarchies outlive the reasons for their emergence, and so frequently does their severity exceed material requirements, that this ideological element is surely crucial to explaining their historical and cultural prevalence.

In addition, the claim that hierarchy is the *only* way to effectively coordinate human action is palpably false. Markets achieve effectiveness in a quite distinct way, as do networks;[77] so there certainly are alternative organisational forms that can coordinate human action and that could be selected in place of hierarchy. The long and complex history of anarchism, for example, mounts a direct challenge to the necessity of hierarchy by appealing to the coordinating capacity of networks. Its bold-faced assertion that 'anarchy is order',[78] indicates the possibility that effectiveness often arises naturally in human networks, and may not require hierarchy at all.

Reasons for the prevalence of hierarchy are, therefore, both material and ideological. We can, therefore – and with some confidence – reject Michels's claim that all organisation requires leadership. This is no scientific law; but rather, a strongly ideological assertion. It is perhaps this ideological leaning that eventually led Michels to declare his support for the Nazi party. We *can* have less hierarchy and more democracy and still achieve organisational effectiveness. What we cannot do, however, is to pretend we can dispense with hierarchy altogether. Still less can we escape its deleterious effects and costs.

Where power is arranged as a ranked tree of asymmetrical status relations – as it so often is – it will continue to corrupt both leaders and followers, and will continue to require careful analysis and management.

In a hierarchy, when A yells at B, and B does what he is told, then A has greater power than B.[79] Such a conception of power focuses on force, on observable behaviour, subjective interests and control over decision-making. It is analogous to the way we impose our will on material objects, and its realistic simplicity perhaps explains why it has long been the most influential view – at least since the political theory of Thomas Hobbes,[80] (who in turn borrowed it from Thucydides[81]). This conception merely asks who prevails, who has more than the other. It shows power as something held by one *over* another.

This is an excessive simplification in two important respects. First, 'power over' concerns settled structures of domination and static institutionalised hierarchies.[82] Yet if hierarchy is a series, or stack, of dominant and subordinate roles, many individuals in the middle of a hierarchy must occupy both a dominant role with their subordinates and a subordinate role with their superiors. It is thus a simplification to assert that hierarchy is characterised merely by dominant and subordinate relationships, or by asymmetrical power. Here, however, our concern to explain how power corrupts has led to an interest in the effects of high relative status on individuals. This is already an arbitrary simplification; even if deployed only to 'freeze frame' the river of human interaction in order to see how it works. In fact, the sheer complexity of an organisational form that is somehow Janus-faced, is overwhelming. Among other things, it requires us to imagine how a single individual might be corrupted by power – both as a leader *and* as a follower *at the same time*; a point to which we shall later return.

The second simplification concerns the dominant/subordinate relation more generally. For power *does* take other forms. It is not, for example, always observable, nor obvious. It can be indirect, subtle and concealed. It can entail not so much force as influence, deeply embedded; and control over ideas, words and decisions that do not appear to be decisions at all. Power can insinuate itself into exclusionary institutional structures that seem entirely natural.[83] How, then are we to fathom the ways in which this kind of power corrupts?

## Ideological power and the myth of autonomy

If power was just about force, status and the raw capacity to coerce, life would be simple and the study of politics would be a science. Across our history, subordinates, slaves, workers and democratic citizens would long ago have swamped the thin layer of elite rulers that sought to keep them down, and social scientists would busy themselves with the accurate measurement of political, economic and personal power. Students of politics might then confine themselves to tweaking what had long ago emerged as *the* solution to politics – perhaps something sensible like 'council democracy' – brought into being by a series of great revolutions. But power is too elusive for that. It slips and disappears and morphs, so that revolutions are delayed, betrayed or merely dissipate. Elites rule not with guns but with ideas. And subordinates collude in their own oppression.

Nothing teaches so effectively as failure, and one of the great lessons of the Twentieth Century was that power is a good deal more complex than at first appears. Indeed, it was precisely in consideration of why revolutions failed, why Fascist and Communist dictatorships emerged and why giving women the vote did not change their social status, that our understanding of the nature of power was so rudely deepened. Critical theory, here including the work of the Frankfurt School and poststructuralism, showed us once and for all that power is not just something deployed by one over another. Instead, as we will explore here, it also designates a general capacity to act, to make and to affect.[84]

In attempting to account for the failure of the socialist revolution and the rise of Fascism, the various theorists of the Frankfurt School drew from Marx, Weber and Freud to explain how power enters individual consciousness via language, norms and routines and how it is implicated in the social construction of knowledge itself.[85] They showed that we are beings who make sense socially and who construct shared worlds of historically specific meaning which we then come to experience as reality. Fully immersed in our own ideological constructions, it can be hard to see out. We thus live in a world not only of money and guns, but also of smoke and mirrors.

Early critical theory oriented itself to finding that invisible ideology, and sought to provide a series of critical tools with which to do so. The resulting project of ideology critique spanned academic disciplines, was critical of existing politics, philosophically rigorous and methodologically self-conscious.[86] It was able to identify and engage with the great developments of history (such as capitalism) *and* to examine empirically particular events, institutions and historical conditions. Finally, it had far stronger cultural and psychological components than did earlier Marxisms. Indeed, early critical theory reached not only for ideology critique, but also for a politically engaged empirical research program, a notion of personal and artistic liberation and a collective and revolutionary politics. When pressed to articulate the psychological element in ideology, the Frankfurt School reached for contemporary advances in what was still a fairly young psychoanalytic theory.

Our understanding of the social and psychological elements of ideology was furthered again by post-structuralism and post modernism. Michel Foucault's analysis moved beyond conceptions of power as something separable from experience, or as something that simply distorted meaning. Certainly, power places 'outposts in the head',[87] and we willingly, if unwittingly, absorb dominant values and collude in our own oppression. But now we understand that power cannot be surgically removed, either from a mind or a situation, in order to reveal the truth. Power is not just a contaminant, but is also constitutive and mixed-in, like an egg in a cake. Conceived in this way, power is always and everywhere constitutive of our social world, of our knowledge of that world and even of our self-understandings.[88] Foucault concentrates on the effects of power, and shows the ways in which power makes meaning and is thus 'productive'. Productive power classifies, organises and orders knowledge in such a way as to maintain political and administrative regimes *and* to control the very concepts with which individuals see themselves.[89] This is not 'power over', but 'power to'. Such a view clearly reveals that power means much more than simply domination. Now we must acknowledge that institutions strongly influence our thinking and are productive of our subjectivities.[90]

'To speak of power', state McKinlay and Starkey, 'is to speak of politics'.[91] With power revealed to be so pervasive in the social world, across our daily organisational lives and in our very thoughts, limiting 'the political' to the traditional institutions of government becomes parochial and absurd.[92] Now, even the contents of our minds are, in part, the result of 'political' struggle, one of which we are only ever dimly aware.

Critical theory shows that we make meaning in social contexts and are influenced in our thinking by the groups, organisations and institutions among which we live. Yet, at the same time, we uphold – as one of our most basic beliefs – that our thoughts are our own, that we think for ourselves, that we are autonomous individuals. Indeed, the valorisation of autonomy in western individualism and across the history of western political thought encourages us to imagine that we are, in our own heads, somehow free from power. To think for oneself, to 'dare to know', were fundamental imperatives of the Enlightenment.[93] And autonomy – defined by Rousseau as the capacity to 'obey a law one made oneself'[94] – has long been the legitimating basis for democracy. We see ourselves as the best judge of our own interests, and so must be consulted as to the form of government we desire.

Here, then, our growing appreciation of the different dimensions of power[95] challenges what amounts to the modernist myth of autonomy. If power is so pervasive, complex and subtle, then it becomes a kind of perceptual cage, one that we cannot see beyond, and indeed, do not even know we inhabit.[96] We do not know how institutions affect our thinking and cannot, therefore, claim to know our own minds. In an important sense, our minds are not our own.

Individual autonomy is heavily compromised both by hierarchic and ideological power. Because of this, if we are to understand how power corrupts, and identify the actual mechanisms by which it does so, we need to examine more closely the interaction of social structure and individual thinking. We must, therefore, move beyond the early forms of psychoanalysis that constrained the theorists of the Frankfurt School, and step up to a more wide-ranging exploration of the complex psychological effects of inhabiting a hierarchic social structure.

In this chapter, we have sought to clarify the meaning of corruption and to show that it affects both elites and subordinates. We have also seen that although corruption by power has not received much direct attention, it *has* been explored as one of the many effects of the hierarchic organisational form. Here, we noted that corruption by power constitutes a long-standing concern in the history of democratic and republican institutions. Hierarchy, however, is not merely a dialectic of master and slave, but a complex stack of oscillating relations of power. Finally, power itself – as critical theory reveals – is not just 'power over', but is also complex and embedded, often hidden and finally, productive of meaning.

And yet, if we could only understand *how* the most simple and synchronic form of power – power over, or dominance – corrupts elites, we would have achieved something of real value. Certainly, power is complex, and affects all those who occupy hierarchic roles. But Acton's famous quote somehow derives its predictive success by claiming merely that asymmetrical status roles corrupt. 'Power over' may be only one of a complex family, but it offers an initial site in which to analyse the process of corruption. So far, however, even this most simple of social relations has escaped the attention it deserves.

How, then, is individual behaviour affected by participation in the hierarchic organisational form?

# 2
# Psychologies of Power

Psychology, as the study of the human mind, tends to begin with the individual and to come to matters social and political as something of an afterthought. The mind is structured in this or that way, people are social, in the social world there are collectives and in those collectives, power comes into play. As a result of this ordinal primacy of the individual, psychology has always struggled to provide insights into the intersubjective world. At best, the discipline has sought to plumb the complex interaction of individual and social processes, and we see this in the development of sociology and social psychology. At worst, it unwittingly adopts a methodological individualism that misses the strange and synergetic effects of groups and simply forgets about power altogether.

While it is by no means clear that collectives are merely aggregates of individuals, neither can we assume that individuals are somehow irrelevant. The problems inherent with beginning, as it were, with the nature of the individual and working up to the social, are mirrored in the explanatory gaps of the more avowedly *social* sciences. So, for example, sociology, political science and even the study of group dynamics, have shown a marked tendency to begin with collectives and to dismiss questions of individual psychology with disdain. Even the relatively recent development of 'political psychology' largely focuses on individual mental activity and its impact on mainstream political judgements. Our present concern, however – to fathom how power corrupts – requires insight into how hierarchic social structures influence individual thought. It might, therefore, be more properly referred to as a study in 'psychological politics' rather than 'political psychology'. Again, we are interested in the thorny problem of how organisations make us think.

When we ask how power corrupts, we are clearly orienting to how individual psychology plays in social and power-saturated collectives, *as well as,* how the social world is a construct of individuals. Here, then, we need to practice thinking two things at once. The relationship between individual and collective is, at least, dialectical; and as we shall see, may be more complex still.

We have already noted the general lack of direct attention paid to the question of how power corrupts. In this chapter, we draw together available insights from related studies of how individuals behave in groups. As we shall see, psychologies of power tend to accord explanatory primacy either to the individual or to the collective. A third category of approaches seeks to reach beyond this division and to examine the very processes by which individual and collective knowledge is co-constructed. We begin, therefore, by raiding studies of individuals in groups, then of groups of individuals and then of the relation of power and knowledge itself.

## Individuals in groups

At their simplest, psychological examinations of power in groups merely observe the 'fact' of asymmetrical abilities: most people are weak and a select few are stronger. It is this that explains the emergence, maintenance – and indeed prevalence – of organisational hierarchy. As both Plato and Aristotle asserted, and as management studies still asserts: some are born to lead and others to follow.[1] The appeal here is to natural capacities, to structures of character and skill internal to the individual. It is personality and individual ability that determine who will provide economic, political and military leadership. If we were to base our understanding of leadership on the books in airport business sections, for example, we would be forced to conclude that the managerial mind is truly something marvellous to behold.

It comes as no surprise, therefore, to note that one of the greatest bodies of knowledge accumulated across the history of ideas is the study of elites. Who they are, how they do it, their special characteristics, their single-handed victories – these are topics that have dominated social scientific and historical studies for generations.[2] As the recovery of social history has shown, however, such an orientation entirely ignores civil society and the lived experience of those beneath the leaders; here in order to highlight exalted individuals and to extract them as autonomous and uniquely functional agents. Quite apart from the evident elitism of such a view – which assumes that it is the actions of special individuals that drive history – groups are treated as mere aggregates of individuals.

Yet a little questioning reveals our general lack of knowledge as to *what* special skills are assumed to be valuable for leadership and our inability to account for why some people have them and others do not.[3] More questions still, and an impatience with the murky world of psychology at last reveals itself. Elitism lacks any clarity about – or even concern to account for – the relative importance of genetic and experiential factors in human learning, the roles played by privilege and class and the tendency of history to be recorded by its victors. Liberal and elite political theory, neo-classical economics and behavioural psychology generally treat the mind as a 'black box' that does not require opening. Huge architectures of explanation are then constructed on the most absurd assumptions about individual psychology. Hobbes, for example, gave us a mechanical man, a mere pin-ball machine, a 'mushroom' that appears full-grown as rational and death-avoiding adult.[4] Work up that 'rationality' into a calculus of pleasure and pain, as in utilitarianism, and we conjure notions of *homo economicus,* the utility-maximising individual, rapacious and isolated. Such characterisations of individual psychology continue to influence contemporary social science, public policy and psephology. According to the social psychologist Janet McIntosh, even Gramsci and Foucault tended to see the mind as merely a 'sponge', a *tabula rasa,* passively absorbing the mental content meted out by hegemonic power.[5] For poststructuralists and those who espouse theories of social constructionism,[6] there are few internal structures to individual psychology; or at least, none that transcend local contexts and parochial regimes of power.

Freud once helpfully remarked that all explanations of human behaviour are ultimately rather silly. Yet his conceptual notation for internal psychological processes remains the most complex and sophisticated available. Psychoanalytic theory sees the individual as buffeted from both within and without. Inside, irrational conflicts,

drives and unconscious symbolic processes require constant management, lest they swamp the individual completely. Freud thus
appeals to a compelling metaphor of internal pressure, a 'hydraulics',
all the time threatening to burst through the ego and superego.
Outside, uncertainty in the environment and the emotional requirements of others continuously demand that individual drives be
moderated. Pressed from both inside and out, human individuals
are looking for all the help they can get.

With great variety, psychoanalytic approaches see relative power
in groups and organisational hierarchy as social structures which
support the self in its ongoing struggle to adjudicate between a rapacious unconscious mind and an insistent external world. Freud
himself suggests that the roles offered by hierarchic organisations
serve to contain and control internal drives.[7] He thus sees high
status in groups as providing additional 'ego function' to those who
require it.[8] Here, then, power structures emerge and stick because
we need them to manage our selves and live successfully in a world
we share with others.

In our efforts to understand how power corrupts – and how individual psychology interacts with groups and organisations – psychoanalytic theory offers a rich and sophisticated set of critical resources.
Yet it also threatens a loss of clarity and defensibility. Two issues in
particular prevent us from freely borrowing its insights. The first
concerns the contentious *ontology* of the internal processes seen to
drive both the dynamics of individual personality and the resulting
account of social power. Though, by training, a scientist and neuro-
physiologist, Freud was also steeped in Hegelian philosophy and
German idealism. His project thus proceeds as one of symbolic
interpretation and a search for hermeneutic, rather than a scientific,
understanding.[9] As a result, his claim to have articulated the *universal* structures of personality is vulnerable to attack on a number
of fronts.

More positivist views of individual psychology dismiss psychoanalysis as little more than an arcane froth of empirically unverifiable
assumptions. It is thus variously charged with being outdated, theo-
logical and unverifiable. In addition, feminist studies have shown
that Freud's interpretations again fall short of universality. His theory
has thus been unmasked as being strongly influenced by its historical and cultural context, particularly when he blindly apes the gender

politics of his time.[10] Other highly publicised *mistakes* include the (purposive?) misinterpretation of infantile sexuality, and his reification of the oedipal complex.[11] A second problem with psychoanalytic theory follows directly upon the first: not only is it of dubious explanatory accuracy, it is also compromised as a rhetorical tool. In our analysis of how power corrupts, we must, therefore, deploy Freudian accounts of internal psychological processes with the utmost care.

At the same time, however, we cannot merely bypass internal psychology just because we lack knowledge of its structure. We need to know *how* the occupation of high status organisational roles interacts with individual psychological processes, and how this somehow serves to provide something to which individuals are drawn. Though we cannot wheel out the full Freudian architectonic, evidence does suggest that *whatever* the nature of mental processes, individuals *do* regularly engage in psychological manoeuvres which are oriented to defending and bolstering the self.[12] Indeed, it is precisely this insight that informed the subsequent development of ego psychology and object relations theory, as well as their empirical validation in developmental psychology.[13] Building on the insight that the self must be defended, Anna Freud identified a series of mechanisms for psychological defence. These included repression, denial, displacement, projection, sublimation and reaction formation.[14] Could it be, therefore, that holding power over others somehow functions as an individual mechanism of ego defence?

One problem with this view is that such defence mechanisms are usually seen as being situated *within* the individual; they are an internal tactic of individual consciousness. Yet, in the case of organisational hierarchy, we are considering the possible psychological assistance that might be provided by a hierarchic social structure. This would constitute an individual defence mechanism that lies *outside* the mind. While it helps us *here*, it is located *over there;* not in the mind but in the social structures that surround us.

If we look more closely, however, we can see that ego defences like symbolic displacement, projection and identification all entail precisely this movement of internal psychological conflict onto external objects. Freud called such 'uses of the world' 'cathexis',[15] which, in keeping with his 'hydraulic' metaphor of internal psychological pressures, he conceived as a discharge of libidinal energy out and onto an object. A psychoanalytics of power thus alerts us to significant complexity in the interaction between internal mental processes and external social structures. When power (in organisations) corrupts, it is thus likely to involve both individual *and* organisational processes. Certainly, it is not just a matter of certain 'special' individuals being able to handle power while others cannot.

A similar internal 'hydraulics', and a similar interaction of internal process and external social structure, informs perhaps the most celebrated psychoanalytic study of organisational hierarchy. The Frankfurt School's research on *The Authoritarian Personality*[16] sought to measure and compare individual attitudes to authority. They thus constructed a psychometric test with an 'f-scale', which quantified an individual's preference for hierarchy and authoritarian leadership over other organisational forms. A high 'f-scale' score was then subjected to a strongly psychoanalytic interpretation which attributed the preference for authoritarianism to an absent or overbearing father in early childhood. Such adults were seen as needing to *identify* with an all-powerful leader,[17] and so constituted fertile ground upon which authoritarianism could grow. Here, again, the help given to the individual by the hierarchic organisation turns on its availability for the identification, displacement and projection of individual processes out and onto an external object.

In psychoanalysis, such 'external' displacement usually targets a family member, or in the case of psychotherapeutic transference, the therapist. But again, we are here considering an ego defence that uses a particular organisational form. By identifying with the authoritarian leader, the impaired ego gains assistance by displacing an acute internal management problem onto something outside the self. In this, hierarchy would seem to be unique among organisational forms, for it can somehow assist the embattled self by offering an external object upon which psychological pressure can be displaced. This is a special capacity indeed, one which enables hierarchy to act as a substitute for other, mostly internal, ways in which the self manages its various conflicts.

We find this complex interaction confirmed when we follow developments in ego psychology, and turn from the evident importance of defending the self to that of actively bolstering it. In the work of Hans Kohut, the building up of the self takes centre stage in the development and individuation of the human personality.[18]

Here again we are treated to an account of internal drives, social-isation and external threats. Yet for Kohut, psychological development is characterised by a gradual building up of the self – by narcissism – now conceived as a normal part of human growth and experience. Capacity, confidence and self-esteem are here layered down, as it were, in the progressively maturing individual. The internal drive of narcissistic need, the internalisation of the empathic responses of caretakers and the reflection of identity by the external world, all combine to build and bolster an always fragile self.[19]

Kohut thus provides us with a fully developed account of how (normal) narcissistic need, or self esteem, is both a product of inter-nalisation and of public recognition. The 'taking in' of familial rela-tionships enables the growing individual to learn how to care for, soothe and feed the self. At the same time, the family begins an expanding zone of 'performance' of the self in public, so that we are first treated to familial reflections of the persona we present to others, which then move into the public spaces of school, work and social relations. Throughout this process of primary and secondary socialisation, the self absorbs a variety of ways to understand and manage its narcissistic drive. According to Kohut, this learning process continues throughout our lives, can be re-learned in therapy and adjusted in light of experience.

The continued 'normality' of the narcissistic drive – or the ongoing need for self-esteem to be both internally managed and externally confirmed – is apparent in the human tendency to be 'hurt' by nega-tive public reflections of the self. Groups and public spaces feed our persona back to us, telling us how we appear to others. When this reflection does not accord with our expectations, or the world fails to recognise our identity, we receive what Kohut calls a 'narcissistic injury'. When we are ignored, or misjudged, or when a capacity we have worked hard to perfect is belittled, we are in receipt of such an 'injury'.[20] While some are more 'thick skinned' than others, most can readily recognise the accuracy of Kohut's insight. Telling the brick-layer that the wall is not straight is to invite a response that more than adequately confirms the very human need to preserve a func-tional level of self esteem. As we shall see, the propensity to mete out 'narcissistic injuries' – both intended and unintended – is a defining characteristic of those corrupted by power.

For Kohut, then, we are indeed individuals in groups; always and necessarily so. Here, however, the processes by which the self is established are at once individual *and* social. The articulation of these processes builds on the more refined and verifiable body of knowledge that emerged from Freud's initial pioneering work – in other words, on object relations and developmental psychology. Kohut thus enables us to put flesh on the bones of our first tentative symptom of corruption by power: that of 'self inflation'. It allows us, for example, to move beyond Minow's allusion to a 'privileging of subjectivity' and towards a more careful, and defensible, account of the role played by perceptions of the self and of others in a process of corruption. Now we can see that the 'growing self-confidence' and 'aggrandisement' of the corrupt leader is indeed a cancerous mushrooming of what is an entirely normal process: that of building and bolstering self esteem.

What then emerges from psychoanalytic approaches to power in organisations is that the occupation of the respective roles of dominance and subordination somehow does psychological work for the individual self. Corruption by power involves a complex interaction between social structure and individual psychological processes. We can say with some surety that the self must develop at the same time as it is buffeted by internal drives and external imperatives. Yet we should not be tempted to over-extend this insight, for once again, we can say little about the precise *nature* of these internal drives. Nor can we easily progress by simply pointing to specific external threats faced by the individual self, and which might, therefore, demand defence.[21] Is corruption by power an escape from internal aggression,[22] terror,[23] anxiety[24] or freedom?[25] Is it a response to contingency, a failure of public recognition, a natural need for leadership, of peer and group pressures, or the material facts of scarcity, informational bottlenecks in organisations[26] or the inevitability of death?[27] Or, perhaps from all of the above?

Psychologies of power that adhere to a methodological individualism thus assist our understanding of how power corrupts, but begin to falter as we focus on the role played in individual mental activity by social and organisational contexts. While it can be argued that individuals are more than sufficiently difficult to comprehend – even in atomised isolation – it is in groups that we live and make meaning, and in groups that we take decisions. More avowedly *social* psychologies that adopt a greater methodological holism are better able to identify – and thus seek to explain – a greater variety of the decidedly strange occurrences that characterise our social interactions, collectives and institutions. Groups, therefore, are more than merely an aggregation of individuals.[28]

## Groups of individuals

We have seen that institutionalised asymmetrical power can deliver organisational effectiveness *and* meet individual psychological needs. But it may also perform more social functions. Indeed, any account of hierarchy would be incomplete if it failed to consider the growing body of knowledge which addresses the social and psychological needs of *groups themselves*.[29] The claim to which we now turn is that there is something about *us when we get together* that brings hierarchic relations of power into being, maintains them and then continues to affect how individuals think.[30]

Holistic approaches in social psychology and group dynamics see social structure as partly an expression of individual psychological need and partly one of *collective* need. Hierarchy here assists both individuals *and* groups as they struggle to manage complex emotional, and indeed psychoanalytic, concerns. Wilfred Bion, for example, describes groups as helping to mediate between individual drives and external reality.[31] Yet where groups are distorted by *collective* psychological dynamics – here in the form of 'basic assumptions' – the collective entity becomes dysfunctional. Basic assumptions are, for Bion, recurrent and disruptive processes that occur *in groups*. Operating beneath individual awareness, they include scapegoating, excessive dependence on the leader, the collective selection and manipulation of a particular pair of individuals and a collective 'fight or flight' response.[32] Here, dysfunctional psychological processes located *in the group itself* are seen to drive the emergence and continuation of institutionalised asymmetries of power.

Clearly, to locate the causal structures for hierarchic relations of power in the 'distinct emotional states of groups',[33] is to raise complex problems of ontology. The group here appears as a collective entity that exhibits emotion and intention and thus resembles a sentient being in its own right; seemingly with internal pressures and structural imperatives of its own. Certainly, in our common conceptions, we often anthropomorphise and naturalise collectives, and groups can appear to take on their own 'character', 'beliefs' and 'culture'; characteristics that can appear unrelated to the individuals of which they are comprised. An institution can thus be 'racist' when its constituent members are not (sic),[34] and collective beings like 'the efficient German midfield' achieve total independence from the way individuals actually play.[35]

Though we can conceive of a group that thinks, and perhaps even of a 'collective mind', clarity around such notions is hard to come by. First, it is by no means obvious *where* the structures and mechanisms that constitute such collective entities *are actually located*, or of what stuff they are made. Second, as Margaret Gilbert so carefully shows, it is only under certain quite constricted conditions that it makes sense to attribute shared beliefs and attitudes to collectives. Certainly, there are such things as 'plural subjects'.[36] They can come into being when a belief is jointly accepted by (most?) members of the group; when that belief has been agreed to by individuals as that which is jointly accepted by the group; and where certain obligations upon accepting a group belief properly pertain.[37] In other words, groups *can* be plural subjects; but only when individuals agree that collective judgements are their own, and continue to do so.

Most groups, organisations and institutions do not meet such stringent conditions. Instead, empirical studies of group-based social inequality and the psychological bases of tyranny show how easily we adopt hierarchies based on the perceived superiority of one class, gender or 'arbitrary set' of individuals, and then come to see that hierarchy as 'natural'.[38] Primitive notions of group superiority thus involve an extrapolation from the *fact* that a particular group has emerged in practice as dominant; first to assert that this group's dominance *must* be fulfilling a collective function, and then to raise a normative claim that this group *should* be dominant *because* it performs that function. Logically, Hume's Fork allows no such derivation of values from facts, and encourages us to resist so naturalistic a fallacy.

Yet even if we resist anthropomorphising collectives and reject unreflective claims to natural sub-group superiority, we cannot deny the prevalence and complexity of power stratifications within and between groups. Indeed, most adults see the world in terms of a 'pyramid of authority', and five minutes in a school playground confirms our collective fascination for intrigue, scapegoating, relative status and relations of power. As we shall see, some researchers even suspect humans have an innate ability to rapidly assess the relations of power that surround us. In an instant, we can recognise the relative status of our own group, our place within it and any possible threats from outside. It is then this 'sixth sense' – what we might call our 'relative power' sense – that enables us to identify available victims, deviants and scapegoats – onto which we can (psychologically) displace our collective needs. In the case of the individual corrupted by power, it would appear that this 'relative power' sense is fully exploited for personal gain.

One approach that seeks to explicate the empirical reality of the power struggles that endlessly occur within and between groups is that of Realistic Group Conflict theory.[39] Here, the preservation of a collective entity, now reified as a 'group' with its own history and identity, *requires* solidarity and cohesion. To function in a cruel and contingent world, groups need norms and boundaries, and thus also, the capacity to exclude those who breach them. Social structure in general and hierarchy in particular is here seen to help groups cohere, fight and prevail. A hierarchy sets everyone in their place, ensures common experience and defines membership.

As with all 'realistic' accounts of social phenomena, conflict-based group theories marshal powerful empirical confirmation that groups are engaged in a zero-sum competition over resources. Groups are then seen to have adopted organisational hierarchy in order to fulfil their own 'psychological' needs and 'identities'. The argument here is that groups prefer hierarchies; they're just funny that way. You can tell they do because hierarchy is so prevalent. Once again, then, we slip into reifying the collective, and move too quickly from identifying a (group) function fulfilled by organisational hierarchy to imagining we have justified that hierarchy – again violating Hume's Fork. In addition, conflict-based intergroup theories are not particularly good at distinguishing individual differences in how people are affected by groups, and are tempted to see group members as homogeneous. Groups then appear as single entities somehow exercising a 'group mind' effect on individuals.[40] With social roles directly determining individual behaviour, conformity becomes passive[41] and any understanding of who, when and how power corrupts disappears over the horizon.

Perhaps social psychology's most concerted and influential explanation for hierarchic social relations and their interaction with individual psychology is that offered by Social Identity theory.[42] Studiously avoiding the pitfalls of collective reification and the simplistic attribution of 'reality' to social interactions, Social Identity theory holds that humans crave, for their own self-esteem, the experience of group membership. Individuals need to *identify* with a group, to define boundaries of 'us and them', to hold their own group in high esteem; and to stereotype, devalue and exclude outsiders. Our individual identity must share a social identity. Groups select and support hierarchy because it provides the group membership individuals crave. Social Identity theory thus presents us with an account of power relations that incorporates psychological *and* social elements, and does so without losing a 'location' for the mechanisms which bring it into being: such mechanisms are located within the individual, and they pertain to the relative status of the group.

Social Identity theory has been strenuously criticised, both for its methodological individualism, its explanatory inconsistencies and for its inability to account for 'the extreme levels of barbarism, brutality, and oppression often found in intergroup relations in the real world'.[43] Yet the strength of Social Identity theory lies not in its analysis of the actual mechanisms that underlie the general psychological need for membership of a high status group. Nor is it particularly able to recognise differences in intensity with which individuals identify with their own ingroup and demonise outgroups.[44] What Social Identity theory does do, however, is to move beyond conceptions of group roles as directly determining behaviour.[45] Conformity is not passive, but active. Power 'over' involves a complex interplay of individual and collective identities. Individual responses to the occupation of a high status role thus vary widely and are sensitive to contexts.[46] For this reason, Social Identity theory is perhaps the most fully articulated *psychological* theory seeking to address questions of power.

It is when the individualistic psychological theory of Social Identity is augmented with a more profoundly *social psychological* approach, however, that we begin to gain real insight into how power corrupts. Seeking to address some of the explanatory lacunae of Social Identity theory, Social Dominance theory sees humans as having what amounts to a biological drive for social inequality.[47] It is our evolutionary past that predisposes us towards hierarchy and to competition between groups. Each of us has a degree of attraction to authoritarian social relations, and a tendency to buy into the

'legitimating myths' deployed to defend them. Of particular interest, however, is that some have more than others.[48] In attempting to
explain why this is the case, Social Dominance theory begins by
making the crucial move towards the incorporation of organisational contexts. Sidanius and Pratto are thus able to assert that,
'one's social status, influence, and power are also a function of one's
group membership and not simply of one's individual abilities
or characteristics'.[49] Indeed, we can here observe that hierarchic
relations of power are 'driven by three proximal processes'. These
include: individual (discriminatory) behaviour, institutional (discriminatory) behaviour and their supporting 'social discourse[s]
(e.g., ideology, attitudes, and stereotypes)'.[50] Here, then, we are at
last playing with all the cards.

According to Social Dominance theory, any given organisational
environment is filled with individuals variously drawn to authoritarianism, as well as organisations variously utilising the hierarchic
organisational form. Both are shot through with 'social discourses'
that support authoritarianism. When they work together, the outcome is corruption by power, mission drift, arbitrary cruelty and
different forms of terror.[51]

The 'Social Dominance Orientation' (SDO) of individuals has been
extensively measured, and responses have been compared across
social groups and cultural contexts. It has been shown that 'men,
Whites, and heterosexuals had higher SDO levels than women,
Hispanics, Afro-Americans, gays, lesbians, and bisexuals'.[52] White
police officers (in both Los Angeles and New Zealand) were found to
have a higher SDO than those who were members of other ethnic
groups, and SDO levels were seen to perfectly mirror the complex
'hierarchic layers of Israeli society'.[53]

Social Dominance theory can also demonstrate empirically that
an individual's attraction to hierarchy tends to increase upon elevation of social status and upon gaining membership of a higher
status groups.[54] This suggests that certain individuals are more strongly
attracted to authoritarian power relations than are others; so that,
when given the right organisational environment and supporting
ideologies, they are particularly vulnerable to corruption by power.
What this empirical data does *not* do, of course, is to 'demonstrate
that holding higher group status *causes* SDO to increase'.[55] Certainly,
we can see that roles with higher social status tend to enhance levels

of SDO,[56] but again, because SDO is driven by individual proclivity in conjunction with particular organisations with particular ideologies, the outcome cannot be attributed to one cause alone. SDO is not, therefore, able to measure corruption by power.

Though Social Dominance theory shows that elevated status correlates positively with acceptance of hierarchy-enhancing ideologies, it also supports Machiavelli and Rousseau's observation that subordinate groups can themselves show high levels of SDO. Though only recently revealed as an element in the explanation of hierarchy, and often criticised for its tendency to blame the victim, subordinate collusion has proven a fruitful line of research.[57] So, for example, the analysis of post-colonial identities and the subtle psychology of oppression[58] illustrate how asymmetrical relations of power are co-created by both elites and subordinates.

According to Sidanius and Pratto, 'subordinates actively participate in and contribute to their own subordination'.[59] Indeed, it is precisely this 'co-creative' element of social hierarchy that is seen to explain its 'remarkable degrees of resiliency, robustness, and stability'.[60] Of particular interest is the observation that sometimes, in the case of subordinate groups, the usual favouritism towards ingroup members is somehow trumped by outgroup favouritism towards those with higher social status.[61] In such cases, subordinates come to believe that those who dominate them are indeed better than themselves. They therefore appear to have internalised the negative stereotypes promulgated by their superiors to the extent that they now judge themselves accordingly. In this way, they see themselves as deserving of their lot. With subordinates becoming, in effect, 'self-debilitating',[62] we again witness the complex interactions of social structure and identity that somehow bring organisational hierarchies into being. Here also, social inequality is seen to generate precisely the ideological blinkers and self-conceptions required for its own preservation.[63]

Social Justification theory takes this notion further still.[64] Here, what we all carry within us is not a basic psychological orientation towards group-based social inequality, but instead, a deep psychological need for the social structures under which we live to be legitimate. We want to support the status quo, and to see it as being there for good reasons.[65] Social Justification theory thus seeks to address the mystery that not *everyone* shows an ingroup bias. As

Social Dominance theory points out, some groups – particularly those of low relative status – often exhibit a bias towards the very out-group that oppresses them, and in this way seem to collude in their own oppression. Individuals – both dominant and subordinate – thus maintain hierarchic social relations by indulging their psychological need for beliefs that serve to maintain hierarchy and to legitimise existing social relations.[66] In this way, Social Justification theory deepens Social Dominance theory's analysis of 'legitimating myths', for it claims that these myths themselves fulfil a basic, individual and psychological need.

The nature of the human mind, and the nature of group inter-actions, thus seems to favour the hierarchic organisational form and serve the interests of dominant elites. In the first chapter of *Capital*, Marx sets out the ways in which capitalism so cleverly conceals the real and exploitative nature of its activities.[67] When the full complexity of this concealment at last reveals itself, Marx steps back and exclaims: 'moneybags must be so lucky!' as to have all these processes working in his favour. Our examination of the complex ways in which hierarchic relations of power insinuate themselves into our minds, interactions, myths and social structures, suggests, similarly, that 'elites must be so lucky', as to have all these processes working to assist them.

This section has explored social psychological approaches that offer a more holistic methodology to the study of how individuals and groups interact. Such approaches again counsel us to note the ways in which group dynamics and social structures both affect – and do psychological work for – individuals. Yet they show a different level of insight into the ontology of group dynamics themselves. At the extreme, notions of collective entities are reified and anthropomorphised. Yet more considered accounts reveal the evident synergetic effects of groups and show that they involve inter-actions between individual and collective that are of extraordinary complexity. In particular, groups provide individuals with a public space through which to perform their identities, to receive feedback, challenge and confirm those identities. Indeed, individual identity here emerges as something that is almost inconceivable as an atomised project. As Wittgenstein so helpfully asserted, there is no private language. Identity is at least in part a social project, one that is intimately tied to the social structures it inhabits. When we ask how power corrupts, therefore, we are always inspecting the 'boundary effects' of individuals and groups.

At the same time, however, internal psychological needs for certain kinds of social structure seem also to be in play. Whether innate or learned, respective individual 'attraction' to organisational hierarchy, and credulity towards its attendant justifications, are varied; and measurably so. They not only differ between individuals, but also between those who come to occupy dominant and subordinate roles.

It is at the boundary of individual and group that identity is co-created, that self-understandings, attitudes and beliefs, are both made and discovered. Clearly, understanding a process as complex as individual corruption by social relations of power requires us to think two things at once – and perhaps even more; for we are here moving closer to inspecting the very construction of meaning itself. Rather than shy away from this implication, however, we must now examine psychologies of power that address the construction of meaning directly, and seek to account for the prevalence and durability of hierarchy by pointing to the very way we come to know.

## Social, rough and reified terrain

The physical world challenges us to gain knowledge of a relatively stable object domain, one apparently independent of the knowing subject. The boiling point of water is not related to the mood of the cook. Physical processes thus invite causal explanations and 'covering' universal laws that apply across social contexts. The same cannot be said for the social world, for here we gaze upon meanings which are contextually specific, differently experienced in different cultures and which seem to be constituted, not by stable and universal facts, but by interrelated symbols and perspectival interpretations.[68] It is of little surprise, then, that social scientists have regularly treated us to accounts of the social world in which it is ontologically distinguished from its physical-objective and aesthetic-subjective counterparts.[69]

The unstable object domain of human affairs thus presents (at least) two significant problems. The first can be referred to as the problem of 'mutual causation', though it is variously referred to in sociological theory as 'concurrent', 'dialectical' or 'bi-directional' causation. We live in a social world, one teeming with symbols and practices which are somehow constructed and maintained by social interaction. Yet while our social activity causes our social world to be what it is, so too, and at the same time, does that social world give us the categories and meanings in which we experience that world. We therefore both *make*, and *are made by*, the social world in which we live. In contrast to the physical world, the ontology of the social is one where 'the product acts back on the producer'.[70] The second epistemological problem generated by the shifting ontology of the social world is that we cannot escape the prospect of its systematic mystification. Once we admit that objective truth eludes us, the possibility that our view is contaminated by power cannot be ruled out. When it comes to human affairs, we thus gaze upon a realm whose actual nature may be distorted and concealed. Here we take each in turn.

The problem of mutual causation arises because we are, in the case of the social world, attempting to gain knowledge of an object which is *not* independent of our attempts to understand it. There is an 'uncertainty principle' in operation here; one that arises from the fact that the social world both causes, and is caused by, the knowing subject. Our understanding of mutual causation was much aided by the linguistic turn in continental philosophy, as language – itself a social construct[71] – confronts the individual as an existing external fact. At the same time, the acquisition of language provides the categories of thought and horizons of understanding of individual experience. Language is thus a powerful example of the mutual causation of the social world.

We might not guess this if we confine ourselves to recent work on knowledge in organisations, particularly that emanating from 'new institutional approaches'.[72] For the most part, these concentrate on a single pole of mutual causation: that of the social construction of the social world – here seen as a network of human-authored institutions. Though such approaches have certainly generated advances in our understanding, Mary Douglas, for example, is scathing of institutionalist inattention to the ways in which individual cognition is affected by institutions,[73] or what she calls the 'social basis of cognition'. Her work stresses the importance of this oft forgotten pole, particularly in understanding how institutions achieve stability and win commitment from their members. She thus highlights the ways in which the social world influences individual memory, recognition and the classification of knowledge.[74]

To recover the social basis of cognition, Douglas resurrects and clarifies Durkheim and Fleck's pioneering theoretical program,[75] in which they sought to overcome the inadequacies of behaviourist psychology.[76] Here, she suggests, we find an extraordinary attempt to grasp both the social construction of reality *and* the reality of social constructions. A crucial part of this research program was precisely to draw attention to the bi-directional ontology of the social world. Douglas recovers this element of their work as a corrective to contemporary social science, which she sees as downplaying this important direction of causation.

Durkheim and Fleck sought to explain how the meanings, actions and understandings which constitute the social world have such extraordinary stability. Indeed, they showed that social constructions can be empirically validated and measured as facts. Sociology should, therefore, 'treat social facts as things'.[77] The 'thought collectives'[78] which construct the social world could meaningfully be studied *as though* they were 'real'. This they attributed to the capacity of social constructions to appear as though their ontology was the same as that of the material world.

However, in Durkheim and Fleck's account of mutual causation, it is not at all clear *where* this 'capacity' is located. Is it, for example, in the socially constructed object, so that the social world actively *mimics* the material? Or is it in the perceiving subject, who cannot tell the difference between a social construction and a material object? If the latter, the *individual* might then be said to have the 'special capacity' – here, to experience social constructions as 'real'. The problem of properly *locating* this capacity resembles the difficulties we encountered when examining conceptions of group processes that seemed to ascribe intention to groups. As with notions of group intention, Durkheim and Fleck at last postulated a collective and sentient entity (in the form of a 'collective consciousness'), at which point most social scientists parted company with their intellectual project.

Psychologies of power – be they methodologically individualistic or holistic – show just how difficult it is to distinguish between individual mental activity and organisational 'culture'. Each affects the other; each influences and is influenced by the other. Our investigation into corruption by power, taking place as it does at this complex interface, demands that we think in both directions at once. Indeed, as research on the individual and social elements in the construction of identity shows, we can barely distinguish between an individual and a collective. The dualism of subject and object, particularly in the intersubjective world of organisations and human symbolic culture, simply does not hold.[79]

One way in which researchers have sought to understand the prevalence of the hierarchic organisational form, and to inspect the complex dynamic that occurs at the boundary of individual and social structure, is thus to focus on the nature of knowledge itself. In these accounts of power in organisations, there is *something about how we know* that endlessly, and inadvertently, brings hierarchic social relations into being. Human epistemology might, therefore, be such as to produce hierarchy as an unintended side-effect of our more general efforts to learn. If this is the case, then corruption by power might itself be an epistemological matter, a twisting and distortion of perception and thus, what amounts to a disorder of knowing.

In effect, such approaches suggest that knowledge is so intimately connected to power that the very (intersubjective) nature of the social world serves to play a series of tricks upon us. Denied objective knowledge, we evince a strong tendency to mythologise the symbolic world in which live.

For example, in Horkheimer and Adorno's extraordinary book, the *Dialectic of Enlightenment*, critical theory steps up to suggest that it is the internal logic of Western reason itself that brings hierarchy into being.[80] By imposing rational analysis upon the world, drawing distinctions and categorising according to similarity and difference, we are seen to express, in vain, our desperate longing for certainty and mastery over our environment. Gradually, ineluctably, we bend all experience and turn all our thoughts, forcing them to conform to the doomed mythical project of being in control.[81] Hierarchy simplifies, it assists control and so is greedily recruited to the cause. Our exquisitely destructive hierarchies thus take the forms they do because they are side-effects of a larger, historically specific, epistemological project known as the Enlightenment.

A similar explanatory move occurs in the philosophy of language, particularly in post-structuralism, where again, the source of hierarchic relations of power is epistemological. Now, though, the driving cause is located in the signs we use to communicate. Language itself, and the boundaries that words place on concepts, determine how we make meaning and how we construct our social and institutional practices.[82] If, as Derrida asserts, the text is all and nothing exists outside of it, then the way language gets used is constitutive of political orders in general and hierarchy in particular. Combine this with Foucault's conception of power as being not just about domination but also as 'productive' of our identities, then hierarchy is at once a social order that is taken deep into the self, and one that we maintain in the very ideas we have about the world.[83]

Blurring the boundary between individual and collective, and conceiving power as a contaminant of social knowledge, raises the question of how conscious we are of such processes. Critical theory and post-structuralism strongly suggest that what passes as individual autonomy and the independence of social structure are myths. The very manner in which we make meaning is concealed from us. For their part, Durkheim and Fleck were quite clear that the social basis of individual cognition is invisible to individuals themselves. 'The individual', Fleck asserts, '...is never, or hardly ever, conscious of the prevailing thought style which almost always exerts an absolutely compulsive force upon his thinking'.[84] Not only is individual cognition influenced by the social world, but this direction of causation takes place beyond individual awareness. Indeed, it is the very invisibility of this causal direction that allows what are, in fact, socially constructed entities to be experienced *as though they were real*.

The suggestion here is that institutions colonise our minds in ways we cannot see. One effect of this is to enable asymmetrical relations of power to *pretend* that they are natural and objectively real. The legitimacy claims of authority trade heavily on this human tendency to 'forget' that our reality is socially constructed. Once a social structure is revealed as merely social construction, its capacity to provide legitimacy is weakened. It is, therefore, imperative for the preservation of authority, states Douglas, that such structures are 'not seen as a socially contrived arrangement',[85] and are kept 'secret'.[86] She then goes on to state that, 'the high triumph of institutional thinking is to make the institutions completely invisible'.[87] In this, Douglas is in agreement with Foucault, who stated the goal of his work to be that of revealing the artificiality and partiality of institutions that *pretend* to be natural and impartial.[88] Being immersed in dominant values and shared meanings enables us to think and see in certain ways, yet that immersion renders other meanings invisible. We can always ask: here and now and within the horizon of our own culture, 'what are the impossible thoughts?'[89] Which of our most cherished beliefs will we later come to recognise as nonsense? Who are we currently oppressing without realising it? Humans are situated epistemological agents, awash in emotion, interaction and a teeming social world.[90] As William Connolly remarks, 'presumptive universals... have grown up like underbrush in and around you', and we inhabit a social world in which 'practices... feel like universals'.[91]

Clearly, accounts which stress mutual causation and reveal the contamination of knowledge by power fly in the face of the long tradition of western individualism. They challenge the enduring fiction that our minds are our own. Experiencing ourselves as knowing subjects, we imagine that our thoughts and feelings are independent of the organisations among which we move. We are individuals first. Only secondarily are we participants in organisations.

This is an intriguing figment. In retrospect, we can clearly see that individuals were once strongly conditioned by their organisational involvements to believe all manner of absurdities, and to imagine that these thoughts were their own. In history, the overwhelming capacity of institutions to determine much of the content of an individual's mind is easier to spot. Ideology is visible in hindsight. So we smile at the King who thought himself 'God's lieutenant'; we shake our heads knowingly when we read the memoirs of slave owners, we are amazed at the cruelties of the past. Looking back, we can recognise the lack of independent thought, the dumb conformity to power, the unreflective acceptance of ideologies that now litter the floor of history; their capacity to motivate and construct the internal world of their adherents long since departed. With hindsight, then, we can see that organisations and institutions once peddled distorted knowledge, and that, all too often, our ancestors were little more than naïve realists. They imagined they gazed directly upon the only possible world; they felt, deep in their hearts, the rightness of their moral values and the legitimacy of their absurdly hierarchic organisations. They did not see what we see now.

Today, we claim to be more reflective and to have risen above such mythical distortions. We have better science, we have representative democracy, human resource management and reflective modernity.[92] Now, therefore, we deny we are naïve realists. However, all previous generations made similar denials. Apparently, quite unlike all who have preceded us across the whole of history, we imagine we at last gaze upon reality. We do not see ideology at play in our own lives. The problem, of course, is that it is at least possible that what is visible in retrospect is still active today. If so, it would, again, be invisible.

The accusation of invisibility: that something exists that is beneath consciousness, is only ever a good argument when made retrospectively; by which time it is redundant. Prior to the object's appearance, the claim appears absurd. Afterwards, when the object is there for all to see, the claim seems obviously, and trivially, true. The fact of ideology's invisibility thus presents difficulties for those who would engage in its critique, for they must point at something that cannot be seen. Invisible ideology cannot be revealed by squinting more carefully. It does not disclose itself to empirical investigation. The racist finds his distorted prejudices confirmed by experience.[93] The misogynist 'sees' that women are worse drivers than men. As with an optical illusion, it is as if the very world itself is habitually lying to us. Where an object is invisible, it has, for the one who cannot see, no existence. The invisible object can enter awareness only when some additional sensory input – formerly excluded or simply unavailable – at last reveals its presence. The disclosure of an object which was formerly invisible to us is, of course, an act of learning. It gives us greater confidence that we are now looking at what is really the case, enables us to identify mere appearance and allows us to theorise as to why we could not see the object before.

That which is out of mind fails to receive critical questioning. We see this in recent accounts of moral judgement. Where something appears to us to be of moral import, such as the suffering of another, we weigh up our actions in moral terms. What should we do? What is the 'right' thing to do? What sort of person am I? It has thus been suggested that serious failures of moral behaviour, such as shown by the likes of Eichmann, Karadic or Sutcliffe, involve incorrect moral *reasoning*. But it would be more accurate to describe this as a *perceptual* error, one that results in a palpable failure to see. Vetlesen, for example, shows that the perception of another's suffering is a *precondition* for moral judgement.[94] Without the emotional response of empathy, he argues, the suffering of another *never appears* as an object of moral import, and consequently, never gets reasoned about at all. Eichmann's moral failure was not, therefore, bad judgement, *qua* bad thinking. It was due, rather, to a complete *absence* of moral judgement.[95] In this case, the suffering of the other is filtered out before any moral questions arise, and the other is effectively dehumanised.

Empathy is the ability to perceive the suffering of another. Failing to empathise renders the humanity of the other invisible and blocks off moral reasoning. This inability turns out to be a recurrent effect of hierarchic and asymmetrical power. When power corrupts, dominants are unable to empathise with subordinates, and so are more likely to harm them with moral impunity.[96] Indeed, returning to the insights offered by Social Dominance theory, we can note that 'the greater one's empathy, the lower one's level of SDO' (social dominance order).[97]

When we watch the rapist, the child molester, or the torturer discussing his crime, we observe the same inability to *see* the suffering he has caused. Lacking empathy – which in moral judgement provides perceptual access to the weal and woe of others – the torturer exhibits the bounded confines of his visible world. And because we see *more* than he, because we can readily witness the other's suffering, we say that his is a false consciousness, that his identity is impoverished; perhaps brutalised by trauma and twisted by mechanisms of defence. In this way, the one who does not see is the exemplar of bad judgement. The quality of moral judgement is thus improved when we overcome perceptual distortions and at last witness the suffering of others. Such a revelation is tantamount to re-humanisation, and in the few cases that it occurs to the murderer or rapist, occasions a devastating flood of remorse.

The social world is a whirl of smoke and mirrors. We can never be sure that our perceptions are accurate, that we are not being manipulated, that our thoughts are really our own. To assist us here, we can again follow Marx, who drew similar conclusions when he sought to reveal the subtle ways in which capitalism deceives its participants, and mystifies and masquerades as objectivity. In particular, he sought to identify two types of perceptual distortion, each generating its own respective form of false consciousness; each enabling capitalism to hide its true nature behind ideology and to disable those who might, if they saw the truth, resist.

First, Marx was much troubled by the problem of limited perspective or partiality of view. At the micro-level, in people's work and daily lives, he argued, capitalism conceals the source of its profits, its apparent super-productivity and even the fact of its exploitation. Only at the macro-level, only in the system as a whole, does profit equate with the total surplus value extracted from the entire working class.[98] Only here, he claimed, could the one who steals the surplus generated by collective labour, be identified,[99] and the truly exploitative nature of capitalism be revealed. Marx's conceptual instrumentation, whether its equations are right or wrong, is designed to show that capitalism is, in reality, a system, a global process, a huge wood. It is not, *as it appears to individuals*, a single tree; no matter how that tree might lie astride our path and dominate our lives.

This first kind of perceptual failure then, which takes the form of a chronic partiality of view, or parochialism, prevents us from seeing the aggregate of our actions, or the big picture. In this way it operates to screen off the *social* costs of labour over-utilisation,[100] of unemployment, of environmental damage and the economic devastation of poorer countries; so allowing capitalism to *appear* efficient. It also debilitates local actors. For them, partiality is a form of blindness. It results in poor political judgement, divisive competition and the inability to effectively coordinate resistance. Yet Marx believed that this kind of deception *could* be overcome, if only by learning to see from a new perspective. Indeed, this was his great and unfulfilled hope: that local actors would pool their knowledge, overcome their partiality and so cast off their chains.

The same cannot be said for the second kind of perceptual distortion he explored: social constructions which *appear* to be physical processes. As social and symbolic beings, as believing beings, our imaginings come to appear real. Marx famously called this our 'religious reflex'.[101] In the opening chapter of *Capital*, he shows how the value of a commodity appears real while being, in fact, 'a mysterious thing',[102] concealing a particular set of social relations. Here, a 'social product'[103] comes to appear as natural,[104] and no amount of evidence to the contrary, nor change in perspective, can ever dispel its deceptive appearance. Capitalism mystifies, it fetishises, it *reifies*, and in so doing, generates illusions which are durable and almost impossible to dispel.[105] Marx used economic and socio-cultural analysis, but he also played with language and literary form in order to tease out such delusions, to demystify social reality, to encourage us to see differently. He tried to show that the value category was a deception, that capitalism's inequalities only *appeared* natural and that its institutions were merely self-legitimising. He knew full well that reification resists empirical falsification, and that, consequently, this kind of illusion was almost inescapable. For in cases such as this, we cannot get behind the immediate evidence of appearance. As with the self-fulfilling prophecy, with paradigm blindness, and with prejudice, we here confront a false world which is somehow self-confirming. Capitalism thus maintains its domination by trading on the fact that, in McIntosh's words, 'human minds are better at representing some things than others'.[106]

Marx's understanding of the perceptual distortions inherent in capitalist ideology has subsequently been deepened in the study of the 'productive' nature of power. Neo-Foucauldian research, though tending towards an idealist view of social structure which lacks the Marxist attention to material forces, provides a sophisticated analysis of the mutual causation that occurs between the individual and the social. Indeed, so subtly is this relation conceived that the individual begins to blend into the social, to be constituted by it and so to finally disappear as a social category. 'After the subject' comes a self-reinforcing perceptual cage from which the now entirely disempowered agent can never hope to escape, or even to think in ways beyond the surrounding regimes of power and knowledge. For Nicholas Rose, for example, the postmodern self has fully internalised the interests of power, to the extent that all possibility of resistance, and even the *thought* of resistance, is effectively removed.[107]

Psychologies of power that direct our attention to epistemological matters serve to highlight the complex ontology of the social world. Mutual causation of individual and collective and the possibility of contamination by power, combine to place objectivity out of reach. In play, here, is the strong human tendency to reify what are, in fact, social constructions. The social world is mystified, its nature concealed; and in ways we cannot see. Beneath our awareness, processes are at work of which we remain blithely unaware. In order to reveal these processes, and thus to identify how power corrupts, we need to understand better how the human mind actually processes knowledge and makes meaning. As we shall see, and as the above quote from McIntosh suggests, our perceptual mechanisms are so structured as to encourage us to make certain kinds of mistakes. These

tists do not engage sufficiently with the current revolution in cognitive psychology, they fail to stipulate the mechanisms which underlie their (merely) functional explanations of social phenomena.[5] In a similar vein, Schott has criticised administrative science for ignoring such developments,[6] and Stein laments their absence in the analysis of power in institutions.[7] Sidanius and Pratto baldly state that 'people in institutional settings have been little studied'.[8] Where cognitive psychology has been used, for example in social theory,[9] behavioural economics[10] and the analysis of persuasion,[11] the engagement has either been rather shallow, distorted by assumptions of rational self-interest or tending to skip any coherent epistemological introduction of the tools being used. Turner himself commits this latter (if rhetorical) mistake; for though he claims that cognitive psychology's identification of the basic building blocks of human thought has profound implications across the social sciences, he does not concern himself with introducing these building blocks. Quickly, cognitive psychologists return their research attention to more technical concerns, just as economists slide back into rational choice. Turner does not bother to defend his assertion that cognitive psychology offers a superior framework for the analysis of social knowledge. Rather, he flatly declares that, 'basic cognitive operations... are universal among human beings'.[12] Such capacities, he states, run 'across all cultures, all histories, all languages, past, passing, and to come'.[13] He shows little awareness of the hard-won suspicion of such 'universal' capacities we find in social theory, and because of this, his work does not translate into the conceptual language of other disciplines.[14]

Cognitive science now dominates the field of psychology, but its claim to species-wide structures of individual information processing remains methodologically distasteful to many social scientists. The identification of universal and structural tendencies for individuals to think in certain ways smacks of determinism and epistemological self-righteousness, and the claim to experimental verification looks like pubescent positivism. Yet when we properly understand the project, and the extraordinary analytic tools it now offers, we must conclude that these are false charges. Certainly, cognitive science suffers from epistemological delusions, is beset with a limiting methodological individualism and remains extraordinarily innocent of power.[15] But once its limitations are recognised – and which academic discipline does not have its own? – it nevertheless provides discerning tools with which to analyse the social construction of knowledge and the effects of institutionalised power on the way individuals think.

Because cognitive psychology remains poorly understood outside its own disciplinary boundaries, this chapter will first provide a brief introduction to, and clarification of, those of its concepts relevant to this investigation. Here, developments in the study of individual cognition are explored, particularly those that stress its selectivity, the knowledge gains such selectivity provides and the processing errors it causes.[16]

## Cognitive tendencies

In the quest for knowledge about how the human mind works, behaviourism offered distinct advantages to psychoanalytic theory. By concentrating on the immediate relation of stimulus to response, behaviourism offered an improved orientation to human action, empirically verifiable theories and concrete practical interventions. To deliver advances in behaviourist theory, the actual contents of the mind were bracketed off to enable the quantitative measurement, and the targeted control of, behaviour. For behaviourists, there was nothing of interest *between* stimulus and response. Indeed, the human mind appeared as little more than a black box, a place-holder, a realm of unnecessary complexity in which Freudians wandered aimlessly across dark, mystical and faintly disgusting plains.

Though entirely dominant in the middle of the last century, the behaviourist paradigm has since been widely discredited. The complexities of mental processes could not, it turned out, be so easily ignored. Early breakthroughs in the identification of cognition as a phenomenon that could be studied experimentally revealed a complex and hidden world *between* stimulus and response, one that belied the 'vulgar empiricism' of behaviourism. Once again, the black box of the mind was prised opened. This time, however, its contents were to be investigated not with psychoanalytic theory but with cognitive science.

Cognitive psychology sees the human mind as an embodied processor of information. Bathed in a 'buzzing-blooming confusion'[17] of sensory input, human consciousness selects relevant data and then operates upon it to generate meaning. Our particular genius, it turns out, is not for the capture of data, but for its systematic reduction and *selection*.[18] Supposedly simple acts, like walking or eating, then emerge as impressive, and largely hidden, triumphs of information selection, processing and integration.

One way to illuminate the concealed world of cognitive processing is examine the common experience of driving down the street and having a word pop unaccountably into one's head. Only when you look around do you realise that the word is written on a shop front or sign post, and that you must have read the word so fast you did not notice you were even doing so. The cognitive skill of reading is learned in childhood. It then becomes 'automated'; meaning that it drops beneath consciousness and operates with extraordinary speed. One can even drive through a complex intersection, obeying lights, avoiding pedestrians and signs, and only latter realise that you were not aware of driving through the intersection at all, and were actually thinking about something quite different. The complex cognition involved in the act of driving, once consciously learned, can now operate entirely beneath awareness.

Though extremely rapid, reading in fact takes time. There is a very small moment of delay between being confronted with a group of squiggles on a page and the recognition of a word that conveys meaning. As with all cognitive processes, this small delay can be accurately measured. Show someone a picture, and then ask them if they have seen that picture before. A moment elapses before they answer, and in that moment, they are doing cognitive work – here examining their memory to check for prior perception of the picture. Such tiny delays are the footprints of cognitive processing. They constitute empirical evidence *against* the passive reception of perceptual stimulus advocated by behaviourism, and *for* the active cognitive operation on sensory data in order to produce meaning.[19] Knowledge is actively constructed by the perceiver, and this construction takes time.

When an individual is wired up to an electro-encephalograph that measures brain activity, the processing of knowledge that occurs during such delays is seen to entail the firing of neural clusters particular to the task at hand. Though humans diverge widely in their experience of the products of cognition, the neurological *form* of that experience is universal. The processing of sensory data here seems part of a cognitive apparatus that we all share. Our brains operate in similar ways, even if the products of cognition vary across cultures and contexts.

Cognitive psychologists are particularly interested in the duration of information processing tasks, in other words, in the tiny yet measurable delays that occur between the reception of data and the generation of meaning. Empirical research shows that the more information processing a given task requires, the longer the delay.[20] So, for example, where someone is asked to imagine a three-dimensional shape and to compare it to a similar shape which has been rotated, the duration of the delay is exactly proportional to the amount of rotation required to map one shape onto the other. In the same way, when an experimental subject is shown a map which is then removed, and is then given instructions to locate places on the map, processing delay has been shown to correlate precisely with the amount of (imaginary) distance required to move from one map location to another.[21] A slightly less technical example is afforded by imagining that the chair in which you now sit be moved to the other side of the room. Now imagine the chair is taken into another room in your house. The respective processing delay required to achieve each imagined outcome (in the mind) is directly proportional to the distance you move the chair.

Not only do such experiments relate the proportionality of delay with the amount of cognitive work required, they also suggest that cognitive representations of reality take the form of spatial models, upon which we operate in much the same way as when acting in a physical world.[22] This has led some researchers to suggest that the human mind cannot (without reflection) distinguish between internal representations and external realities, or between the imagined and the real. In both cases, the cognitive operations and the neurological pathways utilised are similar, and entail the same cognitive delay.[23] This is an important matter, to which we will need to return; but it is worth noting here that this is precisely why sports trainers insist on mental imaging. To rehearse the serving of a tennis ball in your mind improves your real performance, as mental imaging uses precisely the same neural pathways as the activity itself.

It seems, then, that our everyday cognition entails the endless perusal of 'raw' incoming sense data from a spatial and material external world. Of course, with so much active 'cooking' of this raw data taking place, we find, once again, that the nature of 'reality' becomes problematic. This is no more than to say that when meaning construction takes place – and cognitive psychology shows that it takes place all the time – we become uncertain as to whether a given meaning is socially constructed or natural.[24] More accurately, the fact that meaning is partly constructed once again raises the question of *how much* of our experience is being actively made and how much is being passively received. We have already seen, in the previous chapter, that there are good epistemological and ontological reasons why we are unable to answer such questions in regard to the social world, as this is a realm of extraordinary complexity, of bidirectional construction and contamination by power. It will come as no surprise, therefore, that as we explore the explanatory tools on offer from cognitive science, we require a similarly informed scepticism as to the possibility of objective knowledge of the social, rough and reified world in which we live.

How, then, do we construct meaning? What are the mechanisms by which we make sensory data into knowledge? What is it we *do* to that data that it takes a (measurable) amount of time?

Our cognitive apparatus is constructed to solve problems.[25] As a chin-scratching human in the face of a practical difficulty, it is not helpful to be overwhelmed by disorganised sensory data. Consequently, we regularly and massively simplify the torrent of incoming information and select what is relevant to our concerns. The magnificence of human intelligence thus lies not so much in the grasping of knowledge, but in its rejection. We are, it seems, extraordinarily good at ignoring sense data that is irrelevant. The genius of human cognition turns out to be our capacity to 'narrow and concentrate rather than to expand awareness'.[26]

To prevent cognitive overload and focus on the data we need to solve practical problems, individuals in fact (always, everywhere) engage in a set of stages of information processing. Though extremely fast, each stage is, in the laboratory, of measurable duration. The first stage of cognition is a *very general sweep* of the sensory data – a kind of lightning glance around the pub to see if it's generally okay. The second is a rapid and massive *cut* of data deemed irrelevant. From the outset, therefore, we are excluding certain data and lightening the load of cognitive work required to generate knowledge.[27] The third stage is a more detailed *inspection* of surviving data. The fourth integrates data into meaning and usable knowledge.

```
1. The Quick Sweep
2. The Cut
3. The Inspection
4. Integration
```

*Figure 3.1*　The Stages of Individual Cognition

The stages by which we process knowledge reveal just how much active work is required of us in order to wring meaning from sensory data. We are by no means passive recipients, or blank slates.[28] We are not sponges or smooth wax tablets.[29] Instead, we are active *makers* of meaning; constantly operating on, sorting through, selecting from and adding to the data we receive; both from outside and from within.

Choosing among the torrent of incoming data requires selection criteria. These criteria must exist in the mind prior to the encounter with the raw data.[30] Prior knowledge, here in the form of learned selection criteria, thus influences each of our cognitive stages. During the Cut, for example, prior knowledge is particularly involved, for here it informs what will survive to be further operated upon. Before we get anywhere near integrating sense data into meaning, we find ourselves operating with a dataset that has already been massively reduced – and with criteria derived from prior learning.

Human cognition is thus involved in the determination of what we attend to, and then in the construction of meaning. There is much that we never even notice, and, indeed, this is the very source of our genius. When we do select incoming data, however, and successfully integrate it into meaning, our cognition generates a valuable product – which we loosely call 'thinking'. To notice something is to enjoy the end product of a series of cognitive processes. So much for the quick behaviourist skip from stimulus to response.

Not only is much going on between stimulus and response that we do not notice, but we remain oblivious to the distinct stages of our own cognition. As Evans points out, 'subjects are aware of that to which they are attending, but *not* of the selection process directing their attention'.[31] Indeed, he adds that 'a number of significant cognitive processes are not accessible to consciousness', and 'not only may people be unaware of the process underlying their behaviour, but they may also provide a false report upon it'.[32] It is thus possible that we remain unaware of *any* cognitive process, and that we can only ever attend to 'the *product* which it places in consciousness'.[33] Cognitive science here moves close to Kantian theories of mental activity, where phenomena are presented to consciousness by the categories of experience, and we are denied direct access to the 'noumenal' world.[34]

In the previous chapter, our epistemological investigation of power in institutional hierarchies suggested that the 'social element' in cognition is largely invisible to us; that organisations affect us in ways we cannot see. Here, cognitive psychology adds to the list of processes about which we remain blithely unaware. We should not be surprised by this growing list. As one of the most complex objects on the planet, the human mind is the product of a long evolutionary history. It now contains a hundred million neurons and a hundred trillion synapses, and its crenulations have the surface area of a tennis court. While thinking is largely electrical, it is also washed through with a chemical emotional system. The brain is thus a combination of two exquisitely integrated systems. It is made up of three discernible parts, each a layer secreted by its evolutionary history, each encircling the one before. It is also in a body, in a social world and in a biosphere.[35] Yet so does its very ability to rapidly select data and construct meaning result in us not being aware, relatively speaking, of terribly much at all.

Ours is a problem solving cognition; not one overloaded with self-awareness. So effective is our innocence that we are quite capable of learning without knowing we have learned.[36] We have noted that rapid data selection necessitates *pre-attentive* information processing. We thus use a range of heuristic techniques to move rapidly through the world.[37] To save time, these are regularly delegated to our unconscious mind, where they become 'automated'.[38] We will return to 'automated cognition' later, in order to suggest that power corrupts by exploiting invisible cognitive processes and thereby changing what we can see. Here, however, our principle concern is to learn more, from cognitive psychology, about how these hidden heuristic techniques actually function. Only then will we be able to discern the way in which these hard-wired and invisible cognitive processes are recruited by the interests of power in organisations.

To quickly extract relevant information and streamline the process of data selection, we make an (almost) instant scan.[39] We do this by looking for essential features and patterns.[40] Cognitive psychologists have advanced and empirically tested a number of hypotheses to explain how this process works, but all resulting explanations share a reliance on some kind of pre-existing template which the mind holds prior to exposure to sense data and which functions to extract and classify that data into broad types. Whether we call them models,[41] chunks,[42] semantic networks,[43] cognitive or mental maps,[44] scripts[45] or schemas,[46] these templates are the product of prior experience, they are stored knowledge and they therefore exist as a form of memory.

## Schemas

Schema theory, in particular, offers detailed analysis of the role played by such templates. This body of research holds that we carry blocks of general and abstract knowledge, and that the initial data Sweep proceeds as an attempt to find the appropriate generic schema into which specific data can be inserted.[47] As Evans states:

> A schema is something which is elicited from memory and fitted to the current problem by virtue of (a) its domain relevance and (b) its structural similarity. Once elicited, a schema includes procedural knowledge in the form of rules or heuristics which can be applied to the problem in hand.[48]

We therefore have a schema for greeting another person, for getting into a lift, for eating a meal and, indeed, for the full range of everyday events, objects and activities.[49] Schemas function to pick out relevant – or 'schema-consistent' – information from the rush of data we constantly confront. As such, they provide pre-existing search criteria which manage cognitive overload and speed up problem solving.

Evidently, schema theory conceives of knowledge construction as a strongly 'top-down' and active process.[50] In other words, it stresses the importance of what is already in the head of an individual over that emanating from the outside world. Schemas function to rapidly simplify knowledge processing. Experimental evidence confirms that information processing time is reduced when incoming data is 'schema-relevant',[51] and that 'schema-irrelevant' data tends to be filtered out and ignored. While schema theory has its critics,[52] it nevertheless constitutes a significant advance in our understanding of hidden individual knowledge processing.

Our present investigation concerns the politics of thinking, and particularly, the possible influence on cognition by asymmetrical relations of power. We must therefore examine how unconscious and schema-driven knowledge processing might come to be so influenced. Evidently, by selecting and filtering, schemas serve to exclude certain data and thus to control what enters awareness.[53] They constitute repositories of pre-existing knowledge that serve to bias subsequent knowledge selection. Schemas are thus implicated in what we attend to. Two particular issues then arise that require further examination. The first is: where do schemas come from?[54] The second: how do they ever change?

Cognitive psychology's strength is in the empirical study of individual cognitive functioning in the laboratory. Its corresponding weakness lies in its treatment of the social element in knowledge and in its explanations of cognition in settings which exhibit the full complexity of human interaction.[55] It is therefore of little surprise to note that schema theory is notoriously weak on the question of where schemas actually come from,[56] and on the ways in which they arise as part of social and cultural life.

Clearly, schemas are learned during processes of socialisation.[57] As such, they constitute internalised social knowledge,[58] the content of which cannot be taken to be natural or objective.[59] While there may be species-wide capacities to inspect sensory data with heuristic schemas, we should by no means extend this insight to suggest that schemas are similar across different social contexts. This is an important point, and one that will concern us further when we follow cognitive psychology in its foray into organisational knowledge processing.[60] The *content* of schemas is in no way determined by their *form, qua* schema. The presence of species-wide cognitive strategies can never constitute an objective warrant for any actual content of consciousness. To imagine that the science of cognition *could* provide such a warrant is a philosophical category mistake, and a rather dangerous one. For the *products* of species-wide cognitive structures are diverse, personalised, inherently perspectival, context specific, often contaminated by power, driven by emotion and all too often assumed to be objectively real.

When we realise that the content of schemas are different in different contexts and for different identities, that they are affected by early experience and trauma, by familial and social relationships and by surrounding cultural mores, it starts to look as though schema theory may be compatible with psychoanalytic accounts of human personality after all. Indeed, schemas, when seen as having been learned through experience, function rather like the ego defence mechanisms articulated by Anna Freud.[61] In both cases, there is a reduction and selection of data taking place beneath consciousness that defends mental functioning. For Anna Freud, however, and in the subsequent development of ego psychology, the origins of defence mechanisms are well theorised in terms of psychological drives. The first cognitive revolution paid altogether too little attention to the origin of schemas, perhaps reflecting a need to protect the positivist explanatory aspirations of the discipline. It thus sought to avoid being flooded by what it saw as weak interpretative approaches and a great tide of epistemological, and psychoanalytic, uncertainty.

The answer to the question of where schemas come from leads to a second issue: that of the plasticity of schemas. If schemas operate beneath consciousness and are structured to select data that is self-confirming, then the possibility that they become fixed is a serious concern.[62] Schemas are somehow formed, and then become automated, or lowered beneath awareness.[63] Now self-confirming, their origins are forgotten and their products appear in consciousness as common sense.[64] The genius of human intelligence, therefore, lies not only in its use of prior-knowledge in the selection of relevant data, but also in its ability to *change the criteria of selection* in the face of changing circumstances.

Humans learn, both consciously and unconsciously, even when power is actively deployed to prevent their learning.[65] We *can* recover and revise automated knowledge and adapt our schemas. We *can* recognise schema-inconsistent data, even if we tend not to do so. It has even been suggested that we are particularly attuned to picking up changes at the margins of schema consistency (when is a bowl a cup?)[66] and, that this is how we retain our responsiveness to disturbances in our world. Like the human eye, the brain is adept at noticing, in its 'peripheral' vision, movement, difference and change.

Schema theory is thus rather better on what we do when we make meaning than it is on how we learn to make meaning. It is stronger on selectivity than on explaining how selection criteria can change. And indeed, the full complexity of situated human learning would swamp cognitive science, as it does all other explanations of human functioning. What schema theory does do, however, is to illuminate the initial and automated data Cut, the heuristic 'pre-look' of the second stage; the one in which prior knowledge, here in the form of schemas, is active in the construction of knowledge. It reveals the pre-selection of data which regularly occurs beneath awareness, and shows our cognitive tendency to automate the use of selection criteria.[67]

Such automation is clearly adaptive, and is necessary if we are to favour some sensory data over others – something we must do to avoid cognitive overload and solve problems in our everyday lives.[68] Automation reduces cognitive work; it speeds up processing time and, for the most part, delivers effective interpretations. Together, selectivity and automation strongly favour stasis and the reduction of cognitive work. We thus tend to prefer stability, and to settle in our thinking – perhaps to enable us to move our attention to other problems. Schema theory suggests that the human cognitive apparatus is strongly oriented to select for certainty, stasis, problem reduction and cognitive economy. Cognitive psychologists thus frequently refer to us as being 'cognitive misers'.[69] Again, we got where we are today as much by *not* attending to information as by attending to it.

## Bias

The in-built tendency to select for stasis means that we often cheat in our construction of knowledge. Not only do we use pre-learned schemas to rapidly parse incoming data, but we also rely heavily on what amount to automated biases in our cognition. These biases are structural in the human mind, and have received significant study.[70] Sometimes, they are so marked as to cause us to make mistakes of judgement. After all, the great danger of stasis is always a tendency to miss *new* sensory data, to become unresponsive to changes in the environment and, thereby, to fail to learn. In fact, such mistakes – widely referred to as 'cognitive biases' – are not really due to a lack of information,[71] neither to too much information; nor even to insufficient processing time. Indeed, human cognitive biases are not really *processing* mistakes at all. Rather, they are the structural by-products of a cognitive apparatus which, oriented to stasis and the reduction of cognitive work, uses prior knowledge in the automated heuristics of data selection. To understand how organisational and social structures interact with and recruit automated individual cognition – and thereby affect the thinking of individuals – we need a more detailed understanding of cognitive biases. We will here inspect four kinds of cognitive bias, those of simplification, confirmation, affirmation and reification.

We have seen that the act of data selection is, fundamentally, an act of simplification. We save cognitive time and work when we ignore detail and select broadly. We are fastest when we are able to automate the use of schemas, categories and heuristic 'rules of thumb'.[72] Simplification seeks out and selects for similarity, and accentuates difference.[73] The benefits and costs of these tactics are clearly revealed in the study of social stereotyping. A stereotype is a schema – learned from one's social environment – which reduces cognitive work. Its benefit is that it simplifies complex cognitive judgements about people who are different to oneself.[74] Its cost is that it ignores reality and new information, maintains discrimination and perpetuates human suffering. Often automated beneath consciousness, stereotypes are notoriously resistant to change, even in the face of contradictory evidence.[75] Simplification thus reduces cognitive work and increases processing speed. Yet, where micro-changes in data are ignored, judgement can be impaired. Simplification is thus, itself, a kind of cognitive bias.

Similarly, confirmation biases arise when we try too hard to avoid cognitive work and fall back on our existing automated schemas. Numerous studies have shown our strong tendency to seek evidence that validates our prior beliefs. In the laboratory, we can be readily induced to adopt a hypothesis, to collect data that confirms it and to fail to even notice that which suggests our hypothesis is wrong. In such experiments, humans have been caught, time and again, avoiding data which might call their prior beliefs into question.[76] Even when under pressure from contradictory evidence, we still prefer to moderate our existing position rather than to generate a new one.[77] Individual cognition is biased towards the automated confirmation of existing beliefs, to the preservation of those beliefs, and thereby to reaping the benefits of stasis, stability and cognitive repetition. Confirmation bias can reduce work, increase processing speed, give empirical validation and stabilise the environment. Yet it can also lead to complacency, the loss of responsiveness to changing data and, again, to the failure to learn.[78]

Of course, we are not just cognitive misers. We are also responsive to change, and are hardwired to be interested, to relate to others, to learn, invest energy and do cognitive work. Children fall in love with the world and adults strive despite knowledge of their own mortality. Our cognitive apparatus is, therefore, able to seek stasis *and* process new experiences.

Human cognition is more than merely the disinterested processing of knowledge. Indeed, it is emotional, situated and 'hot'.[79] There is a self that processes, and as we have already noted, we evince a whole series of what amount to cognitive biases in our efforts to affirm our self esteem and amplify our personal importance. Such affirmational biases are self-flattering yet false beliefs we hold about our own cognitive processes. They take the form of a consistent overestimation of what we know,[80] and a general overconfidence in our reasoning and judgement.[81] In hindsight, for example, we regularly imagine that our powers of prediction were better than they really were,[82] and in one of the most commonly studied affirmational errors, known as the 'fundamental attributional error', we regularly claim credit for success and deny responsibility for failure.[83] In experimental settings, we tend to blame circumstances when *we* fail at a task, while those observing us tend to blame our character. When the situation is reversed, we attribute another's failure to their character, while they – again – cite circumstances.[84]

These are clearly ego-defensive and esteem-building strategies, designed to provide the slightly rose-tinted glasses necessary for human agency in a time-bound and uncertain world. Lewinsohn et al go so far as to suggest that normal human functioning is characterised by an illusory 'warm glow' in which 'one sees oneself more positively than others see one'.[85] In empirical experimentation, the most accurate self-appraisals of individual cognitive performance are by people who suffer from depression.[86] The 'warm glow', presumably absent in the depressive, seems an integral part of normal human functioning. It is an automated overconfidence, one which assists the ego, accentuates surety and motivates agency. Though overestimating our own capacities can sometimes impede our judgement, for the most part, the bias towards affirmation helps us join the world.

In the previous chapter, we examined ways in which individuals come to experience social constructions as natural, a process we identified as reification. With our understanding of cognition, we can now assert that reification is itself a form of simplification and stabilisation, and thus a way of reducing cognitive work. It serves to reduce the complexities around what is real and what has been constructed. As such, reification may be considered as a type of cognitive bias in its own right, even though it has not received the same detailed treatment in the psychological literature as do the three so far considered.

By conceiving of reification in cognitive terms, we gain significant detail on how it in fact operates as an information processing strategy. Indeed, Marx's concept of reification turns out to be empirically verified by laboratory experimentation in cognitive psychology. Awash in a rich mélange of material and symbolic phenomena, we simply perceive social constructions as natural.[87] We do not, for example, think the value of gold is unreal simply because it is a social construct. Nor do we doubt the import of marriage vows, property rights or the reality of a policeman's power. Yet all of these are what John Searle would call socially constructed or 'institutional facts'.[88] As noted earlier, cognition operates on internal representations – neurologically speaking – in much the same way that it does on phenomena of natural cause. It is this that gives us the structural capacity to rapidly automate schemas and then to attribute the status of objective reality to the cognitive products which ensue. Once again, the benefits of this structural tendency are a reduction in cognitive work and an increase in processing speed.[89] What we can now call the reification bias serves to accentuate certainty, stability and stasis, and, indeed, plays a crucial role in the construction of human culture and history. In particular, reification tends to freeze social constructions, to conceal their causes and to provide self-legitimating narratives for extant social practices.[90]

When we survey the full range of individual cognitive biases, we can see that they all arise from the 'tendency of prior beliefs and attitudes to distort people's reasoning'.[91] In matters of information processing, we cheat. We regularly fool each other and almost always ourselves. Striding blithely through seemingly solid landscapes, we are sure that what we know is objectively the case. Empirical evidence from cognitive psychology thus suggests we have a strongly conservative agenda built into the very structure of our knowledge processing apparatus. The tendency is to routinise and defend, to settle back into what we already know. This is not to say that we cannot learn; only that we often avoid doing so if we can.

Socially constructed schemas are, originally, learned.[92] They are rehearsed, routinised and then they slip silently beneath conscious-ness. Now fully automated, they are experienced as natural. In this sequence, social constructs become common sense and the symbolic becomes material. Now we can reap the benefits of stasis, stability and simplified cognition. Selecting only confirmatory data, we can bathe in the overestimation of our own capacities and the simplified and reified social constructions of our everyday lives. This cognitive strategy enables us to believe, and live, in a symbolic world. It turns out that we are, naturally, structurally and very successfully, *naïve realists*.

As already noted, throughout its development, cognitive science has remained unable to decide whether the inherent selectivity of human cognition makes us lazy work-avoiders or enthralled devour-ers of new knowledge.[93] As with schema theory, focusing on the role played by prior knowledge in the construction of meaning raises questions about how we make new schemas; about how we learn. Cognition is, somehow, oriented *both* to stability and change, to laziness *and* learning, to stasis *and* disturbance. We do not know how much of our automated cognition can be pulled back into aware-ness, scrutinised and changed. Indeed, of any given thought that appears in our mind, we cannot be sure what portion is our own and unique to us as individuals, what portion is determined by our cognitive apparatus, what by the structure of the material world and what by the interests of power.

The fact that *some* portion is determined and universal has been a constant source of confusion in social scientific analysis. As we have seen, in debates around the nature of language, between structural-ists and poststructuralists, between Habermasians and Foucauldians and in the 'rationality debates' in anthropology, we repeatedly observe the difficulties caused by processes of social construction in which both a universal and a contextual element are in play.[94] Certainly, pure universalism is oppressive, denies difference and tempts us to cut off the legs of the individual in order to fit a Procrustean bed. Equally, pure contextualism is oppressive, and leaves us to suffer without recourse to anything beyond what is here and now the case. Lukes's careful analysis of the dynamic interplay between universal and context-dependent criteria of rationality shows the importance of both elements, and reminds us that a structural tendency to make knowledge in a particular way is not some essentialist plot, nor a dastardly act of positivistic homogenisation.[95] Once again, we are reminded of the sophisticated attempts by the early critical theorists, by Durkheim and Fleck and by Berger and Luckmann, to move beyond such one-sided readings of social phenomena and attempt to think of dynamic processes that move in both directions at once.

In some ways, when it comes to being misunderstood, cognitive psychologists have only themselves to blame. In discovering universal structures of human information processing, they *have* tended to underplay the contextual element, and it is this that has required subsequent correction – the 'second' cognitive revolution – by connectionism and situated cognition.[96] The challenge presented to cognitive psychology by its growing encounter with other social sciences is to consider the universal and the contextual in dynamic interaction. This, after all, is precisely what we do every day in practice.[97] When we act, we effortlessly and inescapably combine the universal and the particular, form and content, process and product. There is thus no determinism in cognition. We *do* share certain cognitive *tendencies*, yet these universals are 'empty' or 'thin', and require contextualisation to be complete.[98] 'Biology is not destiny', yet neither should we imagine that our long evolutionary history has not left its mark on the human genome.[99]

Cognitive science offers useful explanatory tools and gives us important detail on the internal structures with which we process information. But it cannot provide a privileged warrant for objective truth regarding the social world. It cannot serve to dictate an objective politics of knowledge. In order to understand how power corrupts, we can gain much from the study of individual cognition. Though schema and bias theory form only a tiny portion of the burgeoning field of cognitive psychology, they do serve to illuminate the processes by which individuals make meaning, and thus begin to reveal the object that is somehow corrupted by power.

We have noted the bi-directionality of social knowledge, and observed that power corrupts at the interface of individual and organisation. The mechanism(s) by which power corrupts is thus not only a matter of individual cognition, but of collective knowledge processing, and it is to this that we now turn. As we shall see, when cognitive science emerges, blinking, from the laboratory, offering tools with which it hopes to investigate '*social*' cognition, it immediately stumbles onto classic problems of social epistemology. Only by sorting through these problems can we delineate the subtle influence of organisational status, location and role occupancy on individual cognition, and thus, finally, articulate the mechanism by which power corrupts.

# 4
# Organisational Knowledge

Our earlier examination of various psychologies of power shows the difficulties encountered when analysis attempts to keep individual and collective knowledge processing apart. The nature of groups, the complex ontology of the social world and the evident interplay of individual and collective knowledge processing all suggest that we cannot separate individuals from their social contexts. Having subsequently explored some of the structural tendencies of our individual cognitive apparatus, we now require a better understanding of how those tendencies interact with processes of collective knowledge processing. After all, individuals do not undertake cognitive activity as solipsists, but learn schemas and gain experience through interaction with others. When it comes to corruption by power, we have, from the outset, known that we are dealing with what amounts to an 'illness of position'.[1] Consequently, we now begin our turn towards the role played by organisational 'position', to collective knowledge processing and to the possibility that organisations themselves are cognitive systems.

## 'Social' cognition?

It was with considerable excitement and expectation that cognitive psychologists first ventured towards the study of organisations. Information processing, here modelled on computing and verified by experimentation, had been successfully charted within the individual. Yet because we think and act together, it must also occur in collectives, groups, work teams, families, organisations, institutions and societies. Indeed, some researchers went so far as to suggest that both individuals *and* organisations think.[2]

Attempts to study 'collective cognition' began, unsurprisingly, with research into leadership styles and the cognitive strategies of managers. Here, management was seen to be in possession of specific skills that somehow delivered sound judgement and effective decision-making. These early studies concentrated on investigating the choices and calculations required of managers in organisational settings.[3] When considering the nature of the collective, early research retained its methodological individualism,[4] and for the most part treated collectives as simple aggregations of individuals.[5] It consequently floundered on the same difficulties as the study of individual cognition, and was decidedly weak on synergic effects,[6] group dynamics, emotion generally and power in particular.

Increasingly informed by epistemological debates over social constructivism, however, cognitive science at last confronted the social element in knowledge, and organisations came to be seen as structures for collective knowledge processing.[7] No longer was 'social' cognition to be conceived as merely the study of the individual cognition of social things. Now, '*social*' cognition focused on groups of cognitive actors and their interactions.[8] Organisations were not to be seen as mere aggregations of individuals, but as pockets of cultural homogeneity, as sealed worlds dominated by what Rousseau would call a 'corporate will'. Organisations thus had a 'nature' of their own, a constructed and social ontology which existed, at least in part, *independently* of individuals.[9] When taken to extremes, such a view saw organisations as 'collective minds', with certain 'cultures',[10] 'characters' and ways of doing things. They 'had' cognitive maps,[11] mental models[12] and normative orders.[13] Organisations 'learn', they store and retrieve knowledge,[14] they make decisions[15] and they act. To early researchers, they thus appeared as discrete cognitive entities, alive and intentional; and collective ones at that.

Yet, as we have already seen, accounts of collective cognition that posit an ontology for the organisation *which is more than the sum of its* parts must demonstrate *where* this added ontology is located. If not in the individual, nor in the interactions between such individuals, then the social remains something deeply mystified. Social theory has long been concerned with the tendency to anthropomorphise such collective entities,[16] and also with their reification.

These difficulties are most clearly apparent in recent studies of how collective knowledge is stored. In the individual cognitive apparatus, knowledge storage usually takes the form of memory. We can thus identify discrete neurological systems corresponding to short and long-term memory, to intellectual and affective memory and observe each system's capacity to store, not only propositional, but also procedural, knowledge.[17] Cognitive social psychologists have thus been tempted to ask: is there such a thing as *collective* memory?[18] Answers have conceived of organisational memory as analogous to that of the individual.[19] Of course, the forms of storage are different, as organisations do not, themselves, have neurons, dendrites and glands. Nor have they evolved through the same developmental stages. Yet organisations do have evolutionary paths.[20] They have facts, data, documents, datasets, machines and intellectual capital.[21] They also store knowledge in their habitual ways of doing things, in procedures, routines, structures and practices. Such procedural knowledge may be tacit, rather than explicit, but it nevertheless constitutes a repository of knowledge gleaned from the past and retrievable in the present. As such, routines and norms must be seen as stored collective knowledge.[22]

Yet, again, it is by no means clear that the collective has the same ontology as the individual,[23] nor that the individual provides, by way of analogy, an accurate model for the apparatus of collective processing.[24] In addition, when we ask how, precisely, something like a norm is stored, and in what *form* such storage occurs, we can only point back at individual cognition and behaviour. Individual memory can hold beliefs and assumptions, but again, an organisation, as something distinct from the individuals that make it up, is not a neurological structure. Information processing certainly occurs at both the individual and the collective level, and both are oriented to problem solving, but significant epistemological problems arise at their interface.[25] It is not at all obvious that we are asking the right question when we start our analysis of knowledge storage in organisations by wondering, as do Sandelands and Stablein, 'what is the organisational counterpart to neural activity in the brain?'[26] Nor can we assert with any confidence that 'the politics of the social organisation and the physiology of the brain share much in common'.[27]

To understand the way organisations process knowledge requires us to identify the *place*, the *form* and the *mechanism,* of knowledge storage. Some organisational knowledge is explicit and frozen in documents, machines and procedures. But some, such as an organisation's 'culture', is stored in the form of tacit ideas, conceptions and beliefs. Such things can only ever be the currency of individual cognition. How, then, does an organisation store its 'culture'? Somehow, the ideas, behaviours and interactions of individuals, when in concert, constitute the knowledge processing of the organisation. Here, processing occurs beneath the consciousness of individuals and is influenced and used by the organisation. We can therefore imagine organisations processing knowledge *through* individuals, and as *giving* individuals certain cognitive habits and routines that in fact constitute the stored knowledge of the organisation.

Individual cognition is selective. It proceeds by glancing at the world, using schemas gained from experience to select information, and only then arranging the surviving data into knowledge. When individuals think in groups, they would appear to *share* schemas, to process knowledge in similar ways, to enjoy common cognitive products.[28] It could be that organisations provide common schemas for their members, and that organisational stability derives from some degree of cognitive homogeneity. It would then follow that organisations survive when they are able to influence how individual members think,[29] particularly by getting them to think the same things. Knowledge storage in organisations occurs in many places and forms, and by a number of mechanisms. One way collective knowledge may be stored is in the unconscious and similar schemas of participating individuals.

Recent advances in the study of social cognition argue that each organisation is best seen as a particular way of constructing meaning and storing knowledge.[30] Each is a 'cognitive community', a shared symbolic world, a perspectival pool of local understanding. These are pockets of common culture, shared schemas and interpretations. They are boundaried areas (symbolically, if not geographically), zones of homogenised meaning; and collective cognition is conceived in terms of *shared* individual cognition. Traditionally, these zones of homogeneous cognition were seen as the only source of coordinated action. Elites, both political and religious, thus sought to standardise the use of certain schemas and to force subordinates to think in the same way.

Subsequent democratisations of knowledge, from the Reformation to the Enlightenment and beyond, encouraged us to realise that collective action could be coordinated not only by 'group think', but also by pluralism – both in politics and markets. When studies in social cognition unreflectively use the word 'shared', then, they reach beyond their own understanding.[31] We do not actually know if effective organisational knowledge processing requires individuals to think in *identical* ways, and thus to have the same mental content. Certainly, an organisation cannot be characterised as homogeneous. Organisations have parts, sub-groups, levels of hierarchy, cross-cutting alliances and networks. They are functionally differentiated, share their members with other organisations and draw from different collective identities.[32] Each dimension of membership has its own community of meaning, each its own favoured schemas.[33] People thus process knowledge in different ways even as they succeed in coordinating their actions. Schemas, it seems, do not *have* to be shared.

In addition, accounts of shared collective cognition must explain why organisational influence on individual cognition so often fails. The apparently paradoxical individual capacities for cognitive stasis *and* disturbance are again evident here, for sometimes, people do not come to share cognition. They fail to internalise the provided norms. They do not reify and automate the required schemas, and so fail miserably to believe.[34] For all the hard-wired ease with which individuals are controlled in organisations, there is also an evident capacity to reject such control, to see through mystifications, to question assumptions and resist organisational influence.

Finally, and epistemologically, to 'share' cognition is to predicate, to an item of cognition, the property of 'sameness'. By this, we indicate that the identical item occurs in the minds of two or more individuals. Ontologically, we add nothing to that item by indicating its multiple occurrences. 'Shared' cognition, like all cognition, occurs within individuals. The fact that it is 'shared' does not mean it has a life independent of individual cognition. As we have already seen, Gilbert's work on plural subjects clarifies the conditions under which shared beliefs *can* be correctly attributed to a collective. One requirement is for conscious individual agreement to 'own' such beliefs, and to make an undertaking toward them. Widespread agreement bequeaths no objective validity to our social knowledge, and indeed, operates more as a pragmatic tactic for managing our lack of objectivity.

We do *not* need to think alike in order to coordinate collective action. All we can safely assert here is that some minimal functional fit, a *compatibility*, arises between individuals.[35] Humans can communicate and coordinate their actions with others, even when they think differently. This may be because 'different individual interpretations... generate similar overt behaviour',[36] or because overt agreement can emerge despite differences in covert judgement.[37] However achieved, we clearly *can* operate together, though this might not be due to our having identical cognition. As with a marriage, it overstretches our understanding to suggest that husband and wife 'share' cognition. All we can say with surety is that there is *some* degree of functional fit; a certain compatibility between the mental content of each spouse.

The analogies of organisational character, memory and thought thus tempt us towards reification. Individuals process knowledge cognitively. Collectives also process knowledge, but not like individuals.[38] There are no collective minds. Organisations do not *think*.[39] To imagine that they do is akin to claiming that organisations eat, simply because goods are carried in through the service entrance; or that they excrete, because rubbish is regularly taken out the back door. Cognition is a form of information processing peculiar to the structures of the human mind. A collective of individuals – an organisation – processes, stores and uses knowledge in very different ways. It is safest, therefore, to say there is no such thing as 'social', 'organisational' or 'collective' cognition, for such phrasing invites epistemological confusion.

While organisations cannot be said to 'have' schemas, it may still be the case that dominant elites push participants into holding certain schemas. The interests of elites would certainly be furthered by the reification and automation of these schemas in the cognition of subordinates. Conveniently, influencing and policing individual schemas would then take place beneath the awareness of the individual. When corporations make their employees rehearse mission statements, wear shirts with tag-lines and pass tests on organisational values, they are clearly attempting to get people to think in particular ways. Repetition, in churches, corporations and armies, is here intended to encourage the adoption, and automation, of standardised schemas. When an evidently miserable teenager slumps through MacDonald's wearing a tee-shirt emblazoned with the words 'I'm loving it', or Marks and Spencer requires employees to state, in an online employment review, whether they have 'succeeded in internalising corporate values', we are reminded just how clumsy organisations are when they attempt to directly influence our thinking. Here, though, we begin to see ways in which dominant interests might benefit from the structural biases and heuristics of individual cognition, even if they are bad at formalising such appropriations.

Organisations certainly use individual biases, but the question then arises as to whether collective knowledge processing can ever be accurately described as being biased. Does the bias of individual cognition have an analogous tendency in collective knowledge processing? Organisations do their knowledge processing through individual thinking; yet to suggest they 'have' schemas is to invite reification. Participating individuals carry schemas, and these can become the subject of a power struggle within the organisation. Here, the organisation and the individual are entwined in a complex embrace, one characterised by significant differences and, also, analogous similarities. Notions such as thinking, schemas and memory do *not* translate from individual cognition to organisational knowledge processing. However, learning and cognitive biases *do* occur within both the individual and the organisation. At the level of the individual, biases arise as a side-effect of the way in which the human cognitive apparatus works. Bias here pertains to how knowledge is processed. Organisations process knowledge. While they do not do so cognitively, they *do* exhibit bias in their processing. Bias in organisations can be affirmational and show marked in-group favouritism. It can be conformational, in that it only recognises certain kinds of knowledge, and thus functions to exclude and de-legitimate 'subjugated knowledges'. Bias can also be reificatory, and this occurs when participating individuals assume organisational schemas to be 'real'. Finally, they can be structurally biased in favour of some individuals over others. It is this that allowed Schnattsneider to assert so tellingly that power in institutions takes the form of a 'mobilisation of bias'.[40]

As we have seen, cognitive psychology cannot drag its usual methodological individualism up to the level of the social and claim that organisations themselves engage in cognition. Organisations are entities of concerted *individual* cognition. They are areas of cognitive compatibility between individuals which, when reified, confront us as ontologically independent. Neither methodological individualism, nor holism, can vault miraculously over the extraordinary complexities of social epistemology.

Cognition is the study of individual information processing structures, and its explanatory tools pertain only to them. Here, however, our concern *is* with the individual. We seek to understand the effects of organisational structure and status on individual cognition. Such an inquiry *can*, therefore, legitimately draw on advances in the study of cognitive science. Of particular importance are the conceptual tools made available by the developments we have been exploring in automated heuristics, schema and bias theory. By keeping our focus on the individual, therefore, we do not so seriously exceed the boundaries of our knowledge about organisations and the ways in which they process knowledge.

When we join an organisation, we must learn, fast. Problems must be solved, ways of doing practised, perfected and automated. Right away, we confront something that appears to be more than the sum of its parts, something that presents to us as an independent being. We are given roles, placed in structures and variously advised by our colleagues. We become part of a community in which information is processed collectively, and in particular ways. There are procedures and structures to learn, tools and etiquette to master, status indicators to be interpreted and rehearsed. Sometimes it is hard to see why things are done in a certain way, and sometimes, no one can tell you why. All the knowledge that has been stored in the practices of an organisation, across its entire history, now constitutes an embedded and settled structure which, though social and symbolic in its ontology, is, nevertheless, independent and beyond the reach of voluntaristic change. This stable zone of experience is at once a social construction *and* a direct influence on individual cognition.

Our new organisation contains complex interpersonal relationships, and these are zones of compatible cognition, areas of functionally coordinated meaning in which we must participate. As we have seen, however, rather than striving for compatibility, organisations usually expend their efforts and resources rather clumsily trying to ensure that cognition is shared and commonly held. Participants are therefore encouraged to make specific kinds of meaning. It is for this reason that, within organisations, individual cognition is a site of considerable interest and intrigue, and there is an ongoing power struggle over what we think. Only dimly visible, far below, this is a hidden and usually silent conflict. Here, the struggle is over interpretive dominance and the control of automated cognition. Organisations are thus extraordinarily political places,[41] and much sacrifice follows their battles over meaning.

Cognitive social psychology enables us to recognise that we are regularly 'pushed' by hierarchic organisations to adopt particular schemas. Once internalised by the individual and installed to run beneath consciousness, such schemas serve to both reduce and redirect our cognitive work. Pushed schemas can include criteria for the selection of information, categories of classification, interpretations, evaluations and behavioural etiquette. When reified, they appear as natural and necessary, and when automated, become invisible and immune from examination. As such, they influence how we conceive of problems, solutions, goals and legitimating narratives.

Individual cognition is subject to structural biases. Whether these arise from dispositions toward simplification, confirmation, affirmation or reification, individuals are prone to make certain kinds of cognitive error. We might, therefore, say that we are 'tugged at', 'tempted' or 'pulled' into these errors by our own cognitive apparatus. In the organisation, pushed schemas and the pull of bias can work together, sometimes to produce 'group think' – often in the service of elites. Here, then, the offer meets a temptation; and a 'fit' occurs between the organisational structure and the cognitive apparatus of the individual. When this is achieved, we win the great prize of organisation: coordinated and motivated intentional action. Any attempt to win this prize must deliver compatible schemas, draw the maximum benefit from the individual cognitive biases and do so beneath individual awareness.[42] It is thus in the interests of dominant elites to encourage such cognition, for it enables subordinate commitment to be appropriated while at the same time concealing that appropriation behind a veil of ideology. Just this kind of cognition occurs frequently in an organisational hierarchy.

To plumb the relation between individual cognition and organisational knowledge processing is thus to stumble upon a continuous political struggle over knowledge in organisations. In our daily organisational lives, there is an ongoing, yet concealed, struggle over the very contents of our minds. Though political scientists have at last torn their gaze from elite institutions, and have been progressively surprised to discover civil society, social capital, new social movements, marginalised voices and collective identities, cognitive psychologists are right: political scientists have not yet reached down far enough. The deeper struggle is personal and organisational, and it pertains to how we think. Organisations should give us spaces for public argument, recognition, display and democracy.[43] Yet they are our ruined agora, choked by hierarchy, wasted and unused.

Across both dominant and subordinate roles, organisations push certain schemas, which then become automated in the individual. These schemas thereby become *both* an item of individual cognition *and* a part of organisational knowledge processing. Fast, automated and largely unreflective, this combination slides effortlessly into the individual mind – lubricated by the structural biases and then concealed by them. Such thinking is entirely natural, and arises from the selective orientation of an otherwise swamped knowledge-seeking individual. And because it is within organisations that we are individually corrupted, how we are affected by power is thus, in part, a matter of where, in the organisational hierarchy, we are located.

## Hierarchy's 'great divide'

Thrown into the world, and denied objective knowledge, we must solve problems and adapt to changes and contingencies we cannot foresee.[44] As information processors under conditions of uncertainty, data rushes towards us, either from 'outside', or from 'within' our own minds. Human cognition is structured so as to manage the directionality of experience. Whatever the nature of the human self, whether physical brain and/or reified social construction, experience seems to approach 'us', to be something through which we move, to be incoming from 'out there'.[45] As cognitive agents, we are always located and situated.[46] To show how our thinking is affected by organisational membership requires us to explore the particular effects, on the individual, of being variously located in a spatial landscape of power.

Where individual cognition finds compatibility with others, we inhabit cross-cutting and overlapping communities of meaning.[47] These contexts are perspectival, relativistic and socially constructed.[48] Yet we experience these contexts as common sense. Indeed, as we have seen, our cognitive structures assist us in doing so. We tend to select and privilege certain schemas, to reify and automate them, to choose data that confirms them and then to use them to affirm our identity. In this way, though we are denied objective truth and essentialist certainty, we function with what Spivak has called a 'strategic essentialism'.[49] The living of life cannot, and need not, wait for the conceptual relation between the universal and the particular to be worked out by philosophy. As situated agents, we negotiate this problematic relation many thousands of times each day.

Because knowledge construction is always situated, it takes place within contexts which already feature a wide variety of stored prior knowledge. Areas of compatible cognition thus confront the individual as ontologically independent, and as incoming from a variety of societal levels. Norms, assumptions and processing schemas are on offer from the micro level of familial and social groups, the meso level of institutions and the macro level of society.[50] Somewhere here is the individual, dropped into organisational worlds characterised by power struggles, damaged information processing and stuck hierarchies.

Hierarchy affects its participants in a variety of ways, though one significant variable is clearly that of relative rank and role.[51] Social psychologists and those who study the psychology of oppression often describe power relations in terms of those who have power and those who do not.[52] As we have already noted, political scientists and sociologists have also, if sometimes simplistically, sought to distinguish between dominance and subordination. Such a distinction is also heuristic, as it serves to begin rudimentary analysis. So too is the distinction synchronic, for it freeze-frames what are complex, layered and dynamic power relations. Its purpose is to provide a working analysis of the complexities of conflicting status roles. Certainly, a more dynamic and diachronic view would reveal the Janus-faced nature of hierarchy, with its offer of rapidly changing roles of dominance and subordination. Yet the synchronic conception of a 'power divide' between dominance and subordination can serve to illuminate the effects of hierarchy on how we think, and how individuals with the same cognitive apparatus can be so differently affected.

The *location* of an individual generates a particular perspective, an agenda for knowledge processing; a partial and simplified view of the organisation. Location also provides a distinct set of self-confirming and self-affirming schemas that are reified and automated, so that individuals come to inhabit discrete symbolic worlds which are experienced as objective.[53] On either side of the 'power divide', these 'real' worlds are different.[54] What domination does is not so much to make people think in the same way, but to make them think in ways *that serve its ends.*

The experience of hierarchic and asymmetrical power thus separates into distinct cognitive projects. This, of course, is one of the oldest critiques of hierarchy, and it has often been noted that elites have a strong tendency to lose sight of what lies beneath them. As Dewey remarks, 'a class of experts is inevitably so removed from the common interests as to become a class with private interests and private knowledge'.[55] Michels described this as a growing *distance* between elites and subordinates; Rousseau saw it in terms of the gradual adoption of distinct types of will; Marx, as the separation of class interests and forms of consciousness. This separation is regularly observable across our organisational lives, and frequently confirmed in psychological experimentation. When Zimbardo made some students guards and others prisoners, it was not long before the guards had constructed a distinct cognitive world, one in which it was acceptable, even enjoyable, to abuse the prisoners, so that the experiment had to be abandoned.[56]

From the point of view of the subordinate, power is experienced as external, as approaching from outside, as something that exists over and apart from their own cognition. In this, the pull of a subordinate's own inherent cognitive biases, which simplify, confirm, affirm and reify, are again in evidence. An individual can respond with an easy internalisation of pushed schemas, and perhaps also with identification and organisational commitment. Yet subordinates can also reject the meanings on offer and question the legitimacy of extant authority. In this case, we find people 'misbehaving' in organisations,[57] and even surreptitiously working against the interests of dominant elites.[58] There is even a sense, here, in which these two realities delineate distinct 'communities of risk', for each faces the other as a source of threat and as a problem requiring management and control. This is no more than to repeat that across all the different experiences that make up an organisation, the respective *locations* of its members generates divergent, and even opposing, cognitive communities.[59]

One of the most important differences on either side of the power divide involves the responsibility for making and implementing decisions. Often, such responsibility lies with the dominant party, and not at all with the subordinate. Where this occurs, the effects on individual cognition are significant, for this particular asymmetry ushers in distinct schemas. In addition, it interacts with individual cognitive biases in different ways. Thus, for example, being responsible for a decision is affirmative of individual capacity, status and worth, and so engages the cognitive bias of affirmation in a positive and narcissistically helpful way. Conversely, lacking responsibility for a decision denies individual capacity, status and worth, and thereby frustrates, or works against, the affirmational bias. In the following chapter, where we relate the effects of organisations on individual cognition to questions around participatory democracy, we will have cause to investigate this matter more fully. Here, however, we should note that responsibility for the decision exerts a profound influence on individual cognition, and that the power divide in organisations ensures that this influence works in very different ways.

Indeed, hierarchy generates a separation of cognitive projects. Organisational structures influence cognition, and hierarchy influences individuals according to their respective locations. It is hierarchy's power divide that cuts, that separates, that brings into being the distinct experience of elites and subordinates and accounts for their being subjected to the pushing of different schemas. In this way, hierarchy generates a progressive uncoupling of elite and subordinate meaning. Now interpreting sensory data in different ways, they become embarked on divergent cognitive projects, at last fashioning their own distinct cognitive zones. Though the organisation requires these zones to themselves be sufficiently compatible to operate together, there is, nevertheless, a discernible separation which serves to create different cultures, groups and communities. This separation is a strong and structural tendency in all hierarchies, and derives, at least in part, from the differing interplay of organisational status and the structural apparatus of individual cognition.

This separation was noted quite early on in the development of cognitive psychology, where it was seen not so much as a manifestation of hierarchy as of organisational roles generally, and the partiality of view in particular. Lawrence and Lorsch identified a process of 'psychological differentiation' which seemed to occur when individuals occupied different roles, worked in different departments and took responsibility for specialised tasks.[60] Walker suggested a series of possible causes for this differentiation, one of which was 'position in the organisational network'.[61] There is thus an existing awareness of the inherent perspectivalism and relativism of individual experience in organisations, one arising from the insight that meaning is, at least in part, a social construction. People certainly experience events like a meeting or an administrative initiative quite differently, and this is because they have made, and are operating within, distinct cognitive worlds. Where meaning so diverges, communication breakdown is inevitable.

Perhaps the most illuminating, and the most chilling, account of the hierarchic separation of cognitive worlds is that afforded by Goffman's studies of the asylum.[62] Drawing on Durkheim's work on the bi-directional causation that occurs in the social world, Goffman charts the terrible divergence and solidification of self-evaluations between patient and psychiatrist, the growing invisibility of the patient's humanity, the resulting breakdown in communication and the casual cruelty of blinkered privilege.

Yet accounts of organisational life that feature the separation of individual and organisational realities seldom move much beyond the general insight that powerholders in organisations seek to push a particular version of reality.[63] Most miss the structural tendency of organisational hierarchy to separate participants into distinct camps and identities, and to do so around a characteristic power divide.[64]

Divergent self-evaluations, distinct collective identities and asymmetrical responsibility all drive a progressive experiential separation within the hierarchic organisation. Gradually, and ineluctably, elites and subordinates begin to mystify each other, lose contact, become blind to the other and reify the other as a coherent out-group. Cognitive separation is a structural tendency of hierarchy, and, if not managed properly, results in mission drift and a debilitating loss of organisational effectiveness. Elite corruption and subordinate collusion, both operating beneath individual awareness, now render subordinate knowledge and capacities entirely invisible, so that the very existence of the hierarchy at last confirms its own necessity. Whether we see this loss of subordinate contribution as a lack of 'perceptual access' to the other, as does Vetlesen, or as the absence of 'enlarged thinking', as does Arendt,[65] the result is the same: hierarchy simplifies, it saves cognitive work, it divides individuals and, as Marx showed, it 'reduces relations among men to those between objects'.

Where this separation is advanced, elites are corrupted and subordinates collude in their own oppression. With cognition so severely simplified and completely automated, it becomes almost impossible to see 'out'. Now, the facts support the necessity of the hierarchy, the boldness of elites can be measured and the foolishness of subordinates can be empirically confirmed. In this way, an existing hierarchy at last achieves – by logical circularity – a status which is self-legitimating and self-perpetuating. Here, then, elites effectively and unknowingly recruit the structures of subordinate cognition to their own ends. This occurs beneath individual awareness, and so constitutes an ideological configuration that is invisible, both to elites and subordinates. This is why Rousseau is able to so effectively criticise Hobbes's characterisation of the state of nature, for Hobbesian man is, by virtue of his repeated experience of domination and subordination, *already* hierarchic. Pull away the carpet of authority, and of course he misbehaves.

Cognitive separation by hierarchy is much in evidence across our everyday organisational lives, where it regularly results in breakdowns in communication. Three particularly damaging separations are those that occur in a representative democracy – between elected officials and citizens; in firms – between managers seeking innovation and those workers who actually innovate[66] and in efforts to increase public engagement – between public managers and community groups.[67]

The interplay of individual and organisational knowledge processing that we have here been exploring serves to illuminate an important side-effect of the hierarchic organisational form, this being its capacity to systematically devalue all other organisational forms. More accurately, as hierarchy divides the experience of dominant and subordinate, it peddles evaluative schemas that coalesce into a self-supporting ideology. This ideology, driven by 'pushed' schemas and the 'pull' of individual cognitive bias, renders the possible effectiveness of other forms invisible. The result is a hard nugget of ideology, one that asserts that hierarchy is the *only* way to achieve organisational effectiveness. This reified equation – between hierarchy and effectiveness – is a significant reason for the prevalence, across history and different cultures, of hierarchic relations of power.

There is thus a schema that equates hierarchy with effectiveness; one that is pushed hard by elites – both at elites and at their subordinates. As a knowledge claim, the equation is endlessly confirmed by the very existence of the hierarchic relations, and operates like a kind of prison around our political imagination. It is self-evident: there can be no other way to coordinate collective action.[68] A ship needs a captain. An army needs a general. A democracy needs a central representative core. When fully reified, automated and invested with affirmational importance, the equation is vigorously defended as a precious symbol of hierarchic power. Indeed, given that it is merely a knowledge claim, the violence and suffering meted out across history by elites (and sometimes even by subordinates) to those who would question it, is extraordinary. Yet we should expect nothing less from an ideological assertion that lies so deep within our hearts, and upon which so much evidently turns.

Robert Michels faithfully replicates the equation of hierarchy with effectiveness when he states that all organisations have a structural tendency towards oligarchy, one which serves to preclude the very possibility of democracy. Earlier, we noted that he was not able to state the causal mechanism for this tendency, nor to indicate where such a mechanism might be located. Now we see that his account, while impressive in its realism, is mistaken in its object. The structural tendency is not *of* organisations *towards* hierarchy. Rather, it is *of* hierarchy *towards* self-legitimation. This structural mechanism is located precisely in the cognitive apparatus of participating individuals placed within existing organisational hierarchies. When Michels studied the German Social Democratic Party, he was inspecting an existing hierarchic organisation. Once in place, hierarchy separates cognition around the power divide and reifies and automates schemas that support that divide. It was *this* that he so faithfully and boldly observed. As such, his 'Iron Law of Oligarchy' amounts to the insight that hierarchy is self-perpetuating. Certainly, illegitimate hierarchic relations of power sit uncomfortably with democracy, where occupation of dominant roles is supposed to be agreed to by participants. In this respect, then, Michels was correct, for cognitive separation is especially damaging when it infects the institutionalised hierarchies of representative democracy.

In an organisational environment characterised by reified hierarchies, more participatory forms of democracy *appear* impossible, and the effective coordination of collective action by agreement and minimal hierarchy seems mere utopia. This is a cognitive distortion, one that results in a significant loss of valuable knowledge, a stunting of political imagination and an incapacity to conceive of meaningful reform. In particular, it denies that the experimentation with network organisational forms now taking place at the margins of political action have anything to offer democracy at all. Not only do we thereby fail to learn from this experimentation, but we also demonise it and define it as non-democratic.[69] It is in the attitude of democratic states to participatory innovation within civil society that our fear of the populace, and thus our profound ambivalence about democracy, at last reveals itself.

So far still at the margins of radical democratic theory and practice, there is a growing orientation to what might be termed an 'anti-institutional' or 'minimally-hierarchic' view of democratic politics. Here, participation is conceived not in terms of voting, but along more deliberative and expressive lines,[70] thus posing problems for its capture in institutional forms.[71] In radical democratic theory, there is a renewed interest in redefining the political and extending it to areas of identity, culture and organisational life. Generally, however, these developments are oriented to the destabilisation of our cultural representations, ways of seeing and conceptions of the self, rather than to the imperatives of power politics.[72] As such, they are largely ignored by mainstream political science. When they do receive attention, they have been strongly admonished for abandoning material questions,[73] for their lack of concrete organisational designs[74] and for their 'utopian' view of citizen capacities.

In the realm of democratic practice, particularly in direct action groups[75] protesting around questions of globalisation, identity[76] and the environment,[77] there is concerted experimentation with new ways of coordinating collective action and a widespread rejection of the vanguardist organisational forms which dominated the radical politics of the past. These experiments are, at this point, extraordinarily widespread, both geographically and in terms of the organisational functions they now address. Across this 'associational revolution', there is a heightened suspicion of state-level institutions and of the formal hierarchies that continue to dominate civil societies. Once again, however, such activities have been heavily criticised and even ridiculed, here for their parochialism, ineffectiveness, political irrelevance and utopianism. As a consequence, networks of flattened hierarchy are not seen as sources of organisational innovation, and we waste what are, in fact, important advances in our understanding of how more participatory networks might be self-organising.

In regard to these practical developments, however, the easy accusation of ineffectiveness does not fit well with the fact that minimal-hierarchic initiatives have been subject to direct physical attack by the police, aggressive surveillance by secret services, disciplinary legislation and close scrutiny by state officials.[78] There is, it seems, a process of assessment at work here which somehow, both dismisses such activities as ineffective while at the same time demonising them as possibly *too* effective, dangerously anti-democratic and thus as developments to be feared.

This incoherence certainly reflects a profound ambivalence about democracy, but is also a result of the thick cloak of ideology that conceals our political order. Once again, we cannot here rely on empirical, or indeed, even historical evidence in order to reveal this ideology. This is forcibly shown in the work of Deleuze and Guattari, who seek to demonstrate how credit for the military innovations of nomadic peoples, such as chariots and cavalry, are subsequently claimed by centralised and sedentary political forms.[79] They describe the terrifying effectiveness of the guerrilla army, the riot, the fast flowing hordes of apparently disorganised barbarians. What emerges from their work is at once the reclamation of an alternative form of action coordination and an account of how that form has been devalued, usurped and rendered invisible.[80]

According to Deleuze and Guattari, the way we understand questions of organisation is systematically restricted and distorted. They argue that we tend to see organisational and political structures in terms of hierarchical arrangements, centralised control and vertical agglomerations of power. The image they use to capture this way of seeing is that of the tree, with its branches spreading upwards from a central trunk. Following their identification of the lack of such centralisation in the nomadic war machine, they begin to explore an alternative form, here using the metaphor of crab-grass, with its matted horizontal connections and concealed labyrinth of rhizomes. What they call 'rhizomatic' action coordination thus takes place along complex neural-like networks,[81] without identifiable nodes of power and across unstructured space. In fact, as Deleuze and Guattari show, these disorganised forms have continually and throughout history challenged the sedentary state, provided it with significant innovations and been variously absorbed and domesticated in what amounts to an ongoing struggle between two quite distinct forms of action coordination.

We find a related approach in the work of Sheldon Wolin, who, by challenging frequently made historical assertions – such as the alleged inability of revolutions to generate democracy – identifies a deep political paradox. Democracy, he argues, is evidenced in moments of participatory and disorganised upheaval, rather than in the more durable periods wherein it is institutionalised.[82] He sees democracy as inherently revolutionary, as challenging of existing institutions, as rhizomatic in its coordination. For this reason, he describes liberal democratic constitutional arrangements as vain attempts to capture and control revolutionary moments. With constitutionalism appearing as the ultimate 'domestication of politics',[83] revolutionary upheaval is revealed as the main source of democratic rights. Were this acknowledged in our historical constructions, he argues, we would be better able to understand that democracy is something that takes place *outside* institutions.

Deleuze and Guattari, and Wolin, are trying to break the ideological strangle-hold exerted by entrenched hierarchy upon our evaluation of political organisation. They remind us of a lost history, one where network and minimal-hierarchic forms were, in fact, highly effective.[84] They suggest that our traditional accounts of the past do not reveal what really occurred, and by extension, neither do we really see what is occurring now. Each holds that the cloak of ideological distortion is so thick that we can no longer even conceive of any possible alternative to liberal democracy. Indeed, so naïve is our realism that we unhesitatingly export our hierarchic interpretation of democracy to other countries,[85] force feeding them the necessary schemas and penalising them if they resist what is so clearly, to us, the truth.

Hierarchy can be a valuable organisational form, but it strongly affects how its members think. It comes with significant and even debilitating hidden costs. One such cost is the tendency for power to corrupt both elites and subordinates; another is its inevitable cognitive separation; still another is its occlusion of different, yet still effective, organisational forms. Such costs are seldom considered when contemplating its use, and it remains common, in meetings across the world, to seek to solve problems by simply appointing a leader. It is this unreflective generation of hierarchy that is responsible for much of the mission drift, ineffectiveness, wasted subordinate knowledge and downright inhumanity we currently observe in so many of our organisations.

Here again, cognitive psychology is able to deepen our understanding of social scientific insights. Hierarchy separates; it is self-legitimating. By focusing on cognition, we can see precisely how it does so.

## Elite corruption

In examining the complex interplay between individual cognition and organisational knowledge processing, we stumble upon the fact that our thoughts are not entirely our own. Here, at the boundary, is a hidden world of political struggle. In an organisational hierarchy, with discernible roles of dominance and subordination, individuals are influenced by organisational knowledge processing in different ways – depending in part upon their relative status in the hierarchy. In this section, we will focus more closely on these differing effects in order to describe the actual mechanisms by which individuals, both dominant and subordinate, are variously corrupted by power. As we shall see, corruption by power turns out to be a pathology of the boundary, a melding of individual and collective, a blurring of one, into and over, the other. At its heart is a process of cognitive substitution.

This process is perhaps most easily observed, in both oneself and others, upon promotion to a higher status role. With new responsibilities and imperatives comes a new space for public recognition and display, and an expanded stage upon which your identity will be performed.[86] Higher status is strongly affirmational.[87] It provides a self-image tinged with pride, and every interaction with subordinates confirms the effect of your higher status on others. As we have already noted, one such effect is the subtle reorientation of interactions with subordinates towards *you*, so that they increasingly reflect *your* needs and *your* psychological processes.[88] This gradual reorientation presents what amount to repeated opportunities for narcissistic self-indulgence and the removal of boundaries upon your behaviour (disinhibition).

Yet so does it require you to orient more fully towards your organisation's goals. You are now an ambassador; you represent your organisation, and are publicly responsible for the coordination of subordinate action towards those goals. Such changes begin the blurring the boundary between yourself and your organisation. Increasingly, you *identify* with the organisation; you bring it into yourself and meld its interests with your own. Slowly but surely, you are becoming a centaur: part individual, part organisation.[89] Any slight against the organisation is now one against your very self.

Rousseau was describing this kind of identification when he said, 'the rich have feelings in every part of their possessions'.[90] Certainly, in the example of Richard Keys with which we began this investigation, the promotion to a high-status role resulted in him 'having feelings in every part of the organisation', particularly with every decision for which he had responsibility. Identification smeared the distinction between himself and the organisation, and it did so to such an extent as to encourage him to confuse his own cognition with the information processing of the organisation. When questioned or threatened with change, this cognitive distortion caused him to become fundamentally defensive in his conceptions, strategies and relationships.[91] This defensiveness was both the product of his psychological investment in the organisation, and of his own cognitive tendencies to affirm his sense of self and confirm the validity of his experience.

Where the self is so intimately bound up with the hierarchic organisation, however, the defensive perimeter can become very wide indeed. Accordingly, Keys became ever more negative in his assessment of subordinates; at last developing a petty preoccupation with even the smallest and most symbolic of challenges to his authority. Now he evinced a reckless willingness to sacrifice everything to retain his power. It may be this defensiveness that makes elites so much more dangerous than the mob. Hobbes was wrong when he claimed that anything was better than his state of nature, for, as Dewey correctly asserts, 'the world has suffered more from leaders and authorities than from the masses'.[92] Similarly, Machiavelli understood that, 'Princes and governments are far more dangerous than are other elements in society'.[93] Once again, tyranny is the greatest cost and most oft repeated critique of the hierarchic organisational form.

What really got to Richard Keys, however, was that the rest of his team seemed to take no responsibility for decision-making. They did not appear to concern themselves with the interests of the organisation. For Keys, who identified so strongly with the organisation and whose internal process was already blurring with that of the collective, this was nothing short of a *personal* rejection. Indeed, it appeared to him as a palpable error of judgement. Subordinate disinterest, and their failure to join him in taking responsibility for decision-making, served to fuel his devaluation of subordinate capacities. In this way, a series of negative evaluative schemas were 'pulled' into his mind, as it were, by his own tendencies towards cognitive bias. Yet these schemas were also 'pushed' at him; here by the hierarchic organisational form itself, and its structural tendency to undervalue subordinate knowledge.

The re-orientation of organisational activities toward the dominating self, increasing identification with the existing hierarchy, downright narcissistic self-indulgence and a growing isolation, all served to remove the psychological boundaries between Keys and his organisation. There now existed a subtle interplay between his own cognition and that of the collective; a fact at once eased and concealed by cognitive bias. Granted an expanding zone of individual cognition and the gradual disappearance of subordinate responsibility, he was systematically encouraged to favour his own interests over those of others. In this, he did no more than fill what had, by now, become an empty space.[94] Seeing no other responsible actor, no possibility for coordination other than hierarchy and no other cognitive world but his own, Keys gradually *substituted* his own cognition for the knowledge processing of the organisation. In his case, there was only faltering awareness of this change, for, aided by his innate tendency to automate cognition, it quickly plunged into his unconscious mind, where it disappeared; leaving him quite unable to distinguish his own self-interest from that of the organisation. Indeed, it became increasingly difficult for him to even perceive any such object as the good of all.

This, then, is how power corrupts the occupant of a high status role: it encourages the individual to substitute his own cognition for that of the collective.[95] Hierarchy simplifies. It favours the use of certain schemas and dovetails with the structural cognitive biases of individuals. In this way, the corrupt leader is lulled into automated cognition and a progressively shrinking world. John Dewey said that 'all special privilege in some way limits the outlook of those who possess it'.[96] Here, we see that this limitation of outlook derives from individual cognitive tendencies and their interaction with the power saturated organisational form of hierarchy itself. Janet McIntosh is thus correct in her assertion that, 'our innate tendencies to think in certain ways... are... *parasitised* by local power formations and *used* in their service'.[97]

The leader substitutes his individual cognition *for* organisational information processing. This is a 'taking over', a taking in; a subsumption. Hierarchic perceptual distortion affects managers, elites, leaders and, indeed, almost anyone with any 'special privilege' at all. Such distortions are incremental, outside awareness and self-perpetuating. The progressive simplification provided by organisational hierarchy and individual cognitive biases – working in tandem – at last reduce the cognitive field to that of elite self-interest; here genuinely experienced as the interests of the organisation. Increasingly isolated, the leader comes to make decisions alone. As he does so, he gazes upon what amounts to a separate, and profoundly narcissistic, reality. This is the ideology of elitism, and it is invisible. In the case of corruption by power, it enables us to genuinely deny that we are subject to any such distortion.

This is why we cannot say, of Richard Keys, that he was lying. When he claimed to know best, to be punishing subordinates for good reason and to be making difficult and correct decisions, he believed it. Yet the paucity of his perception, and his evident inability to rise above his growing cognitive disorder, explained why he felt, in his very bones, that he was right. For organisational elites – no matter how carefully they squint – their own superiority is plain to see. While the degree of corruption by power varies according to individual susceptibility and the extent of status inequality, in its most advanced manifestations, it is a psychotic disorder, for it involves a profound disconnect with reality.

## Subordinate corruption

The effects of hierarchy on individual cognition are very different for subordinates; yet they too receive significant benefits, and they do so, once again, via a process of cognitive substitution. Though it may be lonely at the top, corruption by power is lucrative, and the indulgence of narcissistic need is usually pleasurable. However, while the leader substitutes his own cognition for that of the collective, and so inflates his own self-interest to the exclusion of all else, the subordinate substitutes collective information processing *for his own*. It is this substitution of cognition, facilitated and 'pulled' at by individual cognitive bias, which results in the unwitting collusion with oppression.

To illustrate, let us consider the following: you are situated in a hierarchic organisation and you have a low-status role. Faced with incumbent power, you need to stay alive, gain carrots, avoid sticks and generally defend yourself. To do so, you must have knowledge, and this is provided according to your role. An inescapable partiality of view and an exclusion from decision-making responsibility are here part of a general simplification and reduction of cognitive work offered you by the hierarchic organisational form.

At the same time, hierarchic organisations endlessly dose subordinates with particular schemas, which they intend subordinates to use in their construction of meaning. Pushed schemas include norms, routines and rules, but they also feature powerful assertions about the necessity of hierarchy and the paucity of subordinate capacities. Regularly drilled and rehearsed, these schemas are then eased into subordinate cognition by the biases towards confirmation and reification. When fully automated, this influence operates beneath awareness, and individual cognition can be effectively coordinated to deliver organisational goals. Here, then, subordinates are encouraged to directly *cede* portions of their own cognition to the hierarchic organisation. It is this 'giving over' of cognition to a hierarchy that serves to reduce the cognitive work required of the individual.

This reduction in work has its costs, chief among them being what has been called 'learned helplessness'.[98] Subordinates are awash with pushed schemas that systematically devalue their capacities. These schemas are then pulled at by their own individual cognitive biases, enabling them to slip easily and silently into everyday information processing. In addition, subordinates are severely limited in their affirmational identification with the organisation, most particularly by being denied responsibility for decision-making. When they finally relinquish a portion of their cognition to a hierarchy, they achieve a psychological dependency which is self-confirming. Helplessness – a social construction taking place beneath the awareness of the individual – can now be empirically verified by elites as objective fact. In this way, subordinates are effectively self-debilitating. Their collusion contributes to the maintenance of hierarchy, and allows their individual cognition to be managed in the interests of elite domination.[99]

This 'taking-on' of organisational information processing by the individual accounts for the many descriptions of subordinate collusion which see it in terms of the internalisation of power.[100] Our use of tools from cognitive psychology suggests it is more appropriately characterised as a substitution – here of hierarchic information processing *for* individual cognition. Subordinates 'out-source' or *cede* a portion of their cognitive work to the organisational hierarchy, and do so beneath awareness. It is not, therefore, correct to suggest, as do many hegemony theorists, that we are mere psychological 'sponges', able to directly absorb into ourselves the cultural products of a purposefully deceitful ruling class. Rather, what power offers us is a form of *proxy* cognition, a stand-in, a water carrier; one willing to share the burden of information processing and psychological defence. Upon joining a hierarchy, then, you are not only force-fed ways of thinking. You are also invited, by the very structure of individual cognition itself, to *alienate* portions of your thinking to the organisation.[101]

One of the problems we identified with notions of internalisation, say of disciplinary power, is that it closes off any chance of seeing things in a different way, of overcoming the *productivity* of power so as to even conceive of resistance. This does not sit well with Foucault's assertion of the inevitability of resistance. Foucault presents us, on the one hand, with structural reasons why there will always be resistance; and on the other, with structural reasons why this can never be achieved. Much turns on this paradox, not least, our fears for the future. *How*, then, does power generate resistance? Where is this structural mechanism upon which we rest our hope that we will not, one day, be entirely controlled, our meanings administered, our privacy constantly surveyed?

When we looked at psychoanalytic attempts to describe the mechanisms of ego defence, we noted the capacity of internal psychological process to 'flip' or invert, and so take the form, not of the schema on offer, but of a 'conversion reaction', or reversal, of that schema. We noted a similar propensity for human cognition to overcome innate cognitive bias in order to question and change schemas; and thereby to learn. In their responses to the endless pushing of schemas to which they are subject in a hierarchy, subordinates can be believers or cynics. Either way, they must make their individual cognition functionally compatible with that of the hierarchic organisation: they must *use* the schemas on offer, whether they believe them legitimate or not.

Nor is it of any real consequence to elites if subordinates collude out of a genuine and willing identification with the organisation, or out of a cynical and begrudging acceptance. What *is* vital, however, is that hierarchy preserves the fiction of its unique capacity to coordinate individual action. In our previous analysis of cognition in organisations, we saw that it is not necessary for cognition to be shared, or identical, for the coordination of collective action to occur. It is only necessary that cognition be functionally compatible. Indeed, this was as far as the available explanatory tools were able to take us. Even when actively managed by the special interests in a hierarchy, the minimal requirement of compatible cognition suggests that subordinates can be variously motivated to obey, as long as they *do* obey.

One of the advances made available by studies of postcolonialism is that subordinates often obey, *not* because they believe in the schemas being pushed at them, but simply for instrumental reasons. Pushed schemas are here taken up and used, but only because the carrots and sticks applied to subordinates demand that this be so. Beneath the appearance of obedience, there is room for significant resistance to the interests of power, as long as it is carefully concealed. As George Elliot agreed with her father: she would attend church on the condition that she was allowed to think whatever she wanted while she did so.

There are, of course, dangers inherent in the frequent rehearsal of 'pushed' schemas, particularly so when individual cognitive biases start to 'pull' at them, thus automating their use. Postcolonialism is at its most powerful when it analyses the political struggle over schemas, particularly where such schemas deliver negative assessments of subordinate capacities.[102] Yet, nevertheless, hierarchic organisations, by insisting on merely the *appearance* of obedience, create hidden spaces in which subordinate identities can construct themselves, beyond the gaze of elites and in opposition to their interests.

In his work on slave and feudal societies, James Scott inspects these ongoing and carefully concealed spaces of resistance. Once beyond surveillance, slaves grumble and ridicule their masters and workers rumour and carry out anonymous, and often petty, acts of vandalism.[103] These are hidden cultures of resistance,[104] with their own ways of communicating, their own spaces where they can interact freely; unseen by elites. Such interactions coordinate collective action, and they do so by informal networks which are horizontal and largely devoid of hierarchical structure. These networks pass information at tremendous speed. Always simmering beneath the surface, they only occasionally billow up, challenge dominant power and become visible. Scott invites us to peer into this different world, acknowledging that it is a hard one to see.

Its invisibility is, according to Scott, quite purposeful.[105] Indeed, it is important that subordinates use different forms of communication and action and that they hide them. Only when this hidden world becomes too vital and explosive for existing elites to contain does it at last reveal itself.[106] In such moments, coordinated resistance suddenly appears, and truth is finally spoken to power.[107] Across history, these occasional eruptions have torn freedoms, resources and rights from the hands of elites; though later, as hierarchies reassert control, such events are downplayed in official histories.[108] When hierarchic mastery over individual cognition is re-established, networks of coordinated resistance once again disappear from view. They still exist; but are now, once again, hiding among the figments of homogeneity.

The very fact that humans can learn at all attests to the ongoing possibility that, for any given subordinate in any given hierarchy, inversion of pushed schemas can occur and automated cognition can be hauled back into consciousness and recovered from the organisation. Hierarchy exists all around us. It emerged in response to a combination of material and psychological causes. But its preservation relies inescapably on the individual cognition of its members. It is here, therefore, that the battle for justification occurs. This is the power struggle over meaning: an ongoing conflict over the very contents of our minds. The politics of thinking in organisations takes place, for the most part, beneath the awareness, and beyond even the intention, of individuals. Only when we see *how* hierarchy uses individual cognitive bias to preserve the interests of elites can we show how power corrupts, and how subordinates effectively collude in the construction of their own dependency.

To be corrupted by power as a subordinate, is to cede a portion of one's cognition to a hierarchy. Here, organisational structure reaches directly into individual cognition, offering plausible cognitive strategies and work-reducing schemas. This kind of cognition is self-reinforcing, and when in full cry, results in the best and worst excesses of individuals within organisations. Stanley Milgram filmed it in his famous experiment: two-thirds of us can be made to administer a fatal electric shock to another, merely by being encouraged to do so by actors wearing white coats and carrying clip-boards.[109]

There is a terrible passivity in obedience. To have a portion of one's thinking invisibly colonised is not an admirable quality in a democratic citizen. Most of us do not aspire to be sheep. So important is this kind of cognition, and so destructive its effects upon our history, that we should note its three principle qualities and give it a suitable name.

Where individual cognition is:

1. *also* a part of organisational knowledge processing,
2. automated beneath individual awareness and
3. serves the interests of dominant elites,

we will refer to it as 'battery' cognition. This captures the sense in which this type of thinking is invisibly taken over, managed and *farmed* for its productive efficiency in the interests of power. Battery cognition is a poor stand-in for autonomy, and a profound threat to our individuality. It is certainly an example of undemocratic thinking. As such, it reflects Rousseau's infamous critique of representative government: that the alienation of sovereignty to a proxy constitutes a serious violation of autonomy.[110]

Though battery cognition is undemocratic thinking, it should not be conceived as an intentional plot perpetrated by leaders upon their subordinates – although it can be. Rather, it is more usually a way of thinking that strongly affects *all* members of an organisation, most of the time and in different ways. Battery cognition is thus a common component in everyday organisational knowledge processing. For participating individuals – be they dominant, subordinate or some combination of the two – it is almost wholly invisible. But it is also the most dangerous kind of cognition in which we ever engage. For what is being automated here can serve dominant interests, and do so beneath awareness. Battery cognition thus amounts to blind obedience.

We can now add to our analysis of organisational hierarchy the fact that it has a strong tendency toward elite and subordinate cognitive substitution. Just as subordinates alienate their cognition *to* a hierarchy, so is that hierarchy taken over by the cognitive and psychological processes of elites. This circle of substitutions serves to exchange individual and collective information processing for elite cognition. Indeed, where organisational information processing is already reduced to the self-interest of the leader, subordinates are effectively ceding their own thinking to the narcissistic process of another individual. This circle of substitutions is constitutive of hierarchy, and results, in its most advanced forms, in outright authoritarianism, subordinate adoration of the 'charismatic' leader, corruption by power and organisational sclerosis. In this way, hierarchy serves to exchange autonomous individual cognition for the projected narcissism of leadership.

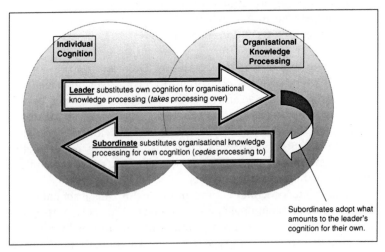

*Figure 4.1*  Corruption as a Circle of Substitutions

In our investigation into how power corrupts, we have noted that conceiving of the relationship between leaders and followers in a hierarchy merely in terms of 'power over' involves a simplification of the complex power relations that actually pertain in organisations. We have indulged this simplification in order to tease out the cognitive dimension of corruption by power, and to show that its distinct effects turn on an individual's location in a hierarchy. However, because hierarchies involve multiple layers of status, most of us are sometimes leaders and sometimes followers. It is thus possible, in the same day at the office and from one meeting to another, to be at one moment dominant, and in the next, subordinate. Most leaders – when they turn around to face their own bosses – are at the same time followers. Corruption by power affects dominants and subordinates in quite distinct ways. It is therefore likely that an individual will be corrupted by power *both* as leader *and* as follower. Where this occurs, we are confronted by the need to understand a circle of cognitive substitution in which elites both take over *and* cede their own cognition; like a tiger chasing its tail.

This degree of complexity is beyond capture in the frozen frame we have been scrutinising, but that is not to detract from the gains made available by this model. The fact that we are both leaders and followers does not mean there is no such thing as 'power over'. As Bertrand Russell said, 'the existence of twilight does not mean there is no difference between night and day'. Rather, our twilight indicates that the full complexity of power relations in organisations, the interplay of individual cognition and organisational knowledge processing and the psychological effects of rapid exchange of relative status roles, continue to evade our understanding. One area in which we can observe this strange mixture of elite and subordinate corruption, however, is in the area of what have been termed 'crimes of obedience'.

First defined during the Nuremberg trials and subsequently deepened in court argumentation following the My Lai massacre in the Vietnam War, crimes of obedience involve following orders that are immoral and should not be followed. They are thus, *at once*, acts of domination over victims *and* subservience to superiors. In crimes of obedience, corrupted subordinates act – momentarily and parochially – like corrupted leaders. Such crimes have resulted in the most desperate acts of cruelty, but they also occur in less dramatic form across our daily organisational lives. We see this when we become swept up by group processes to scapegoat others, when we officiously enforce an absurd bureaucratic rule or carelessly turn away a job applicant. Apparently minor acts of obedience can constitute the most serious crimes many of us commit. Crimes of obedience entail a failure to question immoral orders. They are profound acts of moral blindness, of battery cognition and the abnegation of our capacity to think for ourselves.

We can now summarise our study of the clinical indicators for corruption by power as follows:

1. ***Self Inflation:*** growing self-confidence and the gradual privileging of own perspective; progression from more usual methods of maintaining self esteem to an (unusual) narcissistic aggrandisement; automated reification of one's own superiority as natural; widespread confirmation and affirmational bias; increasingly subjective conception of the public good and subordination of the public good to one's own psychological needs; strong identification with the organisation and substitution of organisational knowledge processing by own cognition; evidence of battery cognition and increased proclivity for crimes of obedience; heightened attraction to hierarchic management philosophy and its attendant justifications and schemas; arrogance and disinhibition; defensive hardening degenerating eventually into the inability to learn.

2. ***Devaluation of Subordinates:*** automated reification of subordinate incapacities as natural; increased adoption, automation and reification of negative schemas regarding subordinates; stereotyping of subordinates as a free-riding and coherent out-group that has abnegated decision-making responsibility – and thus as requiring disciplinary control and paternalistic guidance; dehumanisation of, and a loss of empathy for, subordinates; increased narcissistic injury to subordinates (conscious and unconscious); increased proclivity for crimes of obedience; contempt; arbitrary cruelty.

3. ***Separation:*** emergence of a *cognitive* divide between leader and subordinate, reflecting their respective directions of cognitive substitution.

   For the leader 'taking over' organisational knowledge processing: a growing inability to take other perspectives on board; selection of advisors who support the leader's views; widespread confirmation bias and adoption of automated and static schemas resulting in shrinking sources of knowledge; progressive isolation and cognitive immunisation.

   For subordinates 'ceding' their cognition: increased awareness of, and orientation to, the leader's needs; automated reification and internalisation of own incapacities; collusion; self-debilitation; resentment and resistance; increased proclivity for battery cognition and crimes of obedience.

   For both leader and subordinate: increased automated reification of the hierarchic organisational form and its supporting ideological schemas; communication breakdown.

4. ***Invisibility:*** obtains when the above three behavioural changes take place outside the conscious awareness of affected individuals, and do so through a process of reification bias and automation. Though corruption by power entails an interaction between individual and group, the social influence on individual thinking remains invisible. Corruption is thus a perceptual distortion. It is a disorder of cognition and epistemology, and is parasitic on the invisibility of the processes by which meaning is constructed.

*Figure 4.2*   The Clinical Indicators for Corruption by Power

Corruption by power is a process of cognitive substitution that arises when an individual takes a high status role in an organisation. It involves a parasitic interplay between individual cognitive structures and the knowledge processing of collectives. As such, it is a boundary pathology; an 'illness of position'.[111] It thus affects individuals in distinct ways, depending not only on individual character, but also on their respective location within a hierarchy. Our attempt to identify and describe the mechanisms by which power corrupts has borrowed heavily from cognitive psychology in order to begin to show *how* it actually works. In this, we have tried to move beyond Acton's compelling yet merely functional observation that corruption regularly occurs when individuals are given higher status than their peers. The tools made available by the study of cognition have also helped to delineate the *ways* in which corruption manifests itself; here in terms of self inflation, the devaluation of subordinates, the separation and isolation of cognitive cultures and the loss of awareness and visibility.

Finally, we should note again that the strong human tendency towards corruption by power cannot be attributed to a structural mechanism *within the organisation*. Ontologically speaking, its causal structure is situated within the cognitive apparatus of individuals. *This* apparatus is structurally biased, and is thus the location of the causal mechanism by which power corrupts. Individual cognition tends to simplify, confirm, affirm and reify. In this way, the structure of the human mind favours the artificial maintenance of the hierarchic organisational form. Hierarchy is natural, as is corruption by power, subordinate collusion and the degeneration of political orders. It may even be that domination and subordination constitute the most primordial of all the organisational forms. But like individual cognitive bias, it is not determinate, nor inescapable. We have the evident ability both for bias and for the overcoming of bias. We can allow our individual cognition to be recruited into the service of dominant interests, yet so can we raise consciousness, haul automated cognition into the light and subject it to critical questioning.

The costs of adopting hierarchic relations of power are thus both dramatic and hidden. We have been exploring these costs in some detail, noting how they often occur outside the awareness of participants and analysing the cognitive mechanisms by which they take place. Certainly, the following are often incurred by the hierarchic organisational form:

- Cognitive separation
- Subordinate self-debilitation and alienation
- Wasted subordinate knowledge
- Degeneration of elite knowledge
- Communication breakdown
- Mission drift
- Invisibility of other organisational forms
- General failure of organisational learning
- Tyranny and terror

*Figure 4.3*   The Costs of Hierarchy

The active management of hierarchy's costs – which we earlier identified as a fundamentally *democratic* interest – amounts to an attempt to reduce its negative cognitive effects, to take back responsibility for decision-making and to hold power to account. In this way, we come closer to thinking for ourselves. The preferred treatment for corruption by power, and for the active management of the hierarchic organisational form, is democracy.

Though it may be of little consequence whether we call our political order 'representative democracy' or 'oligarchic turn-taking', democracy in organisations is of a great deal more importance. States are vulnerable to their constituent organisations being democratised underneath them, and in contemporary developments in new social movements, this is again beginning to occur. When a democratic organisation seeks to minimise hierarchy, and balance its gains and costs, the management problems presented by this organisational form must be fully understood if corruption by power is to be avoided.

Instead, we remain constrained within a conception of democracy as little more than an administrative procedure occasionally employed by a nation state. It thus takes a representative form that runs alongside inadequately managed markets. We vote as autonomous citizens; we give our informed consent by ceding decision-making to a professional class – after which we return to our more immediate and private concerns. In such a 'democracy', the costs of hierarchy are denied, endemic, progressive and debilitating.

# 5
# Democratic Conclusions

If politics concerns the question of 'what should we do?' then democracy holds that we should consult the citizenry, empower selected agents to govern effectively and guard against the concentration of power. Since liberalism's attack on religious dogma and the absolutist state, we have learned to refrain from dictating the good for others and resolved to ask individuals for their own conception of the good. As Jürgen Habermas so cogently asserts, 'all things considered, the best judge of individual interests is the individual themselves'.[1] Democracy is not, therefore, a universal truth to be imposed on others, but is, instead, a practice evolved to *prevent the imposition* of a universal truth.[2] We thus do democracy not because we know, but because we do not.

David Owen is right to assert that democracy is the preferred treatment for corruption by power. But his overriding interest is in elite corruption, in *hubris*. His fascination with leadership aligns with his failure to acknowledge that the word 'democracy' might mean more than the current set of treasured state institutions, virtually unchanged in a century and a half. *This* kind of democracy is unable to manage the costs of hierarchy. Electoral democracy today not only fails to treat corruption by power; it actively fosters it. We can use the cognitive account of how power corrupts to see why this occurs.

## The cognitive critique of representation

Our contemporary political order, with its distinctive roles of professional politicians and occasional electors, is both a division of political labour and an extant hierarchy. As such, it makes much of its distinguished record in the coordination of collective action. Yet so is it subject to the organisational tendency towards cognitive separation around the power-divide inherent in all hierarchies. Today, we see this in citizen disengagement with mainstream politics, in the wildly divergent perceptions of public services evinced by politicians and service users, in the hermetically sealed 'gentlemen's club of Westminster' and in the regular top-down bungling of initiatives to increase public engagement. Certainly, current levels of apathy and political disengagement across the liberal democracies suggests the process of cognitive separation is historically embedded and well advanced. The recent inability of elected officials to perceive any wrongdoing in their expense claims attests again to the profoundly isolated world in which they move.

The threat posed by this 'cognitive' separation was clearly observed during the European revolutions by anarchist thinkers and activists. Proudhon, for example, remarked that:

> as soon as I set foot in the parliamentary Sinai, I ceased to be in touch with the masses... I entirely lost sight of the current of events. I know nothing, either of the situation of the national workshop, or the policy of the government... one must have lived in that isolator which is called a National Assembly to realise how the men who are most completely ignorant of the state of the country are almost always those who represent it.[3]

Bakunin saw it too. 'The ruling class', he declared, 'is completely different and separate from the mass of the governed... their longings [are] diametrically opposite'. He attributed the growing conservativism of his radical colleagues upon promotion to a 'change in position and hence of perspective'.[4] Anarchism has continued to point out – at its peril – that cognitive separation presents particular problems for vanguard revolutionary parties. The Soviet history of corruption by power, and the scale of its organised cruelty, attests to the hierarchic tendency towards separation, and the seemingly endless capacity of elites to construct an isolated and self-confirming world.

But so does cognitive separation threaten representational democracy. We have noted the tendency of hierarchic power relations to corrupt both leaders and subordinates, and to affect the latter in ways that stimulate their incapacity and dependency. Now we can see that modern liberal democracy, with its division of political labour, attenuation of active participation and systematic depoliticisation of the public sphere effectively relegates citizens to roles of spectator and subordinate. Responsibility for decision-making is removed from them. Here, then, our analysis of how power corrupts leads to a *cognitive* validation of critiques of representative government, for it shows how a small group of elected officials will become progressively isolated, their narcissism over-indulged and their awareness occluded.

Foremost among the critiques of representative government is that advanced by Rousseau. He claimed that representation entailed an alienation of sovereignty to a proxy, and that this was an unacceptable violation of personal autonomy.[5] Rousseau's critique is a largely normative rejection: for government to be legitimate, popular sovereignty *should* be retained by the autonomous individual.[6] As such, the claim is open to the practical objection from those seeking to defend representation: that autonomy, while a worthy ideal, is simply impractical, and too difficult to sustain in the modern world. In this way, democratic theory has, behind a veil of assumed realism, shrugged its shoulders and accepted the necessity of a centralised representative hierarchy – with all the dangers of corruption that entails and little attention to its costs.

It is widely assumed that a more deliberative politics is simply impractical in massive nation states facing highly complex policy issues.[7] Seldom is this assumption properly scrutinised; still less is it the subject of creative and practical experimentation. Having thus 'established' the inescapable necessity of such a representative core,[8] democratic theorists proceed to design institutional plumbing by which participatory input to the core might be increased.[9] Yet, almost always, such reforms are concerned to preserve the stability and effectiveness of the representative core by protecting it from excessive participatory input. Habermas, for example, has argued that democracy should be deliberative in nature, and that governments are only legitimate when based on the open and discursive agreement of citizens. Yet, cold-footed, he then pulls back, and states that 'discourses do not rule'. Rather, the deliberative fora of the public sphere should 'influence' government; not usurp it.

Citizens in deliberation are therefore required to be 'self-limiting'.[10] Time and again, democratic theorists say they want more democracy, yet remain profoundly ambivalent about more *participation*. Apparently radical calls for deliberative democracy founder when confronted with the brute need for effective government. And they do so because they share, with their elitist counterparts, the assumption that effectiveness can only ever derive from hierarchic institutions.

Rousseau's critique, however, carefully distinguishes between the unacceptability of alienating sovereignty to a representative, and the occasional necessity of delegating power to another.[11] Where the injunction against representation is intended to show the illegitimacy of elected governments, delegation here serves to ensure that the sovereign citizen assembly is organisationally effective. This combination – of a mass legislature and a small executive which is subordinate to the legislature – is a characteristic of mixed republican governmental forms throughout history. But Rousseau's distinction also highlights the profound difference between ceding (substituting) responsibility for decision-making to another, and knowingly and autonomously assigning time-bound tasks to the agents of the people – and then watching them like hawks.

What is at stake here is the difference between an unexamined political hierarchy, and a hierarchy knowingly entered into in order to meet specific challenges by drawing on specific skills. The difference is one between political power and sapiential (knowledge-based) power, and serves to remind us that organisations *can* divide specialist labour, and use hierarchies; provided they scrutinise them fully, manage them aggressively and limit their duration. Though this level of hands-on control of corruption is conceivable in a participatory democracy, it bears little resemblance to what we have today. Liberal democracy can only offer occasional elections. Between elections, and in the name of organisational effectiveness, it insulates public officials to the point that they evade accountability, exclude the populace, over-indulge their narcissistic needs and take over responsibility for decision-making. In Rousseau's words, representatives become fixated on their own 'corporate will', so that 'between elections, the population is again enslaved'.

The informed use of hierarchy requires a full awareness of its costs – many of which arise because power corrupts, and absolute power corrupts absolutely. If we look back to the time-bound dictatorships of the ancient republics – as we did earlier with the example of Cincinnatus – we can regularly observe citizens' awareness of the costs of hierarchy and the vigilance with which they sought to guard against the tendency of power to corrupt. Lacking such vigilance today, the corruption of citizens is actively stimulated by the removal of their responsibility for decision-making and by the cognitive separation occasioned by the hierarchic structures of representative government. Rousseau's infamous critique of representation is thus validated by recent developments in cognitive psychology.

To the charge that we have a representational division of labour out of necessity – in other words, that it is unavoidable because hierarchy is the only effective organisational form – we can reply that the exclusive equation of hierarchy and effectiveness is *itself* an effect of corruption by power. For, as we have seen, the effectiveness of more participatory forms is rendered invisible by cognitive automation and reification, hierarchy-confirming schemas and their self-confirmation by cognitive bias. Representative democracy is, in this way, both the product and the purveyor of corruption.

## Democracies of mind and organisation

If John Dewey is right, and 'the treatment for problems in democracy is more democracy', then we should celebrate democracy's apparent capacity to address the costs of organisational hierarchy. Democracy, however misconceived and endangered, has been repeatedly shown to overcome cognitive separation, reduce subordination and control the corruption of tyrannical elites. It is also the best way to manage the shifting epistemological sands of the social world.

Democracy is an organisational knowledge-gaining strategy. It is a form of collective knowledge processing; one uniquely adapted to contingent, perspectival and complex environments. Once again, we do not know the good, and so must search for it. We do not know whether a particular knowledge claim is produced by the material world, socially constructed and reified, distorted by our prior knowledge, shot-through with invisible power or all of the above – and so we use democracy to do the best we can. The collective search for knowledge is here conceived along skeptical, fallibilistic and dialogic lines. Confronted by contingency and a chronic lack of knowledge, we *can do no better* than involve multiple voices, benefit from difference and deliberate.[12]

This epistemological argument for democracy[13] rests on prag-matist philosophy, particularly Charles Peirce's equation of scientific truth with the 'eventual' consensus of enquirers.[14] We see it again in Karl Popper's 'open society'[15] and in the various strains of communicative ethics now on offer from Apel and Habermas.[16] Democratic theorists like Stanley Cavell, Hilary Putnam and John Dewey, all see democracy as superior to other political orders as a knowledge-gaining strategy, and Putnam has described democracy as 'the pre-condition for the full application of intelligence to the solution of social problems'.[17] With agreement as the goal, attention shifts to the process of debate and the 'fairness' of procedure. Deliberation should be open and fair because the collective search for knowledge works best that way. A similar epistemological strategy informs current debates in management studies around notions of the 'learning organisation'.[18] All such developments claim democracy to be a uniquely effective form of organisational knowledge processing.

Until they become clogged by corruption. Stuck hierarchies, inflated leaders and disengaged subordinates serve to shut down the know-ledge-processing engine and render the organisation ineffective. Intrusive leadership, cognitive separation and communication break-down, rituals of verification,[19] alienated and resentful participants, rampant battery cognition and chronic mission drift all serve to prevent organisations from gaining knowledge. The corrupting organ-isation starts to turn inward; it fails to interact with its environment. As a consequence, it stops learning.

A stuck hierarchy features corrupted power-holders and disengaged subordinates. These stand in stark contrast to democracy's evident need for active and uncorrupted citizens.[20] Instead, the public is fre-quently seen as stupid, lazy[21] and prone to a dangerous instability of preference. This lack of citizen capacity can even be measured as empirical fact. It has been demonstrated, for example, that while most people call for more participation in public services, far less are actually willing to participate themselves.[22] We simply *are* apathetic; *ergo* we need leadership.

Of course, being able to measure something does not mean it is real. Empirical examination does not reveal ontology – at least not in the social, rough and reified terrain we are currently exploring.

Sometimes, facts lie. We can, for example, use a sundial to accurately measure the rotation of the sun around the earth, even though the sun is *not* rotating around the earth. Similarly, we can measure low serotonin levels in the brains of depressed psychiatric patients, but that does not disclose whether the low serotonin is *causing* the depression or the other way around. When we measure political apathy, we are inspecting an object so reified, so shot-through with power, so beyond our ken that we should be decidedly humble in our interpretations of the data. The empirical fact that we are apathetic tells us nothing about citizen capacity, and might be due to other causes.

One clinical indicator for corruption by power is the systematic devaluation of subordinate capacities. Another is that corruption takes place beneath awareness. It is therefore possible that the easy assumption of citizen incapacity is a pushed, negative and decidedly ideological schema that is now automated and internalised by both elites and citizen/subordinates. Fully reified, it can even be measured empirically.

Apathy is an age-old problem in the history of democracy, and classically takes the form of two distinct and competing explanations.[23] Elitist democratic theory holds that apathy is due to the 'fact' that ordinary citizens possess neither the wit nor the will to participate effectively. Participatory democrats blame the failure of government to provide adequate institutions for participation. What we can now see is that, in the liberal democracies, apathy is a form of subordinate corruption by power. It involves the parasitic interplay of individual cognitive tendencies and stuck, hierarchic and corrupting institutions. Apathy further reduces knowledge exchange, and so exacerbates cognitive separation. It thereby detracts from democracy's ability to process knowledge effectively. It tells us little about citizen capacities.

Just as we can empirically measure our widespread apathy, so could we gather research demonstrating that citizen capacities improve with practice.[24] From John Stuart Mill's notion of participation as the 'school of public policy'[25] to the contemporary analysis of small group participation,[26] citizens have shown themselves quite able to grasp complex issues[27] and radically improve the quality of their collective decisions.[28] The proposition that people benefit and learn more effectively when they are involved, empowered and responsible is supported by studies showing improved functioning of psychiatric patients upon involvement in the design and delivery of mental health services[29] and research on participatory forms of childhood education.[30]

Participation educates; but it is by no means clear that the *kind* of participation offered us in the liberal democracies is the most effective teacher. Occasional voting, writing letters to MPs, signing a petition or donating to charity are less effective in improving participatory skills than are more 'deliberative' forms of engagement. Where participation is interactive, and characterised by open argumentation and the informing of preferences, individual preferences *change*.[31] So, for example, asking citizens about increasing police foot patrols results in a resounding 'yes'. Now show those same citizens the budgetary constraints upon such patrols, and they begin to 'refine' and 'modify' their responses.[32] Similarly, when citizens deliberate about their fear of crime, their preferences change again. As the planning theorist John Forrester has argued, and Tetlock's experimentation has empirically confirmed, learning increases with deliberative involvement, personal investment, ownership of, and responsibility for, decisions.[33]

It is in discussion that we both discover and create our needs.[34] If we are to deepen our democracy and consult and engage the public in governance, we must empower fora in which preferences can be formed and refined in deliberation with others and in the light of accurate information. Only then can we gain knowledge of user needs and arrange services that are responsive to them. It is for this reason that so many of the practical democratic 'designs' for organisations advanced by contemporary researchers are deliberative in form. Both Gaventa and Fung are then able to survey the many different types of deliberative fora, or 'micropublics', in order to identify the relative merits of each.[35]

Deliberative decision-making gives a public space for the display and affirmation of identity. It thereby empowers participants, increases knowledge through the sharing of insights, stimulates a collective rejection of negative schemas of subordinates and reduces dependency. Talking is a subversive act. It is for this reason that those corrupted by power are so gifted – almost by reflex – at *limiting* deliberation. Public discussion challenges privilege, and nothing terrifies elites more than open information, public scrutiny and the attentions of a politicised citizenry.

Situated within a power-saturated organisational environment, characterised by badly managed hierarchies, corruption and wasted knowledge, the democrat must be as difficult to recruit to the interests of power, as it is possible to be. This is because – everyday – significant resources are expended to win the political struggle over individual cognition. Schemas are systematically force-fed to participants, and we are particularly encouraged to unquestioningly equate organisational effectiveness with hierarchy. Yet merely to question and resist these schemas is not enough, for it is the combination of 'pushed' schemas and the 'pull' of cognitive bias that results in our unknowing recruitment into serving the interests of power. When our thinking is fully colonised and automated beneath awareness, the result is battery cognition. Here, then, we serve power even when we imagine we are autonomous, and so come to think in ways that work against our interests. We achieve simplicity of understanding and stabilisation of expectation. We avoid cognitive work. In this way, we are used.

Such usage is readily observed in the gangster organisational form. The gang pushes self-affirming schemas – of respect, hierarchy, empathy avoidance and the capacity for violence – that are taken up by the individual cognitive biases and automated beneath awareness. In this way, cruelty is valorised as rule-breaking. In the belief that they are wildly free from societal constraints, gang members are, in fact, the most blindly obedient of subordinates.

Democratic citizens do not so easily do as they are told. First, they demand reasons for the hierarchies and leaders that dominate their lives. Sometimes those reasons are good. But where hierarchy is defensible *only* by recourse to ideological obfuscation, it is open to challenge. Second, they at least attempt to treat their own corruption. They try to recognise their cognitive biases, and to question and update the schemas they use. They work to reject ideological intrusion when it appears in their own minds. In this way, democracy pertains not only to organisations, but also to our own thinking.

There are, at the same time, limits to how much automated cognition can be raised into awareness. Quite apart from the threat of cognitive overload, power is productive of subjectivity. As Foucault shows, the cage of domination is a perceptual one. There is no 'outside of power',[36] and the prison of ideology offers no escape.[37] Deliberations are seldom fair.[38] We can, therefore, never entirely remove the effects of corruption.

But what better way to manage this than more democracy? Democracy is an effective knowledge-gaining strategy for those thrown into a contingent environment and denied objective truth. It raises citizen consciousness, and empowers subordinates to resist their own corruption. When mobilised, this collective force can restrain elites, and may indeed, be the only force that can.

Democracy here reveals one of its many clever ways of managing power: the corruption of elites is finally prevented only by the mobilised populace. Corruption by power is a disorder affecting both leaders and subordinates, and fittingly, the democratic treatment engages both. But the agent of recovery is the subordinate. Only after subordinates *refuse* do they have the capacity to restrain the corruption of elites.

We know so much more about power than we did formerly. Contemporary work on difference, discourse, the relation of power to knowledge and the colonisation of individual cognition, all alert us to the tremendous subtlety of power and to its concealed capacity to influence and construct experience. Democrats thus wield the weapon of ideology critique. Alone, this is not an alternative politics; for it has no organisational form. But a crucial element of political organisation *is* personal. Democracy entails a willingness to question, a disbelief, a mistrust of any claim to the legitimacy of power and a vital and skeptical ethics of suspicion.[39] Voltaire ended all his letters with the words 'wipe out the infamy!' and Kant encouraged us to 'dare to know!' In the same spirit, democrats reject being inadvertently recruited to service the interests of dominant elites and draw on democracy as their fighting creed.

This, of course, is not the 'democracy' David Owen has in mind when he administers it to his corrupt patient.[40] Instead, its closest relative is what McCormick calls 'ferocious populism', an image he takes from Machiavelli.[41] Populism is a much disputed concept, and is almost always used pejoratively.[42] It calls forth a series of negative schemas that suggest the dangerous manipulation of foolish and hot-headed citizens. Yet Machiavelli spent most of his intellectual life arguing that a radical and indeed ferocious populism was precisely the source of the Roman Republics' longevity and dynamism. Its citizens were, as he continually pointed out, vigilant in defence of their freedom and suspicious of those attracted to power. Meeting regularly in a network of assemblies, they argued in public and practiced their participatory skills. They demanded information concerning the governance of the growing empire and achieved a series of constitutional reforms that culminated in the Tribunate. Machiavelli then takes a powerful rhetorical step – common in the Renaissance: he insists that ancient commentators, like Titus Livy, agreed with him. Machiavelli thereby argued that in the Roman Republic, class conflict between the patricians and the plebs was cleverly institutionalised. Openly expressed, such conflict became *productive*. Patricians had the senate; the plebs their Tribunes, with the latter empowered to veto all legislation. To achieve the Tribunate and its power of veto, the plebs had twice to evacuate the city *en masse*, and to camp beyond the walls until they got their way. Each time the Tribunes vetoed legislation that favoured the patricians, or held a patrician to account, it was a dramatic, noisy and public display, and a powerful symbolic victory. In such moments, the entire political order received a stark clarification: *this* is popular sovereignty. Tribune elections, public accusations and uses of the veto were profoundly educational, and so reduced the corruption of the plebs. Empowered citizens then acted to reduce the corruption of the patricians.[43]

Machiavelli uses stories. He raids history, collecting provocative examples and lively evidence. The resulting political images are designed to evoke something other than the usual elitist orientation towards controlling the people; and to ease us into the republican concern: to control elites. Republicanism sees leaders as the greater threat to liberty and has, historically, sought to reject their domination, divide their powers and limit their corruption. Its long history of adjusting constitutions so as to empower forms of participation more expressive than the vote offers a wide array of practical innovations. Republicanism is the clever institutionalisation of elite and citizen relations. Part of its cleverness lies in its awareness that power corrupts.

And it does; not always, but too often. It corrupts in discernible ways, and cognitive psychology can begin to reveal the mechanisms by which it does so. We have used the story of cognition to move beyond the merely functional observation that power corrupts. This has provided a *cognitive* verification of certain concepts in political philosophy, notably Marx's theory of reification and Rousseau's critique of representation. It has also given insight into current political debates around organisational knowledge, political apathy and deliberative democracy. Bringing cognitive psychology together with political philosophy also assisted in the application of cognitive tools to more democratic ends than has so far been attempted. Our investigation has led across social scientific disciplines, through the complex relations of individual cognition and collective knowledge processing, and finally, to matters of democratic organisational design. Long histories and hard cognitive science can evoke a vibrant, noisy and suspicious public sphere, one where citizens are networked by new information technologies and can swarm to reduce corruption. This spells lightning-fast trouble for incompetent elites.

To ask how power corrupts is to illuminate what is usually concealed. For a moment, it may be possible to glimpse the unending power struggle over the very content of our minds. To the side looms our collective addiction to the hierarchic organisational form. Ours is a cult of leadership; a damaging social construction and a constraining myth. It denies awareness of the costs of hierarchy and feeds on the invisible structures of individual cognition.

There is so much outside awareness that democracy will always be required: democracy of knowledge, of organisation and of mind; ideology critique and the avoidance of blind obedience; these are weapons against corruption by power. Surely, the degeneration we have brought upon ourselves requires us to use them.

# Notes

## Introduction

1  Ashforth, B.E., 'Petty Tyranny Organizations', *Human Relations*, 1994, 47: 755–778; Thompson, V.A., *Modern Organisations*, New York: Alfred Knopf, 1961.

2  Offe, C., 'Bindings, Shackles, Brakes: On Self-Limitation Strategies', in Honneth, A., McCarthy, T., Offe, C., Wellmer, A. (eds), *Cultural-Political Interventions in the Unfinished Project of Enlightenment*, Cambridge, MA: MIT Press, 1992; Jones, B.D., *Politics and the Architecture of Choice: Bounded Rationality and Governance*, Chicago: University of Chicago Press, 2001, refers to 'error-correcting procedures' at p. 192.

3  Weber, M., 'Bureaucracy', in Gerth, H.H., Wright Mills, C. (eds) *From Max Weber: Essays in Sociology*, New York: Oxford University Press, 1946; Gay du, P., *In Praise of Bureaucracy: Weber, Organization, Ethics*, London: Sage, 2000.

4  Kershaw, I., *Hitler, 1889–1936: Hubris*, Harmondsworth: Penguin, 2001.

5  Lukes, S., *Power: A Radical View*, New York: New York University Press, 2004.

6  Gandhi, M., *The Collected Works*, Vol. 24, p. 87, New Delhi: Ministry of Information, 1921.

7  The image is from Ahrne, G., *Social Organisations: Interactions Inside, Outside and Between Organisations*, London: Sage, 1994, p. viii; see also, Schott, R.L., 'Administrative and Organisational Behaviour: Insights from Cognitive Psychology', *Administration and Society*, 1991, 23/1: 54–73, p. 66.

8  Owen, D., *The Hubris Syndrome: Bush, Blair and the Intoxication of Power*, London: Politico's, 2007.

9  Owen, 2007, p. 3.

10  Owen, 2007, p. x.

11  For a review of new books on neuroscience, see Rose, S., 'In Search of the God Neuron', *The Guardian*, 27/12/08, p. 8.

12  Searle, J.R., *Freedom and Neurobiology: Reflections on Free Will, Language, and Political Power*, New York: Columbia University Press, 2004.

13  Anderson, J.R., *Cognitive Psychology and its Implications*, p. 3, New York: Freeman, 1995; see also, Turner, S. 'Social Theory as Cognitive Neuroscience', *European Journal of Social Theory*, 2007, 10/3: 357–374, here at pp. 358–359.

14  Turner, M., *Cognitive Dimensions of Social Science*, p. 11, New York: Oxford University Press, 2001.

15  Elster, J., *Explaining Technical Change*, Cambridge: Cambridge University Press, 1983.

16  Thaler, R.H., Sunstein, C.R., *Nudge: Improving Decisions about Health, Wealth, and Happiness*, New Haven: Yale University Press, 2008; Cialdini, R.B.,

119

*Influence: The Psychology of Persuasion*, New York: HarperCollins, 2007; Jones, 2001.
17  Thaler and Sunstein, 2008, p. 5.

## Chapter 1  Corruption, Power and Democracy

1  Barrett, A.A., *Caligula: The Corruption of Power*, p. 145, London: Routledge, 1989.
2  Kipnis, D., Rind, B., 'Changes in self-perceptions as a result of successfully persuading others', *Journal of Social Issues*, 1999; Keltner, D., Gruenfeld, D.H., Anderson, C., 'Power, Approach, and Inhibition', *Psychological Review*, 2003, 110/2: 265–284.
3  Kipnis & Rind, 1999.
4  Kipnis, D., *The Powerholders*, Chicago: Chicago University Press, 1976.
5  Keltner et al., 2003, p. 269.
6  Keltner et al., 2003.
7  Keltner et al., 2003.
8  Keltner et al., 2003, p. 272.
9  Defining an organisation, and distinguishing it from an institution, is notoriously problematic. Katz, D. and Kahn, R.L., in *The Social Psychology of Organisations*, New York: Wiley, 1966 see organisations as social systems that coordinate collective action with norms, values and roles, and do so towards a common goal; Schotter, A., presents an informational account of institutions in *The Economic Theory of Social Institutions*, Cambridge: Cambridge University Press, 1981; Wicks, A.C. and Freeman, R.E. in 'Organisation Studies and the New Pragmatism: Positivism, Anti-Positivism and the Search for Ethics', *Organisation Science*, 9/2, 1998: 123–140, describe an organisation as a construct of signs and things which coordinates distributed agency; Daft, R.J., Weick, K.E. describe an organisation as a human artefact, a symbolic structure which makes, processes and maintains meaning, in 'Toward a Model of Organisations as Interpretation Systems', *Academy of Management Review*, 1984, 9: 284–295; Stein, J. in 'How Institutions Learn: A Socio-Cognitive Perspective', *Journal of Economic Issues*, 1997, 31/3: 729–740, here at p. 730, follows Douglas, M., who distinguishes the institution by its reach over many organisations, in *How Institutions Think*, London: Routledge, 1986, pp. 46–47; see also Jones, 2001, p. 189 on the distinction between organisations and institutions.
10  Minow, M., *Making All the Difference: Inclusion, Exclusion and American Law*, Ithaca: Cornell University Press, 1990.
11  Shapiro, I., *Democratic Justice*, p. 42, New Haven: Yale University Press, 1999.
12  Shapiro, 1999, p. 45.
13  Owen, 2007, pp. 1–2; see also the useful discussion of identification in Jones, 2001, p. 135.
14  Owen, 2007, p. 73.

15 See Baron, H., *The Crisis in the Early Italian Renaissance*, Princeton: Princeton University Press, 1966.

16 George Washington was commonly referred to as being the 'new Cincinnatus'.

17 Baron, 1966.

18 Seligman, M.E.P., *Helplessness: On Depression, Development, and Death*, San Francisco: Freeman & Co., 1977.

19 Rousseau, J.J., *The Social Contract*, Harmondsworth: Penguin, 1968.

20 Rousseau, J.J., *Discourse on the Origins of Inequality*, p. 78, 1984.

21 Pettit, P., *Republicanism: A Theory of Freedom and Government*, Oxford: Oxford University Press, 1999.

22 Hegel, G.W.F., *The Phenomenology of Spirit*, 1977, pp. 115–118.

23 Hegel, 1977, p. 116; Hyppolite, 1974, pp. 173–174.

24 Keltner et al., 2003.

25 Hegel, 1977, p. 117.

26 Lauer, 1976, pp. 107–109, 113, 119.

27 Hegel, 1977, p. 116.

28 Keltner et al., 2003, p. 269.

29 Snodgrass, S.E., Hecht, M.A., Ploutz-Snyder, R., 'Interpersonal Sensitivity: Expressivity or Perceptivity?', *Journal of Personality and Social Psychology*, 1988, 69: 797–811; Dépret, E.F., Fiske, S.T., 'Social Cognition and Power: Some Cognitive Consequences of Social Structure as a Source of Control Deprivation', in Gleicher, W.F. and Marsh, K. (eds) *Control Motivation and Social Cognition*, pp. 176–202, New York: Springer-Verlag, 1993.

30 Snodgrass, 1988.

31 Gamson, W., *Talking Politics*, Cambridge: Cambridge University Press, 1992; see also, Ryfe, 2005, p. 57.

32 This section draws on research presented in Blaug, R. 'Why is there Hierarchy? Democracy and Organisational Form', *Critical Review of International Social and Political Philosophy*, Vol. 11/3, 2009.

33 Lenski, G.E., *Power and Privilege: A Theory of Social Stratification*, Chapel Hill, NC: University of North Carolina Press, 1984.

34 Sidanius, J., Pratto, F., *Social Dominance: An Intergroup Theory of Social Hierarchy and Oppression*, p. 35, Cambridge: Cambridge University Press, 1999.

35 Patrides, C.A., *The Phoenix and the Ladder: The Rise and Decline of the Christian View of History*, Berkeley: Berkeley University Press, 1964.

36 Radner, R., 'Hierarchy: The Economics of Managing', *Journal of Economic Literature*, 1992, 30: 1382–1415, here at p. 1390.

37 Cloke and Goldsmith, 2002, p. 83.

38 Braithwaite, for example, explores circular chains of Principal/agent relations in Dowdle, M.W. (ed.), *Public Accountability: Designs, Dilemmas and Experiences*, Cambridge: CUP, 2006, p. 39.

39 Douglas, *How Institutions Think*, 1986.

40 *The Iliad*, VIII: 19–27.

41 *Genesis*, 28: 10–15.

42 Lovejoy, A.O., *The Great Chain of Being: A Study in the History of an Idea*, Cambridge, MA.: Harvard University Press, 1990.

43  Morgan, G., *Images of Organisation*, London: Sage, 1997, p. 71.
44  Bookchin, M., *The Ecology of Freedom: The Emergence and Dissolution of Hierarchy*, Palo Alto, CA: Cheshire Books, 1982.
45  An analogy used by Plato, and also Engels, for which see *The Marx-Engels Reader*, in Tucker, R.C. (ed.), New York: W.W. Norton & Co., 1978, p. 29.
46  See, on this division in management, Radner, 'Hierarchy: The Economics of Managing', p. 1388.
47  Mill. J.S., *Considerations on Representative Government*, describes this as a necessary distinction between 'doers' and 'controllers', while Milbrath, L.W., *Political Participation: How and Why Do People Get Involved in Politics?* Chicago: Rand McNally, 1965, calls them 'gladiators' and 'spectators'.
48  Hastings, B.M., Shaffer, B., 'Authoritarianism: The Role of Threat, Evolutionary Psychology, and the Will to Power', *Theory and Psychology*, 2008, 18/3: 423–440.
49  See, for example, Worsley, P., 'The practice of politics and the study of Australian kinship', in Gaily, C.W. (ed.), *The Politics of Culture and Creativity*, Gainesville: University of Florida Press, 1992.
50  In their analysis of the emergence and perseverance of hierarchy, both Marx and Weber favour material structures which evolve over time, and sought to show how current hierarchies reflect the historically specific economic development of capitalism or the organisational structures brought on by modernist rationalisation, respectively. For which, see Marx, K., *Capital*, Vol. 1, New York: International Publishers, 1974b and Weber, M., *Economy and Society*, Berkeley: University of California Press, 1978.
51  Machiavelli, N., 1979; Cloke & Goldsmith, 2002, p. 95; Morgan, 1997, p. 114.
52  Wilkinson, 2006; Marmot, 2005; Sennett, 1977.
53  Bowles & Gintis, 1987.
54  Milgram, 1974; Fiske, 1997.
55  Seligman, 1977.
56  Gemmill & Oakley, 1992.
57  Körösényi, 2005; Schumpeter, 1958; Michels, 1958.
58  For an examination of these debates, see Blaug, 2008.
59  Douglas, 1986.
60  Phillips, A., *Engendering Democracy*, Cambridge: Polity Press, 1991, describes women's movement struggles to prevent the media and the police from selecting 'stars' to interview and negotiate.
61  On the ineffectiveness of structurelessness, and its tendency to allow inequalities to continue, see Freeman, J., *The Tyranny of Structurelessness*, London: Dark Star/Rebel Press, 1984.
62  Burke, E., 'Speech at the conclusion of the Poll', Bristol, November 1774.
63  Such agreement can be conceived in terms of discursive redemption, for which see Blaug, R., *Democracy, Real and Ideal: Discourse Ethics and Radical Politics*, New York: SUNY, 1999.

64 Michels, R., *Political Parties: A Sociological Study of the Oligarchical Tendencies of Modern Democracy*, Glencoe, Illinois: Free Press, [1915], 1958.
65 Michels, 1958, p. 70.
66 Michels, 1958, p. 79.
67 Michels, 1958, p. 81.
68 Dahl, R.A., *Democracy and its Critics*, New Haven and London: Yale University Press, 1989; Schwarzmantel, J., *Structures of Power*, London: Prentice Hall, 1987.
69 Williamson, O.E., *Markets and Hierarchies: Analysis and Antitrust Implications*, New York: Free Press, 1975; Radner, 'Hierarchy: The Economics of Managing', pp. 1392, 1412.
70 The social psychologists Sidanius and Pratto note 'the ease of communication among [ruling elite's] relatively few members'. Sidanius and Pratto, 1999, here at p. 23.
71 Landes, p. 597; Dewey makes the point that stabilisation lowers costs, when he asserts that 'habits economise', *The Public and its Problems*, Carbondale: Southern Illinois University Press, 1988.
72 Bureaucracy, as a kind of historically specific hierarchy, also stresses simplification, for which, see *From Max Weber: Essays in Sociology*, Gerth, H.H. Wright Mills, C. (eds), New York: Oxford University Press, 1946, pp. 196–266.
73 Shapiro, 1999, pp. 42–44.
74 Douglas, 1986.
75 Bourdieu, 1990.
76 David, 1975.
77 Thompson et al., 1996; Castells, 1996; Blaug, 1998.
78 Kropotkin, 1972.
79 This formulation follows that of Robert Dahl.
80 Hindess, 1996.
81 Klosko, G., Rice, D., 'Thucydides and Hobbes's State of Nature', *History of Political Thought*, 1985, 6/3: 405–409. Hobbes' first publication was a translation of Thucydides' *Peloponnesian War* and there are telling parallels between Hobbes' state of nature in the *Leviathan* and Thucydides' account in the 'Civil War in Corcyra'.
82 Hindess, 1996, pp. 103–104.
83 Lukes, 2004.
84 Patton, P. 'Ethics and the Subject of Politics', in Moss, J. (ed.), *The Later Foucault*, London: Sage, 1998, pp. 64–77, here at p. 67.
85 Jay, M. *The Dialectical Imagination*, Boston: Little Brown, 1973; Wiggershaus, R., *The Frankfurt School: Its History, Theories and Political Significance*, Cambridge: Polity Press, 1994.
86 Horkheimer, Inaugural Address, *What is Critical Theory?*
87 Kempton, S., *Esquire*, 1970.
88 Foucault, M., *The History of Sexuality: The Will To Knowledge*, Vol. 1, London: Penguin, 2004; Foucault, M., *Power/Knowledge*, New York: Random House, 1980.

89   Foucault, M., *Discipline and Punish: The Birth of the Prison*, Harmondsworth: Penguin, 1977.
90   Foucault, M., *The History of Sexuality: The Will To Knowledge*, Vol. 1, London: Penguin, 2004.
91   McKinlay, A., Starkey, K., 'Managing Foucault: Foucault, Management and Organisation Theory', in *Foucault, Management and Organisation Theory*, McKinlay & Starkey (eds), Thousand Oaks: Sage, 1998, p. 4.
92   Hindess, B., 'Politics and Liberation', in Moss, J. (ed.), *The Later Foucault*, London: Sage, 1998, pp. 50–62; on new forms of power emerging in modern organisations, see Starkey, K., *How Organisations Learn*, Boston, MA: International Thompson Business Press, 1996, p. 151; McKinlay & Starkey, 'Managing Foucault', p. 10; and Burrell, G., 'Modernism, Postmodernism and Organisational Analysis: The Contribution of Michel Foucault', pp. 14–28, 1998, here at p. 21, both in *Foucault, Management and Organisation Theory*, McKinlay, A., Starkey, K. (eds), Thousand Oaks: Sage, 1998.
93   Kant, I. 'What is Enlightenment?'
94   Rousseau, J.J., *The Social Contract*.
95   Lukes, 2004.
96   Rose, N., 'Government, Authority and Expertise in Advanced Liberalism', *Economy and Society*, 1993, 22: 283–299.

## Chapter 2   Psychologies of Power

1   Aristotle, *Nicomachean Ethics*, New York: Bobbs-Merrill, [~330 BC], 1962; see also the absurd yet captivating Nicholson, N., *Executive Instinct*, New York: Crown Business, 2000.
2   Scott, J. (ed.), *The Sociology of Elites*, Volumes 1–3, Cheltenham: Edward Elgar, 1990.
3   Ridgeway, C.L., 'The Emergence of Status Beliefs: From Structural Inequality to Legitimizing Ideology', in Jost, J.T., Major, B. (eds), *The Psychology of Legitimacy: Emerging Perspectives on Ideology, Justice, and Intergroup Relations*, Cambridge: Cambridge University Press, 2001, pp. 176–204, here at p. 263.
4   For the communitarian critique of this suspiciously 'unencumbered self', see Sandel, M.J., 'The Procedural Republic and the Unencumbered Self', *Political Theory*, 1984, 12/1: 81–96.
5   See the outstanding McIntosh, J., 'Symbolism, Cognition, and Political Orders', *Science and Society*, 1998, 62/4: 557–568, p. 561.
6   Barnes, B., Bloor, D., Henry, J., *Scientific Knowledge: A Sociological Analysis*, London: Athlone, 1996.
7   Freud, S., *Civilisation and Its Discontents*, New York: W.W. Norton, 1961.
8   The ego is that part of the tripartite personality structure (id, ego, superego) which is charged with the onerous task of adjudication between the internal and the external world; see also, Major, B., Schmader, T.,

'Legitimacy and the Construal of Social Disadvantage', in Jost, J.T., Major, B. (eds), *The Psychology of Legitimacy: Emerging Perspectives on Ideology, Justice, and Intergroup Relations*, Cambridge: Cambridge University Press, 2001, pp. 176–204, here at p. 177.

9    Dilthey, W., *Selected Writings*, Rickman, H.P. (ed.), Cambridge: Cambridge University Press, 1976; on the ontology of Freud's interpretations, see Wollheim, R., Hopkins. J., *Philosophical Essays on Freud*, Cambridge: Cambridge University Press, 1982.

10   See, for example, *In Dora's Case: Freud, Hysteria, Feminism*, Bernheimer, C., Kahane, C. (eds), London: Virago, 1985.

11   See the excellent Malcolm, J., *In the Freud Archives*, New York: Vintage Books, 2001.

12   See Argyris, C., Schön, D., *Theory in Practice*, San Francisco: Jossey-Bass, 1974, for their discussion of 'defensive routines in organisations'; also, Morgan, G., *Images of Organisation*, p. 93.

13   Kline, M., 'Our Adult World and its Roots in Infancy', *Human Relations*, 1959, 12: 291–303.

14   Freud, A., *The Ego and the Mechanisms of Defence*, New York: International Universities Press, 1961.

15   See, 'On Narcissism', in the *Collected Papers of Sigmund Freud*, Vol. 4, p. 43; also Cohen, S., who strongly features the defence mechanism of denial in his analysis of how we witness the suffering of others, and his provocative suggestion that hierarchy offers individuals the much valued posture of obedience, in *States of Denial: Knowing about Atrocities and Suffering*, Cambridge: Polity Press, 2001, p. 89.

16   Adorno, T.W., *The Authoritarian Personality*, New York: Harper & Row, 1950.

17   On Adorno's F scale, see Feldman, S., 'Enforcing Social Conformity: A Theory of Authoritarianism', *Political Psychology*, 2003, 24/1: 41–74; Sidanius and Pratto's *Social Dominance* effectively updates this project and seeks to quantify authoritarian tendencies in each individual. Our resulting 'Social Dominance Orientation' expresses our individual preference for hierarchy. For a full discussion, see Sidanius and Pratto, 'Social Dominance Theory and the Dynamics of Inequality', pp. 207–213; Turner, J.C., Reynolds, K.J., 'Why Social Dominance Theory has been falsified', pp. 199–206; Schmitt, M.T., Branscombe, N.R., Kappen, D.M., 'Attitudes Toward Group-Based Inequality: Social Dominance or Social Identity?', pp. 161–186, all in the *British Journal of Social Psychology*, 2003, volume 42.

18   Kohut, H., *The Analysis of the Self*, New York: International Universities Press, 1971.

19   Elson, M., *Self Psychology in Clinical Social Work*, New York: Norton, 1986; Chessick, R.D., *Psychology of the Self and the Treatment of Narcissism*, Northvale, NJ: Jason Aronson, 1985.

20   Honneth, A., *The Struggle for Recognition: The Moral Grammar of Social Conflicts*, Cambridge: Polity Press, 1996.

21   Hastings and Shaffer, 2008.

22 Dollard, J.W., Miller, N.E., Doob, l.W., Mowrer, O.H., Sears, R.R., *Frustration and Aggression*, New Haven, CT Yale University Press, 1937.
23 Soloman, D., Greenberg, J., Pyszczynski, T., 'A Terror Management Theory of Social Behavior: The Psychological Functions of Self-Esteem and Cultural World Views', in Zanna, M.P. (ed.), *Advances in Experimental Social Psychology*, Vol. 24, pp. 93–159, San Diego: Academic.
24 Menzies Lyth, I., 'The Functioning of Social Systems as a Defence against Anxiety', in *Containing Anxiety in Institutions: Selected Essays*, London: Free Association Books, 1988, pp. 43–85.
25 Fromm, E., *Escape from Freedom*, New York: Rinehart, 1941.
26 Morgan, *Images of Organisation*, p. 392; Hutchins, E., *In Search of Navigators*, New York: Wiley, 1987.
27 Morgan, *Images of Organisation*, p. 228.
28 Gilbert, M., *On Social Facts*, Princeton, NJ: Princeton University Press, 1989, p. 3.
29 Yalom, I.D., *The Theory and Practice of Group Psychotherapy*, London: Basic Books, 2004.
30 Durkheim, E., *The Rules of Sociological Method*, London: Macmillan, 1982; Schatzki, T.R., 'Introduction: Practice Theory', in Schatzki, T.R., Cetina, K.K., von Savigny, E. (eds), *The Practice Turn in Contemporary Theory*, London: Routledge, 2001.
31 de Board, R., *The Psychoanalysis of Organisations*, London: Tavistock, 1978, p. 42.
32 Bion, W.R., Richman, J., 'Intergroup Tensions in Therapy', *Lancet*, 27: 478–481, 1961.
33 Bion and Richman, 1961, p. 478.
34 See the Stephen Lawrence inquiry and its accusation of 'institutional racism'.
35 Gilbert makes reference to this particular collective entity.
36 Gilbert, 1989.
37 Gilbert, 1989, p. 306.
38 Haslam, S.A., *Psychology in Organizations: A Social Identity Approach*, London: Sage, 2001; Sidanius and Pratto, 1999, p. 33ff.
39 Sherif, M., Harvey, O.J., White, B.J., Hood, W.R., Sherif, C., *Intergroup Conflict and Cooperation: The Robbers' Cave Experiment*, Norman: University of Oklahoma, 1961.
40 Janis, I.L., *Victims of Groupthink*, Boston: Houghton Mifflin, 1972.
41 Turner, J.C., 'Tyranny, Freedom and Social Structure: Escaping our Theoretical Prisons', *British Journal of Social Psychology*, 2006, 45: 41–46, here p. 43; classically, Asch, S., 'Studies of Independence and Conformity: A Minority of One Against a Unanimous Majority', *Psychological Monographs: General and Applied Social Psychology*, Vol. 70, 1956.
42 Tajfel, H., Turner, J.C., Worchel, S., Austin, W.G., *The Psychology of Intergroup Relations*, Washington: Nelson Hall, 1986; Haslam, 2001.
43 Sidanius and Pratto, 1999, p. 19; Spears, R., Jetten, J., Doosje, B., 'The (Ill)legitimacy of Ingroup Bias: From Social Reality to Social Resistance', in *The Psychology of Legitimacy: Emerging Perspectives on Ideology, Justice,*

*and Intergroup Relations*, Jost, J.T., Major, B. (eds), Cambridge: Cambridge University Press, 2001, pp. 332–362, here p. 333.

44 Huddy, L., 'Contrasting Theoretical Approaches to Intergroup Relations', *Political Psychology*, 2004, 25/6: 947–967, here p. 954.

45 Reicher, S., Haslam, S.A., 'Rethinking the Psychology of Tyranny: The BBC Prison Study', *British Journal of Social Psychology*, 2006, 45: 1–40.

46 Schmitt, M.T., Branscombe, N.R., Kappen, D.M., 'Attitudes Toward Group-Based Inequality: Social Dominance or Social Identity?', *British Journal of Social Psychology*, 2003, 42: 161–186.

47 Sidanius and Pratto, 2003.

48 Sidanius and Pratto, 1999, p. 45; Schmitt et al., 2003, p. 162.

49 Sidanius and Pratto, 1999, p. 32; see also p. 56.

50 Sidanius and Pratto, 1999, pp. 38–39.

51 Sidanius and Pratto, 1999, pp. 41–42.

52 Sidanius and Pratto, 1999, p. 77.

53 Sidanius and Pratto, 1999, pp. 77–78.

54 Sidanius and Pratto, 1999, here at p. 45.

55 Sidanius and Pratto, 1999, p. 79, emphasis theirs.

56 Sidanius and Pratto, 1999, p. 94.

57 Seligman, 1977 on 'learned helplessness'.

58 Prilleltensky, I., Gonick, L., 'Polities Change, Oppression Remains: On the Psychology and Politics of Oppression', *Political Psychology*, 1996, 17/1: 127–148; Moore-Gilbert, B., Stanton, G., Maley, W., *Postcolonial Criticism*, London: Longman, 1997; Spivak, G.C., 'Can the Subaltern Speak?', in Nelson, C., Grossberg, L. (eds), *Marxism and the Interpretation of Culture*, Urbana: University of Illinois Press, 1988; Foucault, M., *The History of Sexuality*, London: Allen Lane, 1979; Jost, J.T. and Major, B. (eds), *The Psychology of Legitimacy: Emerging Perspectives on Ideology, Justice and Intergroup Relations*, Cambridge: Cambridge University Press, 2001.

59 Sidanius and Pratto, 1999, p. 43.

60 Sidanius and Pratto, 1999, p. 44.

61 Sidanius and Pratto, 1999, p. 44.

62 Sidanius and Pratto, 1999, p. 44.

63 Huddy, 2004, p. 948.

64 Jost and Benaji, 1994.

65 Jost et al., in Jost, J.T., Major, B. (eds), *The Psychology of Legitimacy: Emerging Perspectives on Ideology, Justice, and Intergroup Relations*, Cambridge: Cambridge University Press, 2001, pp. 363–388, here p. 383.

66 Huddy, 2004, p. 948.

67 Wolff, R.P., *Moneybags Must Be So Lucky: On the Literary Structure of Capital*, Amherst, MA: University of Massachusetts Press, 1988.

68 This is a significant difficulty in the early work of Newell and Simon, who assumed (and represented in diagrammatic form) that the external environment was stable and, by virtue of scientific knowledge, objectively knowable. Distortions of rationality and sense perception could thus be compared to this objective reality. The same cannot be said of the social world. Newell and Simon, 1972, p. 20.

69    Such as Dilthey's distinction between the 'natural' and 'symbolic' realms, Popper's three world theory: Popper K., *The Logic of Scientific Discovery*, London: Hutchinson, 1959; or Weber's value differentiation thesis: Weber. M., *Objectivity in Social Science and Social Policy*, 1904, pp. 49–112; see also Habermas, J., *Knowledge and Human Interest*, Boston: Beacon Press, 1968.

70    Berger, P., Luckmann, T. *The Social Construction of Reality*, New York: Doubleday, 1967, p. 61.

71    Berger and Luckmann, 1967, p. 38; on semantic fields, p. 41.

72    See the introduction to Goodin, R.E. (ed.), *The Theory of Institutional Design*, Cambridge: Cambridge University Press, 1998.

73    Douglas, 1986, pp. ix, x; see also Gilbert, 1989.

74    Douglas, 1986, pp. 3, 8, 67, 72, 92, 109, 112, 124.

75    Durkheim, E., *The Rules of Sociological Method*, Lukes, S. (ed.), London: Macmillan, 1982; Fleck, L., *The Genesis and Development of a Scientific Fact*, Chicago: University of Chicago Press, 1979.

76    Augoustinos, M., Walker, I., *Social Cognition*, London: Sage, 1996.

77    Durkheim, 1982, p. 14; Gilbert, 1989, p. 244.

78    Douglas, 1986, p. 15.

79    Ryfe, 2005, p. 58.

80    Horkheimer, M., Adorno, T., *The Dialectic of Enlightenment*, New York: Seabury Press, 1972.

81    See the introduction in, Bauman, Z., *Intimations of Postmodernity*, London: Routledge, 1992.

82    Lyotard, J.F., *The Postmodern Condition: A Report on Knowledge*, Minneapolis: University of Minnesota Press, 1984.

83    Foucault, M., *The History of Sexuality: The Will To Knowledge*, Vol. 1, London: Penguin, 2004; Moss, J. (ed.), *The Later Foucault*, London: Sage, 1998.

84    Fleck, 1935, cited in Douglas, 1986, p. 13.

85    Douglas, 1986, p. 48.

86    Douglas, 1986, p. 53.

87    Douglas, 1986, p. 99.

88    Best, S., Kellner, D., *Postmodern Theory: Critical Interrogations*. London: Macmillan, 1991, p. 44.

89    Douglas, 1986, citing Merton, p. 76.

90    Haslam, S.A., *Psychology in Organisations: The Social Identity Approach*, Thousand Oaks, CA: Sage, 2001, p. 19.

91    Connolly, W., 'Cross-State Citizen Networks: A Response to Dallmayr', *Millennium: Journal of International Studies*, 2001, 30/2, p. 5.

92    Beck, U., Giddens, A., Lash, S., *Reflexive Modernisation: Politics, Tradition and Aesthetics in the Modern Social Order*, Cambridge: Polity Press, 1994.

93    Snyder, M., Uranowitz, S.W. 'Reconstructing the Past: Some Cognitive Consequences of Person Perception', *Journal of Personality and Social Psychology*, 1978, 36: 941–950.

94  Vetlesen, A.J., *Perception, Empathy, and Judgment: An Inquiry into the Preconditions of Moral Performance*, Pennsylvania: Pennsylvania State University Press, 1994.
95  Arendt, H., *Eichmann in Jerusalem*, Harmondsworth: Penguin, 1964.
96  Altemeyer, B., 'The Other "Authoritarian Personality"', in Zanna, M.P. (ed.), *Advances in Experimental Social Psychology*, 1998, 30: 48–92, New York: Academic Press.
97  Sidanius and Pratto, 1999, p. 49; see also Pratto, F., Sidanius, J., Stallworth, L.M., Malle, B.F., 'Social Dominance Orientation: A Personality Variable Predicting Social and Political Attitudes', *Journal of Personality and Social Psychology*, 1994, 67: 741–763; Halabi, S., Dovidio, J.F., Nadler, A., 'When and How Do High Status Group Members Offer Help: Effects of Social Dominance Orientation and Status Threat', *Political Psychology*, 29/6: P 841–858.
98  Wolff, R.P., *Understanding Marx: A Reconstruction and Critique of Capital*, Princeton: Princeton University Press, 1984, p. 129.
99  Marx, *Capital*, Vol. 1, New York: International Publishers, 1974b, p. 322.
100  Marx, *Capital*, p. 270.
101  Marx, *Capital*, Chapter One, Section Four.
102  Marx, *Capital*, p. 72.
103  Marx, *Capital*, p. 74.
104  Geras, N., 'Marx and the Critique of Political Economy', in *Ideology in the Social Sciences*, Blackburn, R. (ed.), London: Pantheon Books, 1972, p. 288.
105  Marx, 1974; Lukács, 1971; Gemmill and Oakley, 1992; Douglas, 1986, p. 48.
106  McIntosh, 1998, p. 565.
107  Rose, 1993; Frankel, B., 'Confronting Neoliberal Regimes: The Post-Marxist Embrace of Populism and Realpolitik', *New Left Review*, 1997, 226: 57–92, here at p. 85.

## Chapter 3   Individual Cognition

1  Indeed, more than one, as the second revolution generated connectionism, and then three dimensions of connectionism, see Clark, A., *Mindware: An Introduction to the Philosophy of Cognitive Science*, Oxford: Oxford University Press, 2001, p. 84 and Harré, 2002, p. 63, describe a gradual refinement of cognitive science towards more situational, affective, embodied and particular cognition.
2  Anderson, J.R., *Cognitive Psychology and its Implications*, New York: Freeman, 1995, p. 3.
3  Perhaps the best known is the information-processing approach in behavioural economics pioneered by Allen Newell and Herbert Simon, for which see Newell A., Simon, H.A., *Human Problem Solving*, Englewood Cliffs, N.J.: Prentice-Hall, 1972.

4  Turner, M., *Cognitive Dimensions of Social Science*, New York: Oxford University Press, 2001, p. 11.

5  Elster, J., *Explaining Technical Change*, Cambridge: Cambridge University Press, 1983.

6  Schott, R.L., 'Administrative and Organisational Behaviour: Some Insights from Cognitive Psychology', *Administration and Society*, 1991, 23/1: 54–73, here at p. 55.

7  Stein, J., 'How Institutions Learn: A Socio-Cognitive Perspective', *Journal of Economic Issues*, 1997, 31/3: 729–740, here at p. 729.

8  Sidanius and Pratto, 1999, here at p. 14.

9  Strydom, P. 'Introduction: A Cartography of Contemporary Cognitive Social Theory', *European Journal of Social Theory*, 2007, 10/3: 339–356, gives an excellent overview of current activity.

10  Newell and Simon, 1972; Jones, 2001, pp. 87–88.

11  Cialdini, R.B., *Influence: The Psychology of Persuasion*, New York: Harper-Collins, 2007.

12  Turner, 2001, p. 15.

13  Turner, 2001, p. 20

14  McIntosh, 1998, shows a good deal more awareness of these difficulties; see also, Strydom, 2007 for the altogether more substantive engagement now underway in cognitive social theory; also Stoler, A., 'On Political and Psychological Essentialism', *Ethos: Journal of the Society for Psychological Anthropology*, 1997, 25/1.

15  Pfeffer, J., *New Directions for Organisational Theory: Problems and Prospects*, New York: Oxford University Press, 1997; McIntosh, 1998.

16  This section extents research presented in Blaug, R., 'Cognition in a Hierarchy', *Contemporary Political Theory*, 6/1: 24–44, 2007.

17  James, W., *The Principles of Psychology*, Cambridge: Harvard University Press, [1890], 1983.

18  Schott, 1991, p. 58.

19  See Sternberg, R.J., *Intelligence, Information Processing, and Analogical Reasoning*, Hillsdale, NJ: Erlbaum, 1977; and Anderson, 1995, p. 12 on the 'Sternberg Paradigm'.

20  Anderson, 1995, p. 112.

21  Anderson, 1995, p. 115.

22  Anderson, 1995, p. 106

23  Anderson, 1995, p. 135.

24  Schott, 1991, on p. 59, thus states that perception is 'rarely if ever "neutral"'.

25  As Fiske puts it, 'thinking is for doing', cited in Augoustinos and Walker, 1996, p. 285; For definitions of problem solving and delineation of types of problems, see Duncker, K., 'On Problem Solving', *Psychological Monographs*, 1945, 58/5; Newell and Simon, 1972; Hayes, J.R., *Cognitive Psychology: Thinking and Creating*, Homewood, Ill.: Dorsey Press, 1978; Anderson, 1995, pp. 237, 255.

26  Schott, 1991, p. 58; Morgan, G., illustrates this by showing that we are able to pick up a pencil by avoiding *not* picking it up, in *Images of Organisation*, London: Sage, 1997, here at p. 85.

27 Schott, 1991, p. 59.
28 Pinker, S. *The Blank Slate*, London: Penguin, 2002.
29 This is an ancient idea, first propounded by Plato in the *Theatetus* in the section on the Aviary.
30 Augoustinos and Walker, 1996, p. 169.
31 Evans, 1989, J.St.B.T., *Bias in Human Reasoning: Causes and Consequences*, London: Lawrence Erlbaum, 1989, here at p. 16 (emphasis mine).
32 Evans, 1989, p. 92.
33 Evans, 1989, p. 93.
34 Kant, I., *The Critique of Pure Reason*, New York: St. Martin's Press, 1965; Wolff, R.P., *Kant's Theory of Mental Activity*, Cambridge, MA: Harvard University Press, 1963.
35 Rietveld, E., 'The Skillful Body as Concernful System of Possible Actions: Phenomena and Neurodynamics', *Theory and Psychology*, 2008, 18/3: 342–363; van Dijk, J., Kerkhofs, R., van Rooij, I., Haselager, P. 'Can There Be Such a Thing as Embodied Embedded Cognitive Neuroscience?', *Theory and Psychology*, 2008, 18/3: 297–316.
36 Evans, 1989, p. 94.
37 Kahneman, D., Slovic, P., Tversky, A., *Judgment under Uncertainty: Heuristics and Biases*, New York: Cambridge University Press, 1982.
38 Augoustinos and Walker, 1996, p. 67.
39 Anderson, 1995, pp. 72–73.
40 Anderson, 1995, pp. 50, 72–73; Augoustinos and Walker, 1996, p. 165.
41 Johnson-Laird, P., *Mental Models: Towards a Cognitive Science of Language, Inference, and Consciousness*, Cambridge, MA: Harvard University Press, 1983; Schott, 1991, p. 60.
42 Anderson, 1995, p. 124.
43 Anderson, 1995, p. 151.
44 Lawrence, P.R., Lorsch, J.W., *Organisation and Environment*, Cambridge, MA: Harvard University Press, 1967; Anderson, 1995, p. 125; Thau, M., *Consciousness and Cognition*, Oxford: Oxford University Press, 2002.
45 Schank, R.C., Abelson, R.P., *Scripts, Plans, Goals, and Understanding: An Inquiry into Human Knowledge Structures*, Hillsdale, NJ: L. Erlbaum Associates, 1977.
46 Bartlett, F.A., *A Study in Experimental and Social Psychology*, New York: Cambridge University Press, 1932; see also, Augoustinos and Walker, 1996, p. 33.
47 For the abstract nature of schema knowledge and its slot-like structure, see Anderson, 1995, pp. 151, 155; see also Augoustinos and Walker, 1996, p. 5.
48 Evans, 1989, p. 84.
49 Augoustinos and Walker, 1996, p. 41, for types of schema, see p. 5; Schott, 1991, p. 60.
50 This is often referred to as a 'molar', rather than a 'molecular' orientation, for which, see Anderson, p. 164; Schott, 1991, p. 55; Augoustinos and Walker, 1996, pp. 43, 164, 170.

51  Augoustinos and Walker, 1996, p. 170; but p. 171 notes a greater ease of recall for schema-incongruent data.
52  Such as claiming that 'schema theory is weak on social knowledge', Augoustinos and Walker, 1996, pp. 45, 166; that it is 'excessively general', p. 55; 'individualistic', p. 167; hard to falsify, as it can explain any result and its opposite, p. 55; lacks ecological validity, Augoustinos and Walker, 1996, p. 168, that it presupposes rationality of human cognition, p. 170; Remarks in the literature lamenting the lack of attention to affect and intuition are too common to list.
53  Schott, 1991, p. 60.
54  Resnick, L., 'Shared Cognition: Thinking as Social Practice', in *Perspectives on Socially Shared Cognition*, Resnick, L.B., Levine, J.M., Teasley, S.D. (eds), Washington, DC: American Psychological Association, 1993, pp. 1–21, here at pp. 7–8.
55  Rumelhart, D.E., 'Schemata: The Building Blocks of Cognition', in *Theoretical Issues in Reading Comprehension*, Spiro, R.J., Bruce, B.C., Brewer, W.F. (eds), Hillsdale, NJ; Laurence Erlbaum, 1980; Clegg, C., 'Psychology and Information Technology: The Study of Cognition in Organisations', *British Journal of Psychology*, 1994, 85/4: 449–487; Douglas, M., *How Institutions Think*, London: Routledge, 1986; Fiske, S.T., Taylor, S.E., *Social Cognition*, New York: McGraw-Hill, 1991; re the questionable 'ecological validity' of the experimental method, see Schneider, S.C., Angelmar, R., 'Cognition in Organisational Analysis: Who's Minding the Store?', *Organisation Studies*, 1993, 14/3: 347–371; many commentators call for more research on cognition in organisations, for example, Clegg, 'Psychology and Information Technology', 1994, at pp. 449, 468, 472.
56  Augoustinos and Walker, 1996, pp. 51, 170, 175–176; Eiser, J.R., *Social Psychology: Attitudes, Cognition and Social Behaviour*, Cambridge: Cambridge University Press, 1988.
57  Schott, 1991, p. 60.
58  Augoustinos and Walker, 1996, p. 164.
59  Augoustinos and Walker, 1996, p. 107.
60  This is the primary concern of Social Representation Theory, for which see, Moscovici, S., 'On Social Representations', in *Social Cognition: Perspectives on Everyday Understanding*, Forgas, J.P. (ed.), London: Academic Press, 1981; Moscovici, S., 'Notes Towards a Description of Social Representations', *Journal of European Social Psychology*, 1998, 18: 211–250; Augoustinos and Walker, 1996, at p. 137, point out that Moscovici's position is similar to that of Berger and Luckmann.
61  Freud, A., *The Ego and the Mechanisms of Defence*, New York: International Universities Press, 1961; Morgan, *Images of Organisation*, 1997, p. 223.
62  Weber, R., Crocker, J., 'Cognitive Processes in the Revision of Stereotypic Beliefs', *Journal of Personality and Social Psychology*, 1983, 45/5: 961–997; Augoustinos and Walker, 1996, pp. 53, 178; see Evans, 1989, p. 19 for Duncker's concept of 'functional fixity'; Stein, 1997, p. 731 on cognitive inertia; Anderson, 1995, p. 263.
63  Augoustinos and Walker, 1996, p. 67.

64 Augoustinos and Walker, 1996, pp. 52, 166, 168, 178.
65 Evans, 1989, p. 94.
66 Anderson, 1995, p. 159.
67 Evans, 1989, pp. 4, 15.
68 See Stein, 1997, p. 731.
69 Fiske, S.T., 'Controlling Other People: The Impact of Power on Stereo-typing', *American Psychologist*, 1993: 48, pp. 621–628; Fiske, S.T., Taylor, S.E., *Social Cognition*, New York: McGraw-Hill, 1991; Broadbent, D., *Perception and Communication*, London: Pergamon Press, 1958; Kahneman, D., *Attention and Effort*, Englewood Cliffs, NJ: Prentice-Hall, 1973; Clegg, 1994, p. 467; Ryfe, 2005, p. 51.
70 Kahneman, D., Slovic, P., Tversky, A., *Judgment under Uncertainty: Heuristics and Biases*, New York: Cambridge University Press, 1982; Evans, J.St.B.T., *Bias in Human Reasoning: Causes and Consequences*, London: Lawrence Erlbaum, 1989.
71 Augoustinos and Walker, 1996, p. 170.
72 Kahneman, D., Slovic, P., Tversky, A., *Judgment under Uncertainty: Heuristics and Biases*, New York: Cambridge University Press, 1982; Evans, 1989, p. 112; Ryfe, 2005, pp. 51, 55.
73 Sometimes referred to as an 'accentuation effect', Augoustinos and Walker, 1996, p. 106.
74 Stein, 1997, p. 731; Schott, 1991, p. 67.
75 Augoustinos and Walker, 1996, pp. 52, 55; Evans, 1989, p. 63.
76 Evans, 1989, pp. 23, 41, 50, 98; 'Subjects confirm', he states, 'not because they want to, but because they cannot think of the way to falsify', p. 42; On whether we are merely bad Popperians, see pp. 44, 49, 52.
77 Evans, 1989, p. 44.
78 See, on 'cognitive conservativism', Cohen, S., *States of Denial: Knowing about Atrocities and Suffering*, Cambridge: Polity Press, 2001, p. 49.
79 Redlawsk, D.P., Hubby, C.R. 'Hot cognition or cool consideration? Testing the effects of motivated reasoning on political decision making', *Journal of Politics*, 2002, 64: 1021–1044; Kunda, Z., *Social Cognition: Making Sense of People*, Cambridge, MA: MIT Press, 1999.
80 Evans, 1989, p. 97.
81 Evans, 1989, p. 109.
82 Evans, 1989, p. 99.
83 Augoustinos and Walker, 1996, p. 90.
84 Augoustinos and Walker, 1996, p. 170.
85 Cited in Augoustinos and Walker, 1996, p. 93.
86 Augoustinos and Walker, 1996, p. 93.
87 Weick, K., *The Social Psychology of Organising*, Reading, MA: Addison-Wesley, 1979.
88 Searle, J.R., *The Construction of Social Reality*, London: Penguin, 1996.
89 Indeed, reification assists in the construction and maintenance of a coherent self, for which, see Schneider and Angelmar, 1993, p. 6.
90 Rosenberg, N., 'Marx as a Student of Technology', *Monthly Review*, July/August, 1976: pp. 133–158, for Marx on technology as 'frozen knowledge';

Boulding, K.E., 'The Economics of Knowledge and the Knowledge of Economics', *American and Communication*, London: Pergamon Press, 1958, 56/1–2: 1–13.
91  Evans, 1989, p. 45.
92  Schneider and Angelmar, 1993, p. 5.
93  Haslam, S.A., *Psychology in Organisations: The Social Identity Approach*, Thousand Oaks: Sage, 2001, p. 19; see also Ryfe, 2005, p. 56 on the possibility that these are two distinct neurological systems.
94  Wilson, B.R. (ed.), *Rationality*, Oxford: Basil Blackwell, 1970.
95  Lukes, S., 'Some Problems About Rationality', in Wilson, B.R. (ed.), *Rationality*, Oxford: Basil Blackwell, 1970.
96  Clark, 2001; Suchman, L.A., *Plans and Situated Action: The Problem of Human-Machine Communication*, Cambridge: Cambridge University Press, 1987.
97  Schatzki, T.R., Cetina, K.K., von Savigny, E. (eds), *The Practice Turn in Contemporary Theory*, London: Routledge, 2001.
98  Sperber, D., 'Apparently Irrational Beliefs', in *On Anthropological Knowledge*, Cambridge: Cambridge University Press, 1985.
99  McIntosh, 1998, p. 558.

## Chapter 4   Organisational Knowledge

1  Owen, 2007, p. 3.
2  Schneider and Angelmar, 1993, here at p. 7.
3  Meindl, J.R., Stubbart, C., Porac, J.F., *Cognition Within and Between Organisations*, Thousand Oaks: Sage, 1996, p. xi.
4  On methodological individualism in cognitive psychology, see Augoustinos and Walker, 1996, p. 158; Schneider and Angelmar, 1993, p. 2.
5  Schneider and Angelmar, 1993, pp. 7, 9–10.
6  Schneider and Angelmar, 1993, at p. 7, discuss the inability to measure synergies, and how mere aggregation ignores the influence of group dynamics; Gray, B., Bougon, M.G., Donnellon, A., 'Organisations as Constructions and Destructions of Meaning', *Journal of Management*, 1985, 11: 83–98.
7  Schneider and Angelmar, 1993, p. 1; Tushman, M.L., Nadler, D.A., 'Implications of Political Models of Organisation', in Miles, R.H. (ed.), *Resource Book in Macro-Organisational Behaviour*, Santa Monica, CA: Goodyear, 1980, describes 'sets of thinking practices'; Weick, K.E., 'Cognitive Processes in Organisations', in Straw, B.M. (ed.), *Research in Organisational Behaviour*, Greenwich, CT: JA Press, 1979 for 'interpretive systems'; Daft, R.L., Weick, K.E., 'Toward a Model of Organisations as Interpreting Systems', *Academy of Management Review*, 1984, 9/2: 284–295 for organisations as 'minds', and as 'open social systems that seek and interpret information'; Hayes, J., Allinson, C.W., 'Cognitive Style and the Theory and Practice of Individual and Collective Learning in Organisations', *Human Relations*, 1998, 51/7: 847–871, here

at p. 854; Allaire, Y., Firsirotu, M.E., 'Theories of Cognitive Culture', *Organisation Studies*, 1996, 5/3: 193–226 describe organisations as 'social artefacts of shared cognitive maps, or enactments of a collective mind'; Meindl et al., 1996, p. xv.

8 On *social* cognition, see Resnick, 1993, p. 2; Nye, J.L., Brower, A.M. (eds), *What's Social About Social Cognition? Research on Socially Shared Cognition in Small Groups*, Thousand Oaks, CA.: Sage, 1996, 311–323.

9 Sandelands and Stablein, 1987, p. 4, on value of seeing organisations as cultures.

10 Schneider and Angelmar, 1993, p. 3; Hayes and Allinson, 1998, pp. 847–848.

11 Schneider and Angelmar, 1993, p. 8.

12 Hayes and Allinson, 1998, p. 855, where organisations develop 'mental models'.

13 Hutchins, E., *In Search of Navigators*, New York: Wiley, 1987; Resnick, 1993, p. 10; Clegg, 1994, p. 467.

14 Hayes and Allinson, 1998, pp. 847–848, review research on individual and organisational learning.

15 Sandelands and Stablein, 1987, p. 151.

16 Schneider and Angelmar, 1993, pp. 2, 4, 6; Sandelands and Stablein, 1987, p. 5.

17 Individual memory is often seen in terms of 'storage bins', Schneider and Angelmar, 1993, p. 5; Cyert, R.M., March, J.G., *A Behavioural Theory of the Firm*, Englewood Cliffs, NJ: Prentice Hall, 1963, on the encoding of experience in programs and routines.

18 Resnick, 1993, p. 18.

19 Hayes, J., Allinson, C.W., 'Cognitive Style and the Theory and Practice of Individual and Collective Learning in Organisations', *Human Relations*, 1998, 51/7: 847–871, here at pp. 855–856; Daft, R.L., Weick, K.E., 'Toward a Model of Organisations as Interpreting Systems', *Academy of Management Review*, 1984, 9/2: 284–295.

20 Resnick, 1993, p. 7.

21 Dolfsma, W., 'Metaphors of Knowledge in Economics', *Review of Social Economy*, 2000, 159/1: 73–91, here at p. 82, and pp. 86–87; Schneider and Angelmar, 1993, p. 8.

22 Nelson, R.R., Winter, S.G., *An Evolutionary Theory of Economic Change*, Cambridge: Belknap Press, 1982; Schneider and Angelmar, 1993, p. 3; Meindl et al., 1996, p. xv.

23 Schneider and Angelmar, 1993, pp. 5–6; Sandelands and Stablein, 1987 note, at p. 7, the 'marked microfocus' of cognitive science; Schneider and Angelmar, 1993, at pp. 10–11, attribute cognitive phenomena such as beliefs, schemas, information processing, rules, memory and learning *to organisations*.

24 On differences between individual and group learning, see Schneider and Angelmar, 1993, p. 11; Hayes and Allinson, 1998, p. 855; Kim, D.H., 'The Link Between Individual and Organisational Learning', *Sloan Management Review*, 1993, Fall: 37–50, links individual and organisational learning

through mental models; Bandura, A., *Social Foundations of Thought and Action: A Social Cognitive Theory*, Englewood Cliffs, NJ: Prentice-Hall, 1986; Dolfsma, 2000, p. 84; One way organisations and individuals *are* analogous is in the lacunae of research which, again, fails to adequately consider affect, identity and context, for which see Schneider and Angelmar, 1993, p. 2; on the lack of the affective-expressive dimension, and the neglect of the political character of organisations, p. 10; see also, Schott, 1991, p. 56.

25  Schneider and Angelmar, 1993, p. 5.
26  Sandelands and Stablein, 1987, p. 139.
27  Sandelands and Stablein, 1987, pp. 139, 149.
28  On shared assumptions and mental models, see Hayes and Allinson, 1998, p. 853; Swieringa, J., Wierdsma, A., *Becoming a Learning Organisation*, Reading, MA: Addison Wesley, 1992; Schneider and Angelmar, 1993, p. 11; Calder, B.J., Schuur, I., 'Attitudinal Processes in Organisations', in *Research in Organisational Behaviour*, Cummings, L.L., Staw, B.M. (eds), Vol. 3, Greenwich, CT: JAI Press, 1981; March, J.G., Simon, H.A., *Organisations*, New York: Wiley, 1958, pp. 154–158 on group influence on individual schemas.
29  Douglas, M., *How Institutions Think*, London: Routledge, 1986.
30  Strydom, P., 2008, pp. 347–348.
31  On problems with 'shared' cognition, see Resnick, 1993, pp. 11, 13, 18; Schneider and Angelmar, 1993, pp. 8, 13, p. 11 on 'how… individuals within organisations acquire the 'same way of seeing the world?'; Hayes and Allinson, 1998, p. 867, address the desirability of 'like-mindedness'; Walsh, J.P., Henderson, C.M., Deighton, J.A., 'Negotiated Belief Structures and Decision Performance: An Empirical Investigation', *Organisational Behaviour and Human Decision Process*, 1988, 42: 194–216; Sandelands and Stablein, 1987, p. 5 examine shared ideas, meanings and values and how they are held in common; Hayes and Allinson, 1998, pp. 867, 855, on 'convergence'; Sandelands and Stablein, 1987, p. 10; Schneider and Angelmar, 1993, p. 8; Janis, I.L., *Victims of Groupthink*, Boston: Houghton Mifflin, 1972.
32  Schneider and Angelmar, 1993, p. 7; Lawrence, P.R., Lorsch, J.W., *Organisation and Environment*, Cambridge, MA: Harvard University Press, 1967, on different functional experiences see Sandelands and Stablein, 1987, p. 6.
33  Sandelands and Stablein, 1987, p. 7, on 'occupational communities'.
34  Hayes and Allinson, 1998, p. 854, on the triggers for double-loop learning; Schott, 1991, p. 58, on automatic learning, and p. 71 on double loop learning and reflexivity.
35  Resnick, 1993, pp. 13, 15.
36  Schneider and Angelmar, 1993, p. 5.
37  Schneider and Angelmar, 1993, p. 6.
38  See Harré, R., on the ontology of social structure, and the reply by Strydom, P., both in the 'Symposium', *European Journal of Social Theory*, 2002, 5/1: 107–148.

39 On thinking as a metaphor for organisations, see Sims, H.P. Jr., Gioia, D.A., *The Thinking Organisation*, San Francisco, CA: Jossey-Bass, 1986; also, James, L.R., Joyce, W.F., Slocum, J.W., 'Organisations Do Not Cognize', *Academy of Management Review*, 1988, 13/1: 129–132.

40 Schattschneider, E.E., *The Semisovereign People*, Hinsdale: The Dryden Press, 1975.

41 Schott, 1991, p. 55.

42 Morgan, 1997, describes a 'growing realisation ... since the 1980s... that the fundamental task facing leaders and managers rests in creating appropriate systems of shared meaning that can mobilise the efforts of people in pursuit of desired aims and objectives', p. 147, and 'values engineering', p. 150.

43 Japp, K.P., 'Distinguishing Non-Knowledge', *Canadian Journal of Sociology*, 2000, 25/2: 225–238, here at p. 55; See also, Schatzki, T.R., 'Introduction: Practice Theory', in Schatzki, T.R., Cetina, K.K., von Savigny, E. (eds), *The Practice Turn in Contemporary Theory*, London: Routledge, 2001.

44 Clegg, 1994, p. 464; Sandelands and Stablein, 1987, pp. 136–137.

45 James Bashai's unpublished paper 'Erwin Straus' Contribution to Psychology and Psychiatry'.

46 On situated cognition, see Norman, D.A., 'Cognition in the Head and in the World', *Cognitive Science*, 1993, 17: 1–6; Suchman, 1987; see the survey in Clegg, 1994, pp. 464–466.

47 Clegg, 1994, p. 464, speaks of sharing an epistemological commitment to the subjective nature of the world; see also, Resnick, 1993, p. 18.

48 Schott, 1991, p. 66, on organisational experience as perspectical, and thus of 'organisational relativity'; For an epistemological analysis of perspectivalism, see recent feminist work on standpoint epistemology, such as Hartsock, N., 'The Feminist Standpoint: Developing the Ground for a Specifically Feminist Historical Materialism', in *Discovering Reality*, Harding, S., Hintikka, M. (eds), Dordrecht: Reidel, 1983; Harding, S., *Feminism and Methodology*, Bloomington: Indiana University Press, 1987.

49 Spivak, G.C., *The Post-Colonial Critic*, Harasym, S. (ed.), New York: Routledge, 1990.

50 Eder, K., *The New Politics of Class: Social Movements and Cultural Dynamics in Advanced Societies*, London: Sage, 1993.

51 Lenski, 1984; Thompson, 1996.

52 Keltner et al., 2003.

53 Sandelands and Stablein, 1987, pp. 13, 14.

54 Schott, 1991, p. 66.

55 Dewey, J. *The Public and its Problems*, 1988, p. 207.

56 Haney, C., Banks, W. C., Zimbardo, P.G., 'Interpersonal Dynamics in a Simulated Prison', *International Journal of Criminology and Penology*, 1973, 1: 69–97; Zimbardo, P.G. 'On Rethinking the Psychology of Tyranny: The BBC Prison Study', *British Journal of Social Psychology*, 2006, 45: 47–53; Reicher, S., Haslam, S.A. 'Rethinking the Psychology of Tyranny: The BBC Prison Study', *British Journal of Social Psychology*, 2006, 45: 1–40.

57  Ackroyd, S., Thompson, P., *Organisational Misbehaviour*, London: Sage, 1999.
58  Scott, J.C., *Domination and the Arts of Resistance*, New Haven: Yale University Press, 1990.
59  Rousseau terms the collective interest of a powerful group their 'corporate will'. The dominance of corporate will among elite groups is, for him, a significant step towards the corruption of a republic, for which, see *The Social Contract*.
60  Lawrence, P.R., Lorsch, J.W., *Organisation and Environment*, Cambridge, MA: Harvard University Press, 1967; Clegg, C., 1994, 'Psychology and Information Technology: The Study of Cognition in Organisations', *British Journal of Psychology*, 85/4: 449–487, here at p. 469.
61  Walker, G., 'Network Position and Cognition in a Computer Software Firm', *Administrative Science Quarterly*, 30: 103–130, 1985; see also Clegg, 1994, p. 469.
62  Goffman, E., *Asylums*, New York: Doubleday, 1961.
63  Culbert, S.F., McDonough, J., *Radical Management*, New York: Free Press, 1985, p. 96; see also, Schott, R.L., 'Administrative and Organisational Behaviour: Some Insights from Cognitive Psychology', *Administration and Society*, 23/1: 54–73, 1991, here at p. 66.
64  See the discussion in Clegg, 'Psychology and Information Technology', 1994, here at p. 467, in which zones of 'shared' cognition face other, 'discrepant' zones of 'shared' cognition, and that these 'may provide a means of identifying and distinguishing social groups'.
65  Arendt, H., 'Lectures on Kant's Political Philosophy', in Beiner, R. (ed.), *Lectures on Kant's Political Philosophy*, Brighton: Harvester Press, 1982.
66  Lomas, J., *Formalised Informality: An Action Plan to Spread Proven Health Innovations*, Wellington: New Zealand Ministry of Health, 2008.
67  Blaug, R., 'Engineering Democracy', *Political Studies*, 50/1: 102–116, 2002.
68  'It is clear that the scale of the nation-state precludes, just by itself, the possibility of participatory democracy'. Kateb, G., 'Wolin as Critic of Democracy', in Botwinick, A., Connolly, W.E. (eds) *Democracy and Vision: Sheldon Wolin and the Vicissitudes of the Political*, Princeton: Princeton University Press, 2001, pp. 39–57, here at p. 41.
69  Blaug, R., 'Blind Hierarchism and Radical Organisational Forms', *New Political Science*, 2002, 2/3: 379–396, and the exchange with John Ehrenberg in the same issue.
70  Parry, G., Moyser, G., *Political Participation and Democracy in Britain*, Cambridge: Cambridge University Press, 1992, p. 15.
71  Wolin, S., 'Fugitive Democracy', *Constellations*, 1994, 1/1: 11–25.
72  See Cohen, A. *Masquerade Politics*, Oxford: Berg, 1993; Mouffe, C., 'Radical Democracy: Modern or Postmodern', in Ross, A. (ed.), *Universal Abandon? The Politics of Postmodernism*, Edinburgh: Edinburgh University Press, 1988, pp. 31–45; Katsiaficas, G., *The Subversion of Politics: European Autonomous Social Movements and the Decolonization of Everyday Life*, New Jersey: Humanities Press, 1997; Klein, N., *No Logo*, London:

HarperCollins, 2000; Holloway, J., *Change the World Without Taking Power*, London: Pluto Press, 2002.

73 Geras, N. 'Ex-Marxism Without Substance: Being a Reply to Leclau and Mouffe', *New Left Review*, 169, 1988, pp. 34–62.

74 Kymlicka, W., Nelson, W., 'Return of the Citizen: A Survey of Recent Work on Citizenship Theory', *Ethics*, 1994, 104: 352–381, here at p. 369, ft. 21.

75 Epstein, B., 'Radical Democracy and Cultural Politics: What about Class? What about Political Power?' in Trend D. (ed.), *Radical Democracy: Identity, Citizenship, and the State*, London: Routledge, 1996, pp. 127–139.

76 See, for example, *Differences*, Special Issue, Vol. 6, 1994.

77 As so ably documented in ongoing issues of *SchNEWS*, http://www. schnews.org.uk/; see also, Merrick, *Battle for the Trees*, Leeds: godhaven ink, 1998.

78 *SchNEWS* details the harassment to which such initiatives are subject, often through use of provisions in the Criminal Justice and Terrorism Acts, as well as legislation against stalking, harassment and anti-social behaviour.

79 Deleuze and Guattari, 1987, pp. 351–423.

80 Though Deleuze and Guattari would reject the language of action coordination.

81 See, Thompson G. et al. (eds), *Markets, Hierarchies and Networks: The Coordination of Social Life*, London: Sage, 1996.

82 Wolin, 'Fugitive Democracy', 1994; Kateb, 'Wolin as Critic of Democracy', 2001, pp. 39–57, p. 45 argues that Wolin is insufficiently discriminating in regard to institutions, though this amounts to charging fugitive democracy with being, in fact, fugitive; see also, Blaug, R., 'Outbreaks of Democracy', *Socialist Register*, 2000, pp. 145–160.

83 Wolin, 'Fugitive Democracy', 1994, p. 14.

84 Linebaugh, P., Rediker, M. *The Many-Headed Hydra: Sailors, Slaves, Commoners, and the Hidden History of the Revolutionary Atlantic*, London: Verso, 2008.

85 Wolin, S. *The Presence of the Past: Essays on the State and the Constitution*, Baltimore: Johns Hopkins University Press, 1989.

86 Goffman, E., *The Presentation of the Self in Everyday Life*, Harmondsworth: Penguin, 1990; Butler, J., *Bodies that Matter: On the Discursive Limits of Sex*, London: Routledge, 1993.

87 Keltner et al., 2003.

88 Keltner et al., 2003.

89 Again, the image comes from Ahrne, G., *Social Organizations: Interactions Inside, Outside and Between Organizations*, London: Sage, 1994.

90 Rousseau, 1998, *The Social Contract*.

91 Benveniste, 1996.

92 Dewey, J., *The Public and its Problems*, Carbondale: Southern Illinois University Press, 1988, p. 208.

93 Machiavelli, 1979.

94 Keltner et al., 2003, p. 272.

95  It is thus an example of 'privileging subjectivity', for which, see Minow, M., *Making All the Difference: Inclusion, Exclusion and American Law*, Ithaca: Cornell University Press, 1990.

96  Cited in Shusterman, R. 'Putnam and Cavell on the Ethics of Democracy', *Political Theory*, 25/2, 1997: 193–214, here at p. 195.

97  McIntosh, 1998, p. 560. Emphasis mine.

98  Seligman, 1977.

99  Once again, to speak of subordinate collusion is not to excuse elites, nor to blame the victim.

100  As do postmodern theorists, and Berger and Luckmann, 1967.

101  See, for an analysis of this form of alienation, see its use in the critique of religious belief in, Feuerbach, L., *The Essence of Christianity*, New York: Harper, 1957.

102  Spivak, G.C., *The Post-Colonial Critic*, Harasym, S. (ed.), New York: Routledge, 1990.

103  Scott, J.C., *Domination and the Arts of Resistance*, New Haven: Yale University Press, 1990, p. 133.

104  See Mbembe, A., 'The banality of power and the aesthetics of vulgarity in the postcolony', *Public Culture*, 4, 1992, pp. 1–30.

105  Scott, 1990, pp. 4, 32, 40, 132.

106  Scott, 1990, pp. 202–227.

107  Scott himself remains profoundly ambivalent about this outcome, and a good deal of his work is directed against Marxist accounts of ideology. Unfortunately, he does not apply his analysis to neo-liberal regimes.

108  See the 'Nomadology', in Deleuze, G., Guattari, *Thousand Plateaux*, Minneapolis: University of Minnesota Press, 1987; Wolin, S., 'Fugitive Democracy', *Constellations*, 1994, 1/1: 11–25.

109  Milgram, S. *Obedience to Authority: An Experimental View*, New York: Harper Colophon, 1974.

110  Rousseau, *The Social Contract*, 1998, pp. 77–80; Wolff, 1970.

111  Owen, 2007, p. 3.

## Chapter 5    Democratic Conclusions

1  Habermas, *Moral Consciousness and Communicative Action*, 1992.

2  Shapiro, 1999, p. 21.

3  Proudhon, P.J., 'Parliamentary Isolation', in Woodcock, G. (ed.), *The Anarchist Reader*, p. 110.

4  Bakunin, M., 'The Illusion of Universal Suffrage', in Woodcock, G. (ed.), *The Anarchist Reader*, London: Fontana/Collins, 1977, pp. 108–110, here at p. 109.

5  Rousseau, *Social Contract*, pp. 77–80.

6  See, Wolff, R.P., *In Defence of Anarchism*, New York: Harper and Row, 1970.

7  Dahl, 1970; Dahl & Tufte, 1974: 23.

8 Canovan, 1999, p. 13; Beetham, 1992.

9 Hirst, 1994; Budge, 1993; Keane, 1988; Clarke, 1996; Ryfe, 2005, p. 60.

10 Habermas, 1992, p. 453.

11 Rousseau, *The Social Contract.*

12 Habermas, *Moral Consciousness and Communicative Action*, 1992; Botwinick, A. *Wittgenstein, Skepticism and Political Participation*, New York: University Press of America, 1985.

13 Hilary Putnam terms this John Dewey's 'epistemological' justification for democracy, for which, see Shusterman, R., 'Putnam and Cavell on the Ethics of Democracy', *Political Theory*, 1997, 25/2: 193–214, here at p. 194; It is Alvin Goldman's orientation to 'knowledge-gaining practices' that makes his work so important.

14 Pierce conceived of the search for knowledge as a convergence upon 'the opinion which is fated to be ultimately agreed to by all who investigate', *The Collected Papers of Charles Sanders Peirce*, Hartshorne, C., Weiss, P. (eds), Cambridge, MA: Harvard University Press, 1931–5, vols. i–vi: p. 407; see also Goldman's discussion of Peirce, 1999, here at p. 46.

15 Popper, K., *The Open Society and its Enemies*, London: Routledge, 1962.

16 Apel, K.O., *Towards a Transformation of Philosophy*, London: Routledge, 1980; Habermas, J., *The Theory of Communicative Action*, Vol. 1, Cambridge, MA: Beacon Press, 1984; Cohen, J., 'Deliberation and Democratic Legitimacy', in *The Good Polity: Normative Analysis of the State*, Hamlin, A., Pettit P. (eds), Oxford: Basil Blackwell, 1991, pp. 17–34.

17 Putnam, H., 'A Reconsideration of Deweyan Democracy', in *Renewing Philosophy*, Cambridge, MA: Harvard University Press, 1992, p. 180.

18 Senge, P.M., *The Fifth Discipline: The Art and Practice of the Learning Organisation*, Bantam Doubleday, 1994.

19 Power, M., *The Audit Society, Rituals of Verification*, Oxford: Oxford University Press, 1999.

20 As Rousseau said in the *Discourse on the Origins of Inequality*, 'once you have citizens, you have all you need'.

21 Bale, T., Taggart, P., Webb, P., 'You Can't Always Get What You Want: Populism and the Power Inquiry', *The Political Quarterly*, 2006, 77/2, pp. 195–203.

22 McHugh, D., 'Wanting to be Heard But Not Wanting to Act? Addressing Public Disengagement', *Parliamentary Affairs*, 2006: 59/3, pp. 546–552.

23 DeLuca, T. *The Two Faces of Political Apathy*, Philadelphia: Temple University Press, 1995.

24 Ryfe, 2005, p. 52.

25 Mill, J.S., *Considerations on Representative Government*, London: Everyman, 1972.

26 Gastil, J., *Democracy in Small Groups: Participation, Decision-making and Communication*, Gabriola Island: New Society, 1993; Gastil, J., Dillard, J.,

'Increasing Political Sophistication through Public Deliberation', *Political Communication*, 1999, 16: 3–23.

27  Budge, I., 'Direct Democracy: Setting Appropriate Terms of Debate', in *Prospects for Democracy: North, South, East, West*, D. Held (ed.), Cambridge: Polity Press, 1993, pp. 136–155.

28  Pateman, C., *Participation and Democratic Theory*, Cambridge: Cambridge University Press, 1970; Warren, M., 'Democratic Theory and Self-Transformation', *American Political Science Review*, 1992, 86/1: 8–23; Mackie, G., 'Does Democratic Deliberation Change Minds?', *Politics, Philosophy and Economics*, 2006, 5/3: 279–303.

29  Fudge, N., Wolfe, C., McKevitt, C., 'Assessing the promise of user involvement in health service development: ethnographic study', *British Medical Journal*, 2008, 336: 313–317; Simpson, E.L., House, A.O., 'Involving users in the delivery and evaluation of mental health services: systematic review', *British Medical Journal*, 2002, 325: 1265; Mullender, A., Ward, D. *Self-directed Group Work: Users Take Action for Empowerment*, London: Whiting and Birch, 1991.

30  Bath, C., *Learning to Belong: Exploring Young Children's Participation at the Start of School*, London: Routledge, 2009.

31  Fishkin, J.S., *The Dialogue of Justice: Toward a Self-Reflective Society*, New Haven: Yale University Press, 1992; Dryzek, 2002; Elster, 1998; Fishkin, J.S., *Democracy and Deliberation: New Directions for Democratic Reform*, New Haven: Yale University Press, 1991.

32  Luskin, Fishkin & Jowell, 2002.

33  Forrester, J., *The Deliberative Practitioner: Encouraging Participatory Planning Processes*, Cambridge, MA: MIT Press, 1999; Tetlock, P. 'Accountability: A Social Check on the Fundamental Attribution Error', *Social Psychology Quarterly*, 1985, 48: 227–236.

34  Mead, G.H., *Mind, Self, and Society*, Chicago: University of Chicago Press, 1934.

35  Goetz, A.M., Gaventa, J., 'Bringing Citizen Voice and Client Focus into Service Delivery', Brighton: *Institute for Development Studies*, 2001; Fung, A., 'Recipes for Public Spheres: Eight Institutional Design Choices and their Consequences', *Journal of Political Philosophy*, 2003, 11/3: 338–367.

36  Foucault, M., *Power/Knowledge*, New York: Random House, 1980, p. 131.

37  Rose, 1993.

38  This being why Habermas's 'inescapable presuppositions of argumentation' are counterfactual. See also, Boréus, K., 'Discursive Discrimination: A Typology', *European Journal of Social Theory*, 2006, 9/3.

39  See Shapiro, 1999, pp. 42–46; Ricoeur, P., 'Ethics and Culture: Habermas and Gadamer in Dialogue', *Philosophy Today*, 1973, 17: 153–165 and *Freud and Philosophy: An Essay on Interpretation*, New Haven: Yale University Press, 1970.

40  Yet the US and UK are currently discrediting 'democracy' in much the same way as the Soviet Union discredited Marxism.

41 McCormick, J.P., 'Contain the Wealthy and Patrol the Magistrates: Restoring Elite Accountability to Popular Government', *American Political Science Review*, 2006, 100/2: 147–163.

42 Canovan, M., 'Trust the People! Populism and the Two Faces of Democracy', *Political Studies*, 1999, 47/1: 2–16; Laclau, E., 'Populism: What's in a Name?', in F. Panizza (ed.), *Populism and the Mirror of Democracy*, London: Verso, 2005.

43 Elster, J., 'Accountability in Athenian Politics', in Przeworski, A., Stokes, S.C., Manin, B. (eds), *Democracy, Accountability, and Representation*, Cambridge: Cambridge University Press, 1999, pp. 253–278.

# Bibliography

Abrahamson, B., *Bureaucracy or Participation: The Logic of Organization*, London: Sage, 1977.

Ackroyd, S., Thompson, P., *Organizational Misbehaviour*, London: Sage, 1999.

Acton, E.E.D., Lord, 'Letter to Mandell Creighton', April 5, 1887.

Adorno, T.W., *The Authoritarian Personality*, New York: Harper & Row, 1950.

Ahrne, G., 'Civil Society and Uncivil Organizations', in Alexander, J.C. (ed.), *Real Civil Societies: Dilemmas of Institutionalization*, pp. 84–95, London: Sage, 1998.

Ahrne, G., *Social Organizations: Interactions Inside, Outside and Between Organizations*, London: Sage, 1994.

Aldrich, H., *Organizations Evolving*, London: Sage, 2001.

Alinksy, S.D., *Rules for Radicals: A Practical Primer for Realistic Radicals*, New York: Vantage, 1972.

Allaire, Y., Firsirotu, M.E., 'Theories of Cognitive Culture', *Organization Studies*, 1996, 5/3: 193–226.

Allport, F.H., *Social Psychology*, Boston: Houghton-Mifflin, 1924.

Altemeyer, B., 'The Other "Authoritarian Personality"', in Zanna, M.P. (ed.), *Advances in Experimental Social Psychology*, 30: 48–92, New York: Academic, 1998.

Alvesson, M., 'Organizations as Rhetoric: Knowledge Intensive Firms and the Struggle with Ambiguity', *Journal of Management Studies*, 1993, 30: 997–1015.

Anderson, J.R., *Cognitive Psychology and its Implications*, New York: Freeman, 1995.

Apel, K.O., *Towards a Transformation of Philosophy*, London: Routledge, 1980.

Arendt, H., 'Lectures on Kant's Political Philosophy', in Beiner, R. (ed.), *Lectures on Kant's Political Philosophy*, Brighton: Harvester Press, 1982.

Arendt, H., *On Revolution*, Penguin: Harmondsworth, 1973.

Arendt, H., *Eichmann in Jerusalem*, Harmondsworth: Penguin, 1964.

Argyris, C., Schön, D., *Theory in Practice*, San Francisco: Jossey-Bass, 1974.

Aristotle, *Nicomachean Ethics*, New York: Bobbs-Merrill, 1962.

Arquilla, J., Rondfeldt, D. (eds), *Networks and Netwars: The Future of Terror, Crime and Militancy*, Santa Monica, CA: Rand MR-1382-OSD, 2001.

Asch, S., 'Studies of Independence and Conformity: A Minority of One Against a Unanimous Majority', *Psychological Monographs: General and Applied Social Psychology*, Vol. 70, 1956.

Ashenden, S., Owen, D., *Foucault Contra Habermas: Recasting the Dialogue between Genealogy and Critical Theory*, London: Sage, 1999.

Ashforth, B.E., 'Petty Tyranny Organizations', *Human Relations*, 1994, 47: 755–778.

Augoustinos, M., Walker, I., *Social Cognition*, London: Sage, 1996.

Bachelard, G., *The Poetics of Space*, Boston: Beacon, 1964.

Bakhurst, D., 'Pragmatism and Moral Knowledge', *Canadian Journal of Philosophy*, 1998, 14: 227–252.

Bakunin, M., 'The Illusion of Universal Suffrage', in Woodcock, G. (ed.), *The Anarchist Reader*, pp. 108–110, London: Fontana/Collins, 1977.

Bale, T., Taggart, P., Webb, P., 'You Can't Always Get What You Want: Populism and the Power Inquiry', *The Political Quarterly*, 2006, 77/2, pp. 195–203.

Bandura, A., *Social Foundations of Thought and Action: A Social Cognitive Theory*, Englewood Cliffs, NJ: Prentice-Hall, 1986.

Barnes, B., Bloor, D., Henry, J., *Scientific Knowledge: A Sociological Analysis*, London: Athlone, 1996.

Baron, H., *The Crisis in the Early Italian Renaissance*, Princeton: Princeton University Press, 1966.

Barrett, A.A., *Caligula: The Corruption of Power*, London: Routledge, 1989.

Bartlett, F.A., *A Study in Experimental and Social Psychology*, New York: Cambridge University Press, 1932.

Bath, C., *Learning to Belong: Exploring Young Children's Participation at the Start of School*, London: Routledge, 2009.

Bauman, Z., *Liquid Modernity*, Cambridge: Polity Press, 2000.

Bauman, Z., *Intimations of Postmodernity*, London: Routledge, 1992.

Baynes, K., 'Liberal Neutrality, Pluralism, and Deliberative Politics', *Praxis International*, 1992, 12/1: 50–69.

Beck, U., *World Risk Society*, Cambridge: Polity Press, 1999.

Beck, U., Giddens, A., Lash, S., *Reflexive Modernization: Politics, Tradition and Aesthetics in the Modern Social Order*, Cambridge: Polity Press, 1994.

Beetham, D., 'Defining and Justifying Democracy', *Democracy and Human Rights*, Cambridge: Polity, 1999, pp. 1–30.

Beetham, D., 'Liberal Democracy and the Limits of Democratization', *Political Studies*, 1992, XL: 40–53.

Beetham, D., *The Legitimation of Power*, London: Macmillan, 1991.

Benda, V. et al., 'Parallel Polis, or An Independent Society in Central and Eastern Europe: An Inquiry', *Social Research*, 1988, 55: 211–260. *Economic Review*, 1956, 56/1–2: 1–13.

Benhabib, S., *Situating the Self*, Cambridge: Polity Press, 1992.

Benhabib, S. 'The Methodological Illusions of Modern Political Theory: The Case of Rawls and Habermas', *Neue Hefte fur Philosophie*, 21, 1982, pp. 47–74.

Benveniste, G., 'Survival Inside Bureaucracy', in Thompson, G., Frances, J., Levacic, R., Mitchell, J. (eds), *Markets, Hierarchies and Networks: The Coordination of Social Life*, Thousand Oaks: Sage, 1996.

Berger, P., Luckmann, T. *The Social Construction of Reality*, p. 61, New York: Doubleday, 1967.

Bernheimer, C., Kahane, C. (eds), *In Dora's Case: Freud, Hysteria, Feminism*, London: Virago, 1985.

Best, S., Kellner, D., *Postmodern Theory: Critical Interrogations*, London: Macmillan, 1991.

Bion, W.R., Richman, J., 'Intergroup Tensions in Therapy', *Lancet*, 1961, 27: 478–481.

Birchall, J., *Building Communities the Co-operative Way*, London: Routledge, 1988.

Blakeley, G., 'Flamboyant Labels on Empty Luggage? Recent Theorizing on Democracy', *Contemporary Politics*, 2001, 7/4: 331–337.

Blaug, R., 'Why is there Hierarchy? Democracy and Organisational Form', *Critical Review of International Social and Political Philosophy*, 2009, Vol. 11/3.

Blaug, R., 'Direct Accountability at the End', in Leighton, D., White, S. (eds), *Building a Citizen Society: The Emerging Politics of Republican Democracy*, Lawrence & Wishart, 2008.

Blaug, R., 'Cognition in a Hierarchy', *Contemporary Political Theory*, 6/1: 24–44, 2007.

Blaug, R., 'Blind Hierarchism and Radical Organizational Forms', *New Political Science*, 2002, 2/3: 379–396.

Blaug, R., 'Engineering Democracy', *Political Studies*, 2002, 50/1: 102–116.

Blaug, R., 'Outbreaks of Democracy', *Socialist Register*, 2000, pp. 145–160.

Blaug, R., *Democracy, Real and Ideal: Discourse Ethics and Radical Politics*, New York: SUNY Press, 1999.

Blaug, R., 'The Tyranny of the Visible: Problems in the Evaluation of Anti-Institutional Radicalism', *Organization*, 1998, 6/1: 33–56.

Board, de, R., *The Psychoanalysis of Organisations*, London: Tavistock, 1978.

Bookchin, M., *The Ecology of Freedom: The Emergence and Dissolution of Hierarchy*, Palo Alto, CA: Cheshire Books, 1982.

Boréus, K., 'Discursive Discrimination: A Typology', *European Journal of Social Theory*, 2006, 9/3.

Botwinick, A., *Skepticism and Political Participation*, Philadelphia: Temple University Press, 1990.

Botwinick, A., *Wittgenstein, Skepticism and Political Participation*, University Press of America, 1985.

Boulding, K.E., 'The Economics of Knowledge and the Knowledge of Economics', *American and Communication*, London: Pergamon Press, 1958.

Bourdieu, P., *Outline of a Theory of Practice*, Cambridge: Cambridge University Press, 1977.

Bourne, L.E., Dominowski, R.L., Loftus, E.F., Healy, A.F., *Cognitive Processes*, Englewood Cliffs, NJ: Prentice Hall, 1986.

Bowles, S., Gintis, H., Gustafsson, B. (eds), *Markets and Democracy: Participation, Accountability and Efficiency*, Cambridge: Cambridge University Press, 1993.

Broadbent, D., *Perception and Communication*, London: Pergamon Press, 1958.

Brown, M.H., Hosking, D.M., 'Distributed Leadership and Skilled Performance as Successful Organization in Social Movements', *Human Relations*, 1986, 39/1: 65–79.

Bryant, C, Jary, D., *Giddens' Theory of Structuration: A Critical Appreciation*, London: Routledge, 1991.

Budge, I., 'Direct Democracy: Setting Appropriate Terms of Debate', in D. Held (ed.), *Prospects for Democracy: North, South, East, West*, pp. 136–155, Cambridge: Polity Press, 1993.

Bufacchi, V., 'Sceptical Democracy', *Politics*, 2001, 21/1: 23–30.

Burback, R., 'Roots of the Postmodern Rebellion in Chiapas', *New Left Review*, 1994, 205: 113–124.

Burchell, G., Gordon, C., Miller, P., Foucault, M., *The Foucault Effect – Studies in Governmentality*, London: Harvester Wheatsheaf, 1991.

Burke, E., 'Speech at the Conclusion of the Poll', Bristol, November, 1774.

Burke, P., *A Social History of Knowledge*, Cambridge: Polity, 2000.

Burns, D., *Poll Tax Rebellion*, Stirling: AK Press, 1992.

Burrell, G., 'Modernism, Postmodernism and Organizational Analysis: The Contribution of Michel Foucault', in McKinlay, A., Starkey, K. (eds), *Foucault, Management and Organization Theory*, pp. 14–28, Thousand Oaks: Sage, 1998.

Butler, J., *Bodies that Matter: On the Discursive Limits of Sex*, London: Routledge, 1993.

Butler, J., *Gender Trouble: Feminism and the Subversion of Identity*, London: Routledge, 1990.

Calder, B.J., Schuur, 'Attitudinal Processes in Organizations', in Cummings, L.L., Staw, B.M. (eds), *Research in Organizational Behavior*, Vol. 3, Greenwich, CT: JAI Press, 1981.

Callahan, R., Salipante, P.Jr., 'Boundary Spanning Units: Organizational Implications for the Management of Innovation', in Miles, R.H. (ed.), *Resource Book in Macro-Organizational Behavior*, Santa Monica, CA: Goodyear, 1980.

Canovan, M., 'Trust the People! Populism and the Two Faces of Democracy', *Political Studies*, 1999, 47/1: 2–16.

Carter, A., *Direct Action and Liberal Democracy*, New York: Harper, 1973.

Castells, M., *The Rise of the Network Society*, Oxford: Blackwell, 1996.

Cavell, S., *Conditions Handsome and Unhandsome: The Constitution of Emersonian Perfectionism*, Chicago: University of Chicago Press, 1990.

Cavell, S., *The Claim of Reason*, Oxford: Oxford University Press, 1979.

Chandler, A., *Strategy and Structure: Chapters in the History of the American Industrial Enterprise*, Cambridge, MA: MIT Press, 1962.

Chessick, R.D., *Psychology of the Self and the Treatment of Narcissism*, Northvale, NJ: Jason Aronson, 1985.

Chomsky, N., *Language and Mind*, New York : Harcourt Brace Jovanovich, 1972.

Churns, A.B., 'The Principles of Socio-Technical Design', *Human Relations*, 1976, 29: 783–792.

Cialdini, R.B., *Influence: The Psychology of Persuasion*, New York: HarperCollins, 2007.

Clark, A., *Mindware: An Introduction to the Philosophy of Cognitive Science*, Oxford: Oxford University Press, 2001.

Clarke, P.B., *Deep Citizenship*, London: Pluto Press, 1996.

Clegg, C., 'Psychology and Information Technology: The Study of Cognition in Organizations', *British Journal of Psychology*, 1994, 85/4: 449–487.

Clegg, S.R., Palmer, G., *The Politics of Management Knowledge*, London: Sage, 1996.

Clegg, S.R., *Modern Organizations: Organization Studies in the Postmodern World*, London: Sage, 1990.

Cloke, K., Goldsmith, J., *The End of Management and the Rise of Organizational Democracy*, San Francisco: Jossey-Bass, 2002.

Cohen, A., *Masquerade Politics*, Oxford: Berg, 1993.

Cohen, J., 'Reflections on Rousseau: Autonomy and Democracy', *Philosophy and Public Affairs*, 1986, 15/3: 275–297.

Cohen, J., 'Deliberation and Democratic Legitimacy', in Hamlin, A., Pettit, P. (eds), *The Good Polity: Normative Analysis of the State*, pp. 17–34, Oxford: Basil Blackwell, 1991.

Cohen, S., *States of Denial: Knowing about Atrocities and Suffering*, Cambridge: Polity Press, 2001.

Cohn, N., *The Pursuit of the Millennium*, London: Paladin, 1970.

Colby, M., 'The Epistemological Foundations of Practical Reason', *Inquiry*, 1999, 42/1: 25–48.

Connolly, W., 'Cross-State Citizen Networks: A Response to Dallmayr', *Millennium: Journal of International Studies*, 2001, 30/2, p. 5.

Connolly, W.E., *Neuropolitics: Thinking, Culture, Speed*, Minneapolis: University of Minnesota Press, 2002.

Craig, G., Mayo, M., 'Community Participation and Empowerment: The Human Face of Structural Adjustment or Tools for Democratic Transformation?', in Craig, G., Mayo, M. (eds), *Community Empowerment*, pp. 1–11, London: Zed Books, 1995.

Crandall, S.C., Beasley, R.K., 'A Perceptual Theory of Legitimacy: Politics, Prejudice, Social Institutions, and Moral Value', in Jost, J.T., Major, B. (eds), *The Psychology of Legitimacy: Emerging Perspectives on Ideology, Justice, and Intergroup Relations*, pp. 77–102, Cambridge: Cambridge University Press, 2001.

Culbert, S., McDonough, J., *Radical Management*, New York: Free Press, 1985.

Cyert, R.M., March, J.G., *A Behavioral Theory of the Firm*, Englewood Cliffs, NJ: Prentice Hall, 1963.

Daft, R.J., Weick, K.E., 'Toward a Model of Organizations as Interpretation Systems', *Academy of Management Review*, 1984, 9: 284–295.

Dahl, R.A., 'Democracy and the Chinese Boxes', in Kariel, H.S. (ed.), *Frontiers of Democratic Theory*, New York: Harper & Row, 1970.

Dahl, R.A., *Democracy and its Critics*, New Haven and London: Yale University Press, 1989.

Dahl, R.A., Tufte, E., *Size and Democracy*, Stanford: Stanford University Press, 1974.

Dalton, R.J., Kuechler, M. (eds), *Challenging the Political Order*, Cambridge: Polity, 1990.

Daudi, P., *Power in the Organization: The Discourse of Power in Managerial Praxis*, Oxford: Blackwell, 1986.

David, P., *Technical Choice, Innovation and Economic Growth*, Cambridge: Cambridge University Press, 1975.

de Board, R., *The Psychoanalysis of Organisations*, p. 42, London: Tavistock, 1978.

Deleuze, G., Guattari, F., *A Thousand Plateaus*, Minneapolis: University of Minnesota Press, 1987.

DeLuca, T. *The Two Faces of Political Apathy*, Philadelphia: Temple University Press, 1995.

Denzau, A.T., North, D.C., 'Shared Mental Models: Ideologies and Institutions', *Kyklos*, 1994, 47/1: 3–31.

Dépret, E., Fiske, S.T., 'Perceiving the Powerful: Intriguing Individuals versus Threatening Groups', in *Journal of Experimental Psychology*, 1999, 35: 461–480.

Dépret, E.F., Fiske, S.T., 'Social Cognition and Power: Some Cognitive Consequences of Social Structure as a Source of Control Deprivation', in Gleicher, W.F., Marsh, K. (eds), *Control Motivation and Social Cognition*, pp. 176–202, New York: Springer-Verlag, 1993.

Dewey, J., *The Public and its Problems*, Carbondale: Southern Illinois University Press, 1988.

Dilthey, W., *Selected Writings*, Rickman, H.P. (ed.), Cambridge: Cambridge University Press, 1976.

Dolfsma, W., 'Metaphors of Knowledge in Economics', *Review of Social Economy*, 2000, 159/1: 73–91.

Dollard, J.W., Miller, N.E., Doob, l.W., Mowrer, O.H., Sears, R.R., *Frustration and Aggression*, New Haven, CT Yale University Press, 1937.

Donaldson, L., *American Anti-Management Theories of Organization*, Cambridge: Cambridge University Press, 1995.

Douglas, M., *How Institutions Think*, London: Routledge, 1986.

Dowdle, M.W. (ed.), *Public Accountability: Designs, Dilemmas and Experiences*, Cambridge: CUP, 2006.

Downs, A., *An Economic Theory of Democracy*, New York: Harper, 1957.

Dryzek, J., *Deliberative Democracy and Beyond: Liberals, Critics, Contestations*, Oxford: Oxford University Press, 2002.

Duffield, M., *Global Governance and the New Wars*, London: Zed Books, 2001.

Duncan, G., Lukes, S., 'The New Democracy', *Political Studies*, 1963, 11: 156–177.

Duncker, K., 'On Problem Solving', *Psychological Monographs*, 1945, 58/5.

Dunn, J., *Democracy: The Unfinished Journey*, Oxford: Oxford University Press, 1992.

Dunn, J., *Western Political Theory in the Face of the Future*, Cambridge: Cambridge University Press, 1979.

Durkheim, E., *The Rules of Sociological Method*, Lukes, S. (ed.), London: Macmillan, 1982.

Easterby-Smith, M.J., Araujo, J. Burgoyne, J., *Organizational Learning and the Learning Organization: Developments in Theory and Practice*, London: Sage, 1999.

Eder, K., *The New Politics of Class: Social Movements and Cultural Dynamics in Advanced Societies*, London: Sage, 1993.

Eiser, J.R., *Social Psychology: Attitudes, Cognition and Social Behaviour*, Cambridge: Cambridge University Press, 1988.

Elson, M., *Self Psychology in Clinical Social Work*, New York: Norton, 1986.

Elster, J., 'Accountability in Athenian Politics', in Przeworski, A., Stokes, S.C., Manin, B. (eds), *Democracy, Accountability, and Representation*, pp. 253–278, Cambridge: Cambridge University Press, 1999.

Elster, J., *Deliberative Democracy*, Cambridge: Cambridge University Press, 1998.

Elster, J., 'The Market and the Forum: Three Varieties of Political Theory', in Elster, J., Hylland, A. (eds), *Foundations of Social Choice Theory*, pp. 103–132, Cambridge: Cambridge University Press, 1986.

Elster, J., *Explaining Technical Change*, Cambridge: Cambridge University Press, 1983.

Emery, M., *Participative Design for Participative Democracy*, Canberra: Australian National University, 1993.

Epstein, B., 'Radical Democracy and Cultural Politics: What about Class? What about Political Power?', in Trend D. (ed.), *Radical Democracy: Identity, Citizenship, and the State*, pp. 127–139, London: Routledge, 1996.

Evans, J.St.B.T., *Bias in Human Reasoning: Causes and Consequences*, London: Lawrence Erlbaum, 1989.

Feenberg, A., *Critical Theory of Technology*, New York: Oxford University Press, 1991.

Feldman, S., 'Enforcing Social Conformity: A Theory of Authoritarianism', *Political Psychology*, 2003, 24/1: 41–74.

Ferguson, K.E., *The Feminist Case Against Bureaucracy*, Philadelphia: Temple University Press, 1983.

Festenstein, M., 'Fallible Democracy: Comment on Bufacchi', *Politics*, 2002, 22/3: 163–166.

Festenstein, M., 'Putnam, Pragmatism, and Democratic Theory', *The Review of Politics*, 1995, 574: 693–721.

Festinger, L., *A Theory of Cognitive Dissonance*, Stanford: Stanford University Press, 1970.

Feuerbach, L., *The Essence of Christianity*, New York: Harper, 1957.

Fishkin, J.S., *The Dialogue of Justice: Toward a Self-Reflective Society*, New Haven: Yale University Press, 1992.

Fishkin, J.S., *Democracy and Deliberation: New Directions for Democratic Reform*, New Haven: Yale University Press, 1991.

Fiske, S.T., 'Stereotyping, Prejudice, and Discrimination', in Gilbert, D.T., Fiske, S.T., Lindzey, G. (eds), *The Handbook of Social Psychology*, 4th Edition, pp. 357–411, New York: McGraw-Hill, 1997.

Fiske, S.T., 'Controlling Other People: The Impact of Power on Stereotyping', *American Psychologist*, 1993, 48: 621–628.

Fiske, S.T., Taylor, S.E., *Social Cognition*, New York: McGraw-Hill, 1991.

Fleck, L., *The Genesis and Development of a Scientific Fact*, Chicago: University of Chicago Press, 1979.

Forrester, J., *The Deliberative Practitioner: Encouraging Participatory Planning Processes*, Cambridge, MA: MIT Press, 1999.

Forsyth, D.R., Kelley, K.N., 'Heuristic-Based Biases in Estimations of Personal Contributions to Collective Endeavors', in Nye, J.L., Brower, A.M. (eds), *What's Social About Social Cognition? Research on Socially Shared Cognition in Small Groups*, Thousand Oaks, CA: Sage, 1996.

Foucault, M., *The History of Sexuality: The Will To Knowledge*, Vol. 1, London: Penguin, 2004.

Foucault, M., 'Nietzsche, Genealogy, History', in Rabinow, P. (ed.), *The Foucault Reader*, London: Penguin, 1984.

Foucault, M., *Power/Knowledge*, New York: Random House, 1980.

Foucault, M., 'Two Lectures', in Foucault, M. *Power/Knowledge*, pp. 78–109, New York: Random House, 1980.

Foucault, M., *Discipline and Punish: The Birth of the Prison*, Harmondsworth: Penguin, 1977.

Frankel, B., 'Confronting Neoliberal Regimes: The Post-Marxist Embrace of Populism and Realpolitik', *New Left Review*, 1997, 226: 57–92.

Fraser, N., *Unruly Practices: Power, Discourse and Gender in Contemporary Social Theory*, Cambridge: Polity, 1989.

Freeman, J., *The Tyranny of Structurelessness*, London: Dark Star/Rebel Press, 1984.

Freire, P., *Pedagogy of the Oppressed*, New York: Continuum, 1983.

Freud, A., *The Ego and the Mechanisms of Defence*, New York: International Universities Press, 1961.

Freud, S., *Civilization and its Discontents*, New York: W.W. Norton, 1961.

Freud, S., 'On Narcissism', in the *Collected Papers of Sigmund Freud*, Vol. 4, 1959.

Fromm, E., *Escape from Freedom*, New York: Rinehart, 1941.

Fudge, N., Wolfe, C., McKevitt, C., 'Assessing the Promise of User Involvement in Health Service Development: Ethnographic Study', *British Medical Journal*, 2008, 336: 313–317.

Fukuyama, F., 'The End of History?', *The National Interest*, 1989, Summer: 3–18.

Fuller, S., *Knowledge Management Foundations*, Woburn, MA: Butterworth-Heinemann, 2001.

Fung, A. 'Recipes for Public Spheres: Eight Institutional Design Choices and their Consequences', *Journal of Political Philosophy*, 2003, 11/3: 338–367.

Gadamer, H., *Truth and Method*, New York: Seabury Press, 1975.

Gamson, W., *Talking Politics*, Cambridge: Cambridge University Press, 1992.

Gardner, H., *The Mind's New Science: The History of the Cognitive Revolution*, New York: Basic Books, 1987.

Gastil, J. *The Deliberative Democracy Handbook: Strategies for Effective Civic Engagement in the Twenty-first Century*, San Francisco: Jossey Bass, 2005.

Gastil, J., *Democracy in Small Groups: Participation, Decision-making and Communication*, Gabriola Island: New Society, 1993.

Gastil, J., Dillard, J., 'Increasing Political Sophistication through Public Deliberation', *Political Communication*, 1999.

Gavin, H., *The Essence of Cognitive Psychology*, London: Prentice Hall, 1998.

Gay du, P., *In Praise of Bureaucracy: Weber, Organization, Ethics*, London: Sage, 2000.

Gemmill, G., Oakley, J., 'Leadership: An Alienating Social Myth?', in *Human Relations*, 1992, 45: 113–129.

*Genesis*, 28: 10–15.

Georgakis, D., Surkin, M., *Detroit, I Do Mind Dying: A Study in Urban Revolution*, New York: St. Martin's Press, 1975.

Geras, N., 'Ex-Marxism Without Substance: Being a Reply to Leclau and Mouffe', *New Left Review*, 1988, 169: 34–62.

Geras, N., 'Marx and the Critique of Political Economy', in Blackburn, R. (ed.), *Ideology in the Social Sciences*, p. 288, London: Pantheon Books, 1972.

Giddens, A., *The Constitution of Society: Outline of the Theory of Structuration*, Berkeley: University of California Press, 1984.

Gilbert, M. *On Social Facts*, Princeton, NJ: Princeton University Press, 1989.

Gledhill, J., *Power and its Disguises: Anthropological Perspectives on Politics*, London: Pluto Press, 2000.

Goetz, A.M., Gaventa, J. 'Bringing Citizen Voice and Client Focus into Service Delivery', Brighton: *Institute for Development Studies*, 2001.

Goffman, E., *The Presentation of the Self in Everyday Life*, Harmondsworth: Penguin, 1990.

Goffman, E., *Asylums*, New York: Doubleday, 1961.

Goldman, A.I., *Pathways to Knowledge*, Oxford: Oxford University Press, 2002.

Goldman, A.I., *Knowledge in a Social World*, Oxford: Oxford University Press, 1999.

Goldman, A.I., *Epistemology and Cognition*, Cambridge, MA: Harvard University Press, 1986.

Goodin, R.E. (ed.), *The Theory of Institutional Design*, Cambridge: Cambridge University Press, 1998.

Goodwyn, L., 'Organizing Democracy: The Limits of Theory and Practice', *Democracy*, 1981, 1/1: 41–60.

Gramsci, A., *Selections from the Prison Notebooks*, London: Lawrence & Wishart, 1971.

Gray, B., Bougon, M.G., Donnellon, A., 'Organizations as Constructions and Destructions of Meaning', *Journal of Management*, 1985, 11: 83–98.

Gunsteren, H.R., van, *A Theory of Citizenship: Organizing Plurality in Contemporary Democracies*, Oxford: Westview Press, 1998.

Habermas, J., 'Further Reflections on the Public Sphere', in Calhoun, C. (ed.), *Habermas and the Public Sphere*, pp. 421–461, Cambridge, MA: MIT Press, 1992.

Habermas, J., *Moral Consciousness and Communicative Action*, Cambridge: Polity Press, 1992.

Habermas, J., *The Structural Transformation of the Public Sphere*, Cambridge: Polity Press, 1989.

Habermas, J., *The Theory of Communicative Action*, Vol. 2, Cambridge, MA: Beacon Press, 1987.

Habermas, J., *The Theory of Communicative Action*, Vol. 1, Cambridge, MA: Beacon Press, 1984.

Habermas, J., 'Modernity Versus Postmodernity', *New German Critique*, 1981, 22: 3–14.

Habermas, J., 'Legitimation Problems in the Modern State', *Communication and the Evolution of Society*, Cambridge: Polity Press, 1979.

Habermas, J., *Legitimation Crisis*, Cambridge: Polity Press, 1976.

Habermas, J., *Knowledge and Human Interest*, Boston: Beacon Press, 1968.

Haley, J., *Uncommon Therapy*, New York: Norton, 1973.

Hall, S. (ed.), *Representation: Cultural Representations and Signifying Practices*, London: Sage, 1997.

Hamilton, A., Madison, J., Jay, J., *The Federalist Papers*, New York: Mentor Books, 1961.

Hampsher-Monk, I., *A History of Modern Political Thought: Major Political Thinkers from Hobbes to Marx*, Oxford: Blackwell, 1992.

Haney, C., Banks, W. C., Zimbardo, P.G., 'Interpersonal Dynamics in a Simulated Prison', *International Journal of Criminology and Penology*, 1973, 1: 69–97.

Harding, S., *Feminism and Methodology*, Bloomington: Indiana University Press, 1987.

Hardt, M., Negri, A., *Empire*, Cambridge, MA: Harvard University Press, 2000.

Harré, R., *Cognitive Science: A Philosophical Introduction*, London: Sage, 2002.

Harré, R., Strydom, P., 'Symposium', *European Journal of Social Theory*, 2002, 5/1: 107–148.

Hartsock, N., 'The Feminist Standpoint: Developing the Ground for a Specifically Feminist Historical Materialism', in Harding, S., Hintikka, M. (eds), *Discovering Reality*, Dordrecht: Reidel, 1983.

Haslam, S.A., *Psychology in Organizations: A Social Identity Approach*, London: Sage, 2001.

Hastie, R., 'Problems for Judgment and Decision Making', *Annual Review of Psychology*, 2001, 52: 653–683.

Hastings, B.M., Shaffer, B. 'Authoritarianism: The Role of Threat, Evolutionary Psychology, and the Will to Power', *Theory and Psychology*, 2008, 18/3: 423–440.

Hayes, J., Allinson, C.W., 'Cognitive Style and the Theory and Practice of Individual and Collective Learning in Organizations', *Human Relations*, 1998, 51/7: 847–871.

Hayes, J.R., *Cognitive Psychology: Thinking and Creating*, Homewood, Ill.: Dorsey Press, 1978.

Hegel, G.W.F., *The Phenomenology of Spirit*, Oxford: Oxford University Press, 1977.

Hellstrom, T., Raman, S., 'The Commodification of Knowledge about Knowledge: Knowledge Management and the Reification of Epistemology', *Social Epistemology*, 2001, 15/3: 139–154.

Hetherington, S., *Good Knowledge, Bad Knowledge: On Two Dogmas of Epistemology*, Oxford: Clarendon Press, 2001.

Hindess, B., 'Representation Ingrafted upon Democracy?', *Democratization*, 2000, 7/2: 1–18.

Hindess, B., 'Politics and Liberation', in Moss, J. (ed.), *The Later Foucault*, pp. 50–62, London: Sage, 1998.

Hindess, B., *Discourses of Power: From Hobbes to Foucault*, Oxford: Blackwell, 1996.

Hirschhorn, L., *The Workplace Within: Psychodynamics of Organizational Life*, Cambridge, MA: MIT Press, 1988.

Hirschman, A.O., *Exit, Voice and Loyalty*, Cambridge, MA: Harvard University Press, 1970.

Hirst, P., *Associative Democracy: New Forms of Economic and Social Governance*, Cambridge: Polity Press, 1994.

Hobbes, T., *Leviathan*, New York: Bobbs-Merrill, 1958.

Holloway, J., *Change the World Without Taking Power*, London: Pluto Press, 2002.

Holloway, J., 'The Concept of Power and the Zapatistas', www.ecf.cle/yabasta/hollowe.htm, 1996.

Holt, G.R., Morris, A.W., 'Activity Theory and the Analysis of Organizations', *Human Organization*, 1993, 52/1: 97–109.

Honneth, A., 'Integrity and Disrespect: Principles of a Conception of Morality Based on a Theory of Recognition', *Political Theory*, 1992, 20/2: 187–201.

Honneth, A., *The Struggle for Recognition: The Moral Grammar of Social Conflicts*, Cambridge: Polity Press, 1996.

Horkheimer, M., *Between Philosophy and Social Science: Selected Early Writings*, Cambridge MA: MIT Press, 1993.

Horkheimer, M., Adorno, T., *The Dialectic of Enlightenment*, New York: Seabury Press, 1972.

Horkheimer, M., 'Traditional and Critical Theory', *Critical Theory: Selected Essays*, New York: Seabury Press, 1972.

Huddy, L., 'Contrasting Theoretical Approaches to Intergroup Relations', *Political Psychology*, 2004, 25/6: 947–967.

Hutchins, E., *In Search of Navigators*, New York: Wiley, 1987.

Hyppolite, J., *Genesis and Structure of Hegel's Phenomenology of Spirit*, Evanston: Northwestern University Press, 1974.

Iredale, W., Grimston, J., 'Britain Four Meals Away from Anarchy?', *The Sunday Times*, Oct., 2004.

James, L.R., Joyce, W.F., Slocum, J.W., 'Organizations Do Not Cognize', *Academy of Management Review*, 1988, 13/1: 129–132.

James, O., 'Is Your Boss a Psychopath?', *Guardian Newspaper*, 18/4/05.

James, W., *The Principles of Psychology*, Cambridge: Harvard University Press, 1983.

Janis, I.L., *Victims of Groupthink*, Boston: Houghton Mifflin, 1972.

Japp, K.P., 'Distinguishing Non-Knowledge', *Canadian Journal of Sociology*, 2000, 25/2: 225–238.

Jay, M., 'The Debate over Performative Contradiction: Habermas versus the Poststructuralists', in Honneth, A., McCarthy, M., Wellmer, A. (eds), *Philosophical Interventions in the Unfinished Project of Enlightenment*, Cambridge, MA: MIT Press, 1992.

Jay, M., *The Dialectical Imagination*, Boston: Little Brown, 1973.

Johnson-Laird, P., *Mental Models: Towards a Cognitive Science of Language, Inference, and Consciousness*, Cambridge, MA: Harvard University Press, 1983.

Jones, B.D., *Politics and the Architecture of Choice: Bounded Rationality and Governance*, Chicago: University of Chicago Press, 2001.

Jost, J., Benaji, M., 'A Decade of System Justification Theory: Accumulated Evidence of Conscious and Unconscious Bolstering of the Status Quo', *Political Psychology*, 2004, 25/6: 881–919.

Jost, J., Benaji, M., 'The Role of Stereotyping in System Justification and the Production of False Consciousness', *British Journal of Social Psychology*, 1994, 22: 1–27.

Jost, J.T., Burgess, D., Mosso, C.O., 'Conflicts of Legitimation among Self, Group, and System', in Jost, J.T., Major, B. (eds), *The Psychology of Legitimacy: Emerging Perspectives on Ideology, Justice, and Intergroup Relations*, pp. 363–388, Cambridge: Cambridge University Press, 2001.

Kahneman, D., *Attention and Effort*, Englewood Cliffs, NJ: Prentice-Hall, 1973.

Kahneman, D., Slovic, P., Tversky, A., *Judgment under Uncertainty: Heuristics and Biases*, New York: Cambridge University Press, 1982.

Kaldor, M., *Global Civil Society: An Answer to War*, Cambridge: Polity Press, 2003.

Kamal, S.S., *Ethnic Self-Determination and the Break-Up of States*, London: International Institute for Strategic Studies, 1993.

Kant, I., 'An Answer to the Question: What is Enlightenment?', in *Practical Philosophy* (Cambridge Edition of the Works of Immanuel Kant), Cambridge: Cambridge University Press, 1999.

Kant, I., *The Critique of Pure Reason*, New York: St. Martin's Press, 1965.

Kaplan, R.D., 'The Coming Anarchy', *The Atlantic Monthly*, 1994, 273/2: 44–76.

Kateb, G., 'Wolin as Critic of Democracy', in Botwinick, A., Connolly, W.E. (eds), *Democracy and Vision: Sheldon Wolin and the Vicissitudes of the Political*, Princeton: Princeton University Press, 2001, pp. 39–57.

Katsiaficas, G., *The Subversion of Politics: European Autonomous Social Movements and the Decolonization of Everyday Life*, New Jersey: Humanities Press, 1997.

Katz, D., Kahn, R.L., *The Social Psychology of Organizations*, New York: Wiley, 1966.

Keane, J. (ed.), *Civil Society and the State*, London: Verso, 1988.

Kelly, M., *Critique and Power: Recasting the Foucault/Habermas Debate*, Cambridge, MA: MIT Press, 1994.

Keltner, D., Gruenfeld, D.H., Anderson, C., 'Power, Approach, and Inhibition', *Psychological Review*, 2003, 110/2: 265–284.

Kershaw, I., *Hitler, 1889–1936: Hubris*, Harmondsworth: Penguin, 2001.

Kim, D.H. 'The Link Between Individual and Organizational Learning', *Sloan Management Review*, 1993, Fall: 37–50.

Kipnis, D., *The Powerholders*, Chicago: Chicago University Press, 1976.

Kipnis, D., Rind, B., 'Changes in Self-Perceptions as a Result of Successfully Persuading Others', *Journal of Social Issues*, 1999.

Klein, N. *No Logo*, London: HarperCollins, 2000.

Kline, M., 'Our Adult World and its Roots in Infancy', *Human Relations*, 1959, 12: 291–303.

Klosko, G., Rice D., 'Thucydides and Hobbes's State of Nature', *History of Political Thought*, 1985, 6/3: 405–409.

Kohut, H., *The Analysis of the Self*, New York: International Universities Press, 1971.

Körösényi, A., 'Political Representation in Leader Democracy', *Government and Opposition*, 2005, 40/3: 358–378.

Krogh, G. von, *Enabling Knowledge Creation: How to Unlock the Mystery of Tacit Knowledge and Release the Power of Innovation*. Oxford: Oxford University Press, 2000.

Kropotkin, P., *Mutual Aid: A Factor of Evolution*, London: Allen Lane, 1972.

Kunda, Z., *Social Cognition: Making Sense of People*, Cambridge, MA: MIT Press, 1999.

Kymlicka, W., Nelson, W., 'Return of the Citizen: A Survey of Recent Work on Citizenship Theory', *Ethics*, 1994, 104: 352–381.

Laclau, E., 'Populism: What's in a Name?', in F. Panizza (ed.), *Populism and the Mirror of Democracy*, London: Verso, 2005.

Lam, A. 'Tacit Knowledge, Organizational Learning and Societal Institutions', *Organization Studies*, 2000, 21/3: 487–513.

Landes, D.S., 'What Do Bosses Really Do?', *The Journal of Economic History*, 1986, 46/3: 585–623.

Lash, S., Urry, J., *The End of Organized Capitalism*, Cambridge: Polity Press, 1987.

Latour, B., Woolgar, S., *Laboratory Life: The Construction of Scientific Facts*, Princeton, NJ: Princeton University Press, 1986.

Lauer, Q., *A Reading of Hegel's Phenomenology of Spirit*, New York: Fordham University Press, 1976.

Lave, J., *Cognition in Practice*, Cambridge: Cambridge University Press, 1988.

Lawrence, P.R., Lorsch, J.W., *Organization and Environment*, Cambridge, MA: Harvard University Press, 1967.

Lefebvre, H. 'La Commune: derniere fete populaire', in Leith, J.A. (ed.), *Images de La Commune*, pp. 33–45, Montreal: McGill-Queen's University Press, 1971.

Lenski, G.E., *Power and Privilege: A Theory of Social Stratification*, Chapel Hill, NC: University of North Carolina Press, 1984.

Linebaugh, P., Rediker, M. *The Many-Headed Hydra: Sailors, Slaves, Commoners, and the Hidden History of the Revolutionary Atlantic*, London: Verso, 2008.

Livy, *The Early History of Rome*, Harmondsworth: Penguin, 1960.

Locke, J., *The Second Treatise of Government*, Indianapolis: Bobbs-Merrill, 1952.

Locke, J., *Essay Concerning Human Understanding*, 1690, III.

Lomas, J., *Formalised Informality: An Action Plan to Spread Proven Health Innovations*, Wellington: New Zealand Ministry of Health, 2008.

Lord, R.G., Maher, K.J., 'Cognitive Theory in Industrial and Organizational Psychology', in Dunnette, M.D., Hough, L.M. (eds), *Handbook of Industrial and Organizational Psychology*, Palo Alto, CA: Consulting Psychologists Press, 1991.

Love, N.S., 'Foucault & Habermas on Discourse and Democracy', *Polity*, 1989, 22/2: 269–293.

Lovejoy, A.O., *The Great Chain of Being: A Study in the History of an Idea*, Cambridge, MA.: Harvard University Press, 1990.

Lukács, G., *History and Class Consciousness*, London: Merlin, 1971.

Lukes, S., *Power: A Radical View*, New York: New York University Press, 2004.

Lukes, S. (ed.), *Power*, New York: New York University Press, 1986.

Lukes, S., 'Some Problems about Rationality', in Wilson, B. R. (ed.), *Rationality*, Oxford: Basil Blackwell, 1970: 194–213.

Luskin, R.C., Fishkin, J.S., Jowell, R., 'Considered Opinions: Deliberative Polling in Britain', *British Journal of Political Science*, 2002, 32: 455–487.

Lynch, M., 'Against Reflexivity as an Academic Virtue and Source of Privileged Knowledge', *Theory, Culture & Society*, 2000, 17/3: 26–54.

Lyotard, J.F., *The Postmodern Condition: A Report on Knowledge*, Minneapolis: University of Minnesota Press, 1984.

Machiavelli, N., 'The Discourses on Livy', in Bondanella, P., Musa, M. (eds), *The Portable Machiavelli*, Harmondsworth: Penguin, 1979.

Mackie, G. 'Does Democratic Deliberation Change Minds?', *Politics, Philosophy and Economics*, 2006, 5/3: 279–303.

Macpherson, C.B., *The Life and Times of Liberal Democracy*, Oxford: Oxford University Press, 1977.

Major, B., Schmader, T., 'Legitimacy and the Construal of Social Disadvantage', in Jost, J.T., Major, B. (eds), *The Psychology of Legitimacy: Emerging Perspectives on Ideology, Justice, and Intergroup Relations*, pp. 176–204, Cambridge: Cambridge University Press, 2001.

Malcolm, J., *In the Freud Archives*, New York: Vintage Books, 2001.

Mansbridge, J.J., *Beyond Adversary Democracy*, New York: Basic Books, 1980.

March, J.G., *A Primer on Decision Making: How Decisions Happen*, New York: Free Press, 1994.

March, J.G., Simon, H.A., *Organizations*, New York: Wiley, 1958.

Marglin, S.A., 'What Do Bosses Do? The Origins and Functions of Hierarchy in Capitalist Production', in Gorz, A. (ed.), *The Division of Labour: The Labour Process and Class-Struggle in Modern Capitalism*, London: Harvester, 1978: 13–54.

Marmot, M. *The Status Syndrome*, London: Bloomsbury, 2005.

Marx, K., 'The Class Struggles in France: 1848–1850', in Fernbach, D. (ed.), *Surveys from Exile: Marx*, Harmondsworth: Penguin, 1973.

Marx, K., *1844 Manuscripts*, in Tucker, R.C. (ed.), *The Marx-Engels Reader*, New York: Norton, 1974a.

Marx, K., *Capital*, Vol. 1, New York: International Publishers, 1974b.

Mbembe, A. 'The Banality of Power and the Aesthetics of Vulgarity in the Postcolony', *Public Culture*, 1992, 4: 1–30.

McCormick, J.P., 'Contain the Wealthy and Patrol the Magistrates: Restoring Elite Accountability to Popular Government', *American Political Science Review*, 2006, 100/2: 147–163.

McCormick, J.P. 'Machiavellian Democracy: Controlling Elites with Ferocious Populism', *American Political Science Review*, 2001, 95/2: 297–313.

McGraw, K.M., 'Contributions of the Cognitive Approach to Political Psychology', *Political Psychology*, 2000, 21/4: 805–832.

McHugh, D. 'Wanting to be Heard But Not Wanting to Act? Addressing Public Disengagement', *Parliamentary Affairs*, 2006, 59/3: 546–552.

McIntosh, J. 'Symbolism, Cognition, and Political Orders', *Science and Society*, 1998, 62/4: 557–568.

McKay, G. *DiY Culture: Party and Protest in Nineties Britain*, London: Verso, 1998.

McKinlay, A., Starkey, K., 'Managing Foucault: Foucault, Management and Organization Theory', in McKinlay, A., Starkey, K. (eds), *Foucault, Management and Organization Theory*, Thousand Oaks: Sage, 1998.

McLaren, R.I., *Organizational Dilemmas*, New York: John Wiley, 1982.

Mead, G.H., *Mind, Self, and Society*, Chicago: University of Chicago Press, 1934.

Meindl, J.R., Stubbart, C., Porac, J.F., *Cognition Within and Between Organizations*, Thousand Oaks: Sage, 1996.

Melucci, A., *Challenging Codes: Collective Action in the Information Age*, Cambridge: Cambridge University Press, 1996.

Menzies Lyth, I. 'The Functioning of Social Systems as a Defence against Anxiety', *Containing Anxiety in Institutions: Selected Essays*, London: Free Association Books, 1988: 43–85.

Merrick, *Battle for the Trees*, Leeds: godhaven ink, 1998.

Michels, R., *Political Parties: A Sociological Study of the Oligarchical Tendencies of Modern Democracy*, Glencoe, Illinois: Free Press, 1958.

Milbrath, L.W., *Political Participation: How and Why Do People Get Involved in Politics?* Chicago: Rand McNally, 1965.

Milgram, S. *Obedience to Authority: An Experimental View*, New York: Harper Colophon, 1974.

Mill, J.S. *Considerations on Representative Government*, London: Everyman, 1972.

Mill, J.S., 'Essay on Bentham', in Warnock, M. (ed.), *Utilitarianism and Other Writings*, New York: Meridian, 1959.

Minow, M., *Making All the Difference: Inclusion, Exclusion and American Law*, Ithaca: Cornell University Press, 1990.

Moore-Gilbert, B., Stanton, G. and Maley, W., *Postcolonial Criticism*, London: Longman, 1997.

Morgan, G., *Images of Organization*, London: Sage, 1997.

Moscovici, S., 'Notes Towards a Description of Social Representations', *Journal of European Social Psychology*, 1998, 18: 211–250.

Moscovici, S., Doise, W., *Conflict and Consensus: A General Theory of Collective Decisions*, London: Sage, 1994.

Moscovici, S., 'Comment on Potter and Litton', *British Journal of Social Psychology*, 1985, 244: 91–93.

Moscovici, S., 'On Social Representations', in Forgas, J.P. (ed.), *Social Cognition: Perspectives on Everyday Understanding*, London: Academic Press, 1981.

Moss, J. (ed.), *The Later Foucault*, London: Sage, 1998.

Mouffe, C., 'Radical Democracy: Modern or Postmodern', in Ross, A. (ed.), *Universal Abandon? The Politics of Postmodernism*, pp. 31–45, Edinburgh: Edinburgh University Press, 1988.

Muhammad, R.A., 'Participatory Development: Toward Liberation or Co-optation?', in Craig & Mayo, *Community Empowerment*, 1995, pp. 24–32.

Mullender, A., Ward, D. *Self-directed Group Work: Users Take Action for Empowerment*, London: Whiting and Birch, 1991.

Neisser, U., *Cognitive Psychology*, New York: Appleton-Century-Crofts, 1967.

Nelson, R.R., 'Recent Evolutionary Theorizing About Economic Change', *Journal of Economic Literature*, 1995, 33: 48–90.

Nelson, R.R., 'Why Do Firms Differ, and How Does It Matter', *Strategic Management Journal*, 1991, 12: 61–74.

Nelson, R.R., Winter, S.G., *An Evolutionary Theory of Economic Change*, Cambridge: Belknap Press, 1982.

Newell, A., Simon, H.A., *Human Problem-Solving*, Englewood Cliffs, NJ: Prentice-Hall, 1972.

Nicholson, N., *Executive Instinct*, New York: Crown Business, 2000.

Nonaka, I., 'The Knowledge-Creating Company', in Starkey, K. (ed.), *How Organizations Learn*, Boston, MA: International Thompson Business Press, 1996.

Norman, D.A., 'Cognition in the Head and in the World', *Cognitive Science*, 1993, 17: 1–6.

Nye, J.L., Brower, A.M. (eds), *What's Social About Social Cognition? Research on Socially Shared Cognition in Small Groups*, Thousand Oaks, CA: Sage, 1996: 311–323.

Ober, J., *Mass and Elite in Democratic Athens*, Princeton: Princeton University Press, 1989.

Offe, C., 'Bindings, Shackles, Brakes: On Self-Limitation Strategies', in Honneth, A., McCarthy, T., Offe, C., Wellmer, A. (eds), *Cultural-Political Interventions in the Unfinished Project of Enlightenment*, Cambridge, MA: MIT Press, 1992.

Offe, C., *Disorganized Capitalism*, Polity Press, 1985.

Owen, D. *The Hubris Syndrome: Bush, Blair and the Intoxication of Power*, London: Politico's, 2007.

Paine, T,. *Declaration of the Rights of Man and Citizens*, Harmondsworth: Penguin, 1984.

Parry, G., Moyser, G., 'More Participation, More Democracy?', in Beetham, D. (ed.), *Defining and Measuring Democracy*, London: Sage, 1994.

Parry, G., Moyser, G., *Political Participation and Democracy in Britain*, Cambridge: Cambridge University Press, 1992.

Parry, G., *Political Elites*, London: George Allen and Unwin, 1968.

Pateman, C., *Participation and Democratic Theory*, Cambridge: Cambridge University Press, 1970.

Patrides, C.A., *The Phoenix and the Ladder: The Rise and Decline of the Christian View of History*, Berkeley: Berkeley University Press, 1964.

Patterson, M.L., 'Social Behavior and Social Cognition: A Parallel Process Approach in Nye, J.L., Brower, A.M. (eds), *What's Social About Social Cognition? Research on Socially Shared Cognition in Small Groups*, Thousand Oaks, CA: Sage, 1996.

Patton, P., 'Ethics and the Subject of Politics', in Moss, J. (ed.), *The Later Foucault*, London: Sage, 1998, pp. 64–77.

Peet, R., Watts, M. (eds), *Liberation Ecologies: Environment, Development, Social Movements*, London: Routledge, 1996.

Peirce, C., *Collected Papers*, Cambridge, MA: Harvard University Press, 1931–5.

Pettit, P., *Republicanism: A Theory of Freedom and Government*, Oxford: Oxford University Press, 1999.

Pfeffer, J., *New Directions for Organizational Theory: Problems and Prospects*, New York: Oxford University Press, 1997.

Phillips, A., *Engendering Democracy*. Cambridge: Polity Press, 1991.

Pilisuk, M., McAllister, J., Rothman, J. (eds), 'Coming Together for Action: The Challenge of Contemporary Grassroots Community Organizing', *Journal of Social Issues*, 1996, 52/1: 15–38.

Pinker, S., *The Blank Slate*, London: Penguin, 2002.

Pizzorno, A., 'An Introduction to the Theory of Political Participation', *Social Science Information*, 1970, 9/5: 29–61.

Plato, *Theatetus*, Oxford: Clarendon Press, 1983.

Polanyi, M., *The Tacit Dimension*, London: Routledge, 1967.

Popper, K., *The Open Society and its Enemies*, London: Routledge, 1962.

Popper, K., *The Logic of Scientific Discovery*, London: Hutchinson, 1959.

Posner, M.I., Snyder, C.R., 'Attention and Cognitive Control', in Solso, R.L. (ed.), *Information Possessing and Cognition*, Hillsdale, NJ: Erlbaum, 1975.

Powell, W.W., 'Neither Market nor Hierarchy', in Thompson, G.J., Frances, R., Levacic, R., Mitchell, J., *Markets, Hierarchies and Networks: The Coordination of Social Life*, pp. 265–276, Thousand Oaks: Sage, 1996.

Power, M., *The Audit Society, Rituals of Verification*, Oxford: Oxford University Press, 1999.

Presthus, R., *The Organizational Society*, New York: St. Martin's, 1978.

Prilleltensky, I., Gonick, L., 'Polities Change, Oppression Remains: on the Psychology and Politics of Oppression', *Political Psychology*, 1996, 17/1: 127–148.

Proudhon, P.J., 'Parliamentary Isolation', in Woodcock, G. (ed.), *The Anarchist Reader*, London: Fontana/Collins, 1977, p. 110.

Proudhon, P.J., 'The Anarchist View of Democracy', in Woodcock, G. (ed.), *The Anarchist Reader*, 1848.

Prychitko, D.L. and Vanek, J. (eds), *Producer Cooperatives and Labor-Managed Systems*, Cheltenham: Edward Elgar, 1996.

Putnam, H., 'A Reconsideration of Deweyan Democracy', *Renewing Philosophy*, Cambridge, MA: Harvard University Press, 1992: 180–202.

Rabinow, P., Rose, N. (eds), 'Foucault Today', in Rabinow, P., Rose, N. (eds), *The Essential Foucault: Selections from the Essential Works of Foucault, 1954–1984*, New York: New Press, 2003.

Radner, R., 'Hierarchy: The Economics of Managing', *Journal of Economic Literature*, 30, 1992: 1382–1415, here at p. 1390.

Redlawsk, D.P., Hubby, C.R. 'Hot Cognition or Cool Consideration? Testing the Effects of Motivated Reasoning on Political Decision Making', *Journal of Politics*, 2002, 64: 1021–1044.

Reed, S.K., *Cognition: Theory and Applications*, Pacific Grove, CA: Brooks/Cole Publishing, 1988.

Reicher, S., Haslam, S.A. 'Rethinking the Psychology of Tyranny: The BBC Prison Study', *British Journal of Social Psychology*, 2006, 45: 1–40.

Reid, H.G., 'Democratic Theory and the Public Sphere Project: Rethinking Knowledge, Authority and Identity', *New Political Science*, 2001, 23/4: 517–536.

Resnick, L., 'Shared Cognition: Thinking as Social Practice', in Resnick, L.B., Levine, J.M., Teasley, S.D. (eds), *Perspectives on Socially Shared Cognition*, pp. 1–21, Washington, DC: American Psychological Association, 1993.

Ricoeur, P. 'Ethics and Culture: Habermas and Gadamer in Dialogue', *Philosophy Today*, 1973, 17: 153–165.

Ricoeur, P. *Freud and Philosophy: An Essay on Interpretation*, New Haven: Yale University Press, 1970.

Ridgeway, C.L. 'The Emergence of Status Beliefs: From Structural Inequality to Legitimizing Ideology', in Jost, J.T., Major, B. (eds), *The Psychology of Legitimacy: Emerging Perspectives on Ideology, Justice, and Intergroup Relations*, pp. 176–204, Cambridge: Cambridge University Press, 2001.

Rietveld, E., 'The Skillful Body as Concernful System of Possible Actions: Phenomena and Neurodynamics', *Theory and Psychology*, 2008, 18/3: 342–363.

Rose, N., 'Government, Authority and Expertise in Advanced Liberalism', *Economy and Society*, 1993, 22: 283–299.

Rose, S. 'In Search of the God Neuron', *The Guardian*, 27/12/08, p. 8.

Rosenberg, N., 'Adam Smith on the Division of Labour: Two Views or One?', *The Emergence of Economic Ideas: Essays in the History of Economics*, Aldershot: Edward Elgar, 1994.

Rosenberg, N., 'Marx as a Student of Technology', *Monthly Review*, 1976, 28/3: 133–158.

Rosenberg, S.W., *The Not So Common Sense: Differences in How People Judge Social and Political Life*, New Haven: Yale University Press, 2002.

Rousseau, J.J., *Discourse on the Origins and Foundations of Inequality among Men*, Harmondsworth: Penguin, 1984.

Rousseau, J.J., *The Social Contract*, Harmondsworth: Penguin, 1968.

Rumelhart, D.E., 'Schemata: The Building Blocks of Cognition', in Spiro, R.J., Bruce, B.C., Brewer, W.F. (eds), *Theoretical Issues in Reading Comprehension*, Hillsdale, NJ: Laurence Erlbaum, 1980.

Ryfe, D.M., 'Does Deliberative Democracy Work?', *Annual Review of Political Science*, 2005, 8: 49–71.

Ryle, G., 'Knowing How and Knowing That', *Proceedings of the Aristotelian Society*, 1945, pp. 1–16.

Sandel, M.J., 'The Procedural Republic and the Unencumbered Self', *Political Theory*, 1984, 12/1: 81–96.

Sandelands, L.E. and Stablein, R.E., 'The Concept of Organizational Mind', *Research in the Sociology of Organizations*, Greenwich: JAI Press, 1987.

Schank, R.C., Abelson, R.P., *Scripts, Plans, Goals, and Understanding: An Inquiry into Human Knowledge Structures*, Hillsdale, NJ: L. Erlbaum Associates, 1977.

Schattschneider, E.E., *The Semisovereign People*, Hinsdale: The Dryden Press, 1975.

Schatzki, T.R., 'Introduction: Practice Theory', in Schatzki, T.R., Cetina, K.K. and von Savigny, E. (eds), *The Practice Turn in Contemporary Theory*, London: Routledge, 2001.

Scheuerman, W.E. 'Globalization and Exceptional Powers: The Erosion of Liberal Democracy', *Radical Philosophy*, 1999, 93: 14–23.

Schmitt, M.T., Branscombe, N.R., Kappen, D.M. 'Attitudes Toward Group-Based Inequality: Social Dominance or Social Identity?', *British Journal of Social Psychology*, 2003, 42: 161–186.

Schneider, S.C., Angelmar, R., 'Cognition in Organizational Analysis: Who's Minding the Store?', *Organization Studies*, 1993, 14/3: 347–371.

Schott, R.L., 'Administrative and Organizational Behavior: Some Insights from Cognitive Psychology', *Administration and Society*, 1991, 23/1: 54–73.

Schotter, A., *The Economic Theory of Social Institutions*, Cambridge: Cambridge University Press, 1981.

Schumpeter, J.A., *Capitalism, Socialism and Democracy*, London: Allen & Unwin, 1958.

Schwarzmantel, J., *Structures of Power*, London: Prentice Hall, 1987.

Scott, J., *Power*, Cambridge: Polity Press, 2001.

Scott, J.C., *Domination and the Arts of Resistance*, New Haven: Yale University Press, 1990.

Scott, J. (ed.), *The Sociology of Elites*, Volumes 1–3, Cheltenham: Edward Elgar, 1990.

Searle, J.R., *Freedom and Neurobiology: Reflections on Free Will, Language, and Political Power*, New York: Columbia University Press, 2004.

Searle, J.R., *The Construction of Social Reality*, London: Penguin, 1996.

Seligman, M.E.P., *Helplessness: On Depression, Development, and Death*, San Francisco: Freeman & Co., 1977.

Senge, P.M., *The Fifth Discipline: The Art and Practice of the Learning Organisation*, Bantam Doubleday, 1994.

Sennett, R., *The Hidden Injuries of Class*, Cambridge: Cambridge University Press, 1977.

Servaes, J., Jacobson, T.L., White, S.A., *Participatory Communication for Social Change*, London: Sage, 1996, p. 24.

Shapiro, I. *Democratic Justice*, New Haven: Yale University Press, 1999.

Sherif, M., Harvey, O.J., White, B.J., Hood, W.R., Sherif, C., *Intergroup Conflict and Cooperation: The Robbers' Cave Experiment*, Norman: University of Oklahoma, 1961.

Shusterman, R., 'Putnam and Cavell on the Ethics of Democracy', *Political Theory*, 1997, 25/2: 193–214.

Sidanius, J., Pratto, F., 'Social Dominance Theory and the Dynamics of Inequality', *British Journal of Social Psychology*, 2003, 42: 207–213.

Sidanius, J., Pratto. F., *Social Dominance: An Intergroup Theory of Social Hierarchy and Oppression*, Cambridge: Cambridge University Press, 1999.

Simon, H., *Models of Thought*, New Haven: Yale University Press, 1955.

Simons, J., *Foucault and the Political*, London: Routledge, 1995.

Simpson, E.L., House, A.O., 'Involving Users in the Delivery and Evaluation of Mental Health Services: Systematic Review', *British Medical Journal*, 2002, 325: 1265.

Sims, H.P.Jr., Gioia, D.A., *The Thinking Organization*, San Francisco, CA: Jossey-Bass, 1986.

Skinner, Q., 'The Empirical Theorists of Democracy and their Critics: A Plague on Both Their Houses', *Political Theory*, 1973, 1/3: 287–306.

Smith, A., *The Wealth of Nations*, New York: Random House, 1937.

Snodgrass, S.E., Hecht, M.A., Ploutz-Snyder, R., 'Interpersonal Sensitivity: Expressivity or Perceptivity?', *Journal of Personality and Social Psychology*, 1988, 69: 797–811.

Snyder, M., Uranowitz, S.W., 'Reconstructing the Past: Some Cognitive Consequences of Person Perception', *Journal of Personality and Social Psychology*, 1978, 36: 941–950.

Soloman, D., Greenberg, J., Pyszczynski, T., 'A Terror Management Theory of Social Behavior: The Psychological Functions of Self-Esteem and Cultural World Views', in Zanna, M.P. (ed.), *Advances in Experimental Social Psychology*, Vol. 24, pp. 93–159, San Diego: Academic.

Spears, R., Jetten, J., Doosje, B., 'The (Ill)legitimacy of Ingroup Bias: From Social Reality to Social Resistance', in Jost, J.T., Major, B. (eds), *The Psychology of Legitimacy: Emerging Perspectives on Ideology, Justice, and Intergroup Relations*, pp. 332–362, Cambridge: Cambridge University Press, 2001.

Sperber, D., *On Anthropological Knowledge*, Cambridge: Cambridge University Press, 1985.

Spivak, G.C., *The Post-Colonial Critic*, Harasym, S. (ed.), New York: Routledge, 1990.

Spivak, G.C., 'Can the Subaltern Speak?', in Nelson, C., Grossberg, L. (eds), *Marxism and the Interpretation of Culture*, Urbana: University of Illinois Press, 1988.

Spooner, L., 'The Indefensible Constitution', in Woodcock, G. (ed.), *The Anarchist Reader*, pp. 103–108, Glasgow: Fontana, 1977.

Starkey, K., *How Organizations Learn*, Boston, MA: International Thompson Business Press, 1996.

Stein, J., 'How Institutions Learn: A Socio-Cognitive Perspective', *Journal of Economic Issues*, 1997, 31/3: 729–740.

Sternberg, R.J., *Intelligence, Information Processing, and Analogical Reasoning*, Hillsdale, NJ: Erlbaum, 1977.

Stewart, D., 'The Hermeneutics of Suspicion', *Journal of Literature and Theology*, 1989, 3: 296–307.

Stewart, J., 'Thinking Collectively in the Public Domain', *Soundings*, 1996, Autumn/4: 213–223.

Stoler, A., 'On Political and Psychological Essentialism', *Ethos: Journal of the Society for Psychological Anthropology*, 1997, 25/1.

Strydom, P., 'Introduction: A Cartography of Contemporary Cognitive Social Theory', *European Journal of Social Theory*, 2007, 10/3: 339–356 gives an excellent overview of current activity.

Suchman, L.A., *Plans and Situated Action: The Problem of Human-Machine Communication*, Cambridge: Cambridge University Press, 1987.

Surowiecki, J., *The Wisdom of Crowds: Why the Many are Smarter than the Few*, London: Abacus, 2005.

Swieringa, J., Wierdsma, A., *Becoming a Learning Organization*, Reading, MA: Addison Wesley, 1992.

Tajfel, H., Turner, J.C., Worchel, S., Austin, W.G., *The Psychology of Intergroup Relations*, Washington: Nelson Hall, 1986.

Taylor, C., 'Foucault on Freedom and Truth', *Political Theory*, 1984, 12/2: 152–183.

Tetlock, P. 'Accountability: A Social Check on the Fundamental Attribution Error', *Social Psychology Quarterly*, 1985, 48: 227–236.

Thaler, R.H., Sunstein, C.R. *Nudge: Improving Decisions about Health, Wealth, and Happiness*, New Haven: Yale University Press, 2008.

Thapalia, C.F., 'Animation and Leadership', in Servaes, J., Jacobson, T.L., White, S.A., *Participatory Communication for Social Change*, pp. 150–161, 1996.

Thau, M., *Consciousness and Cognition*, Oxford: Oxford University Press, 2002.

*The Iliad*, VIII: 19–27.

Thompson, G., Frances, J., Levacic, R., Mitchell, J., *Markets, Hierarchies and Networks: The Coordination of Social Life*, Thousand Oaks: Sage, 1996.

Thompson, V.A., *Modern Organizations*, New York: Alfred Knopf, 1961.

Tronto, J.C., 'Beyond Gender Difference to a Theory of Care', *Signs: Journal of Women in Culture and Society*, 1987, 12/4: 644–663.

Tsagarousianou, R., Tambini, D. (eds), *Cyberdemocracy: Technology, Cities and Civic Networks*, London: Routledge, 1997.

Turner, J.C., 'Tyranny, Freedom and Social Structure: Escaping our Theoretical Prisons', *British Journal of Social Psychology*, 2006, 45: 41–46.

Turner, J.C., Reynolds, K.J., 'Why Social Dominance Theory has been Falsified', *British Journal of Social Psychology*, 2003, 42: 199–206.

Turner, M., *Cognitive Dimensions of Social Science*, New York: Oxford University Press, 2001.

Turner, S., 'Social Theory as Cognitive Neuroscience', *European Journal of Social Theory*, 2007, 10/3: 357–374.

Tushman, M.L., Nadler, D.A., 'Implications of Political Models of Organization', in Miles, R.H. (ed.), *Resource Book in Macro-Organizational Behavior*, Santa Monica, CA: Goodyear, 1980.

van Dijk, J., Kerkhofs, R., van Rooij, I., Haselager, P. 'Can There Be Such a Thing as Embodied Embedded Cognitive Neuroscience?', *Theory and Psychology*, 2008, 18/3: 297–316.

van Gunsteren, H.R., *A Theory of Citizenship: Organizing Plurality in Contemporary Democracies*, Oxford: Westview Press, 1998.

Vanek, J., *The General Theory of Labor-Managed Market Economies*, Ithaca: Cornell University Press, 1970.

Varela, F.J. 'Neurophenomenology: A Methodological Remedy for the Hard Problem', *Journal of Consciousness Studies*, 1996, 3: 330–349.

Vetlesen, A.J., *Perception, Empathy, and Judgment: An Inquiry into the Preconditions of Moral Performance*, Pennsylvania: Pennsylvania State University Press, 1994.

Vries de, M.K., Miller, D., *The Neurotic Organization*. San Francisco: Jossey-Bass, 1985.

Wainwright, H., *Arguments for a New Left*, Oxford: Blackwell, 1994.

Walker, G., 'Network Position and Cognition in a Computer Software Firm', *Administrative Science Quarterly*, 1985, 30: 103–130.

Walsh, J.P., Henderson, C.M., Deighton, J.A., 'Negotiated Belief Structures and Decision Performance: An Empirical Investigation', *Organizational Behavior and Human Decision Process*, 1988, 42: 194–216.

Walzer, M., 'Liberalism and the Art of Separation', *Political Theory*, 1984, 12/3: 315–330.

Warren, M., 'Democratic Theory and Self-Transformation', *American Political Science Review*, 1992, 86/1: 8–23.

Watzlawick, P., *How Real is Real?* New York: Vintage Books, 1977.

Weber, M., *Economy and Society*, Berkeley: University of California Press, 1978.

Weber, M. 'Bureaucracy', in Gerth, H.H., Wright Mills, C. (eds), *From Max Weber: Essays in Sociology*, New York: Oxford University Press, 1946.

Weber, M., *From Max Weber: Essays in Sociology*, New York: Oxford University Press, 1946.

Weber, M., *Objectivity in Social Science and Social Policy*, 1904: 49–112.

Weber, R., Crocker, J., 'Cognitive Processes in the Revision of Stereotypic Beliefs', *Journal of Personality and Social Psychology*, 1983, 45/5: 961–997.

Weibe, R.H., *Self-Rule: A Cultural History of American Democracy*, Chicago: University of Chicago Press, 1995.

Weick, K.E., *Sensemaking in Organizations*, London: Sage, 1995.

Weick, K.E., 'Cognitive Processes in Organizations', in Straw, B.M. (ed.), *Research in Organizational Behavior*, Greenwich, CT: JA Press, 1979.

Weick, K.E., *The Social Psychology of Organizing*, Reading, MA: Addison-Wesley, 1979.

Wheen, F., *How Mumbo-Jumbo Conquered the World: A Short History of Modern Delusions*, London: Fourth Estate, 2004.

White, E., 'Between Suspicion and Hope: Paul Ricoeur's Vital Hermeneutic', *Journal of Literature and Theology*, 1991, 5: 311–321.

Wicks, A.C., Freeman, R.E., 'Organization Studies and the New Pragmatism: Positivism, Anti-Positivism and the Search for Ethics', *Organization Science*, 1998, 92: 123–140.

Wicks, A.C., Freeman, R.E., 'Organization Studies and the New Pragmatism: Positivism, Anti-Positivism and the Search for Ethics', *Organization Science*, 1998, 9/2: 123–140.

Wiggershaus, R., *The Frankfurt School: Its History, Theories and Political Significance*, Cambridge: Polity Press, 1994.

Wilkinson, R., 'The Impact of Inequality: Empirical Evidence', *Renewal*, 2006, 14/1: 20–26.

Williamson, O.E., *Markets and Hierarchies: Analysis and Antitrust Implications*, New York: Free Press, 1975.

Wilson, B.R. (ed.), *Rationality*, Oxford: Basil Blackwell, 1970.

Wolff, R.P., *Kant's Theory of Mental Activity*, Cambridge, MA: Harvard University Press, 1963.

Wolff, R.P., *In Defence of Anarchism*, New York: Harper and Row, 1970.

Wolff, R.P., *Understanding Marx: A Reconstruction and Critique of Capital*, Princeton: Princeton University Press, 1984.

Wolff, R.P., *Moneybags Must Be So Lucky: On the Literary Structure of Capital*, Amherst, MA: University of Massachusetts Press, 1988.

Wolin, S., *Democracy Incorporated: Managed Democracy and the Spectre of Inverted Totalitarianism*, Princeton: Princeton University Press, 2008.

Wolin, S., 'Fugitive Democracy', *Constellations*, 1994, 1/1: 11–25.

Wolin, S., 'Norm and Form: The Constitutionalizing of Democracy', in Euben, J.P., Wallach, J.R., Ober, J. (eds), *Athenian Political Thought and the Reconstruction of American Democracy*, Ithaca: Cornell University Press, 1994.

Wolin, S., *The Presence of the Past: Essays on the State and the Constitution*, Baltimore: Johns Hopkins University Press, 1989.

Wollheim, R., Hopkins. J., *Philosophical Essays on Freud*, Cambridge: Cambridge University Press, 1982.

Worsley, P., 'The Practice of Politics and the Study of Australian Kinship', in Gaily, C.W. (ed.), *The Politics of Culture and Creativity*, Gainsville: University of Florida Press, 1992.

Wyler, R.S., Srull, T.K., *Handbook of Social Cognition*, Vol. 3, Hillsdale, NJ: Erlbaum, 1983.

Yalom, I.D., *The Theory and Practice of Group Psychotherapy*, London: Basic Books, 2004.

Zimbardo, P.G., 'On Rethinking the Psychology of Tyranny: The BBC Prison Study', *British Journal of Social Psychology*, 2006, 45: 47–53.

# Index